Wife or Worker?

Asia/Pacific/Perspectives

Series Editor: Mark Selden

Wife or Worker?

Asian Women and Migration

Edited by Nicola Piper and Mina Roces

Foreword by Eleonore Kofman

ROWMAN & LITTLEFIELD PUBLISHERS, INC.
Lanham • Boulder • New York • Oxford

#51251733

ROWMAN & LITTLEFIELD PUBLISHERS, INC.

Published in the United States of America
by Rowman & Littlefield Publishers, Inc.
A Member of the Rowman & Littlefield Publishing Group
4501 Forbes Boulevard, Suite 200, Lanham, Maryland 20706
www.rowmanlittlefield.com

P.O. Box 317, Oxford OX2 9RU, United Kingdom

British Library Cataloguing in Publication Information Available

Library of Congress Cataloging-in-Publication Data

Wife or worker? : Asian women and migration / edited by Nicola Piper and
Mina Roces.
        p. cm. — Asia/Pacific/perspectives
Includes bibliographical references and index.
    ISBN 0-7425-2377-2 (cloth : alk. paper) — ISBN 0-7425-2378-0 (pbk. : alk. paper)
    1. Women alien labor—Asia, Southeastern. 2. Women in development—Asia,
Southeastern. 3. Asia, Southeastern—Emigration and immigration—Economic aspects. 4.
Women alien labor—East Asia. 5. Women in development—East Asia. 6. East Asia—
Emigration and immigration—Economic aspects. I. Piper, Nicola. II. Roces, Mina, 1959–
III. Series: Asia/Pacific/perspectives (Rowman and Littlefield, Inc.)
    HD6191 .W54 2003
    304.8'082'0959—dc21

                                                                2002155385

Printed in the United States of America

♾ ™ The paper used in this publication meets the minimum requirements of American
National Standard for Information Sciences—Permanence of Paper for Printed Library
Materials, ANSI/NISO Z39.48-1992.

Contents

Acknowledgments

We owe a huge debt of gratitude to a number of institutions and individuals who have all contributed to this volume. This project was conceived at the Nordic Institute of Asian Studies (NIAS) when Mina Roces was there for a one-month fellowship in November 1999. We would like to thank NIAS and former NIAS Director Robert Cribb (now a reader in history in the Research School of Asian and Pacific Studies at The Australian National University) for providing us with the opportunity and the institutional logistics to begin this project. Professor Mark Selden (series editor for Rowman & Littlefield) should be singled out as the person who has been intimately involved in the project from its beginnings as a book proposal to its final stage. We feel very fortunate to have had Professor Selden's hands-on approach to the book; and the manuscript benefited from his many suggestions, criticisms, and comments. We also appreciate his commitment and dedication to the project during its various stages and for his enthusiastic support and encouragement. We also acknowledge the input of our colleagues who took the time to read some chapters and make constructive comments. In particular we are indebted to Professor Anthony Fielding (University of Sussex), Professor Eleanore Kofman (University of Nottingham), Dr. Anne O'Brien (University of New South Wales) and Associate Professor Beverley Kingston (University of New South Wales).

Our respective institutions gave us much needed financial support in the form of subventions (for copyediting and for camera-ready format) and hence we are very thankful to both the School of History, University of New South Wales, and The Australian National University. We are especially grateful to Professor John Braithwaite, Chair of the Regulatory Institutions Network, Australian National University, for a generous financial contribution which allowed us to employ a professional indexer. The Center for Social Research, Central Queensland University, was generous enough to fund the project on Mount Isa.

We are indebted to the following for technical and artistic help: Alfredo Roces for designing our book cover, Dr. Hamish Graham for formatting the table in chapter 4, Angela Lober for creating the map in chapter 4, Alan Walker for the index, our copyeditor Paulette McGee, production editor April Leo, and Jessica Gribble who helped with the book cover as well. Susan McEachern was a wonderful acquisitions editor, who helped us with the technical side of preparing the manuscript for submission.

An anthology cannot be produced without willing contributors and we thank all the contributors for submitting their chapters on time, responding to the reader's corrections ever so promptly, and for their good nature in the editing process. Finally, we thank all those women and men interviewed for all the chapters in this book; thank you all for your time and your kindness.

Nicola Piper and Mina Roces
Australia, November 2002

Foreword

Eleonore Kofman

The formation of the family has received very little attention within the literature on international migration. One of the main reasons for this neglect is that family migration is considered to be secondary compared to labor migration and is associated with females whose migratory role is limited to that of the dependant or a trailing spouse. Of course, it is wrongly assumed that wives cease to work once married or that they simply seek employment as a supplement to family resources. The scant attention paid to family migration prevails despite the high priority given to family links as criteria in the determination of entry in the classic societies of immigration, such as Australia, Canada, and the United States. In these countries policies have become less nationally restrictive since the mid-1960s, especially in relation to Asian immigration. And much of this migration involves the formation of new families through marriage movements.

Disinterest in family migration also seems at odds with some of the patterns arising from the globalization and diversification of migration. As various chapters in this book highlight, there is increasing movement of unmarried individuals for education, work, and travel. These international movements bring individuals in contact with others of different nationalities, resulting in migration subsequent to marriage.

The relationship of marriage and migration generates different categories and raises a number of issues. There are those who move in search of a husband (Japan, Mount Isa) in contrast to those who move as couples to another country that may be the country of origin of one of the spouses or a third country. There are those who marry in order to obtain a more secure status to escape from poor employment prospects or de-skilling, or to acquire a long-term residence permit (as in the case of Canada and Germany). There are those who bring in spouses as part of family reunion policies, whether it be from their own country or the wider diaspora (intracultural) or from another country (intercultural). There are also those who move for the sake of another member of the family, whether it be for their children's education (as discussed in the case of migration to the United States here) or to look after an elderly relative. Another neglected aspect of family migration and marriage is the scenario of women who have migrated first to work and are then able to bring in other family members (i.e., family reunification initiated by women as the primary migrants). This overturns the stereotyped idea of the imported wife and is becoming more common with the growth of migrant domestic labor in North America, Europe, and Asia. Such a development is in evidence with the maturing of migratory flows to Southern European countries that has meant that some of the established female migrants, such as Filipinas, have brought in husbands in the past decade. The period of absence may have disrupted gender relations and identities that for some leads to divorce.

We thus need to move away from simplistic ideas of marriage as complying with traditional forms and as disempowering. Marriage may be entered into for instrumental purposes and be quite rationally considered in terms of desired objectives. Immigration legislation too tends to force couples to marry in order to migrate since cohabiting is generally not permitted. Some, especially professional women on the other hand, may decide not to get married and seek fulfillment through work and assignments abroad. On the other hand, marriage may enable women to get out of dead-end jobs or achieve greater economic and legal security, especially since the acquisition of citizenship is made easier through marriage. And of course these days marriage does not necessarily entail exiting from the labor market.

The chapters in this book address many of these issues in relation to Asian women who have migrated to other Asian countries, Europe, Australia, and North America. The formation of families across states is becoming of increasing significance and is being addressed in research on transnational migration and the life cycle, especially in relation to the complex movements across the Asia Pacific. It is time that we recognize the significance of family formation and marriage and examine the diverse experiences and strategies pursued by women and men in marrying internationally.

Introduction: Marriage and Migration in an Age of Globalization

Nicola Piper and Mina Roces

A dramatic rise in the number of marriages in the international, or transnational, context has occurred in the final decades of the twentieth century, reflecting deepening globalization processes including increasing numbers of individuals working, studying, and/or traveling abroad. This trend can very well be observed in East and Southeast Asia where intraregional labor migration flows have grown in importance and diversity in recent years (Piper and Ball 2001). Since the 1980s, East and Southeast Asia have become increasingly significant labor-importing regions, overtaking in magnitude Asian migration to the oil-producing economies of the Middle East. This is partly related to an enormous intensification of Asian regionalism measured by intra-Asian FDI, trade, capital and financial flows—and migration. Substantial numbers of Asian women are part of these intraregional as well as global migration flows.

Although there has been a long tradition of female cross-border migration in the Asia Pacific region, women are increasingly dominating migration flows (OECD 1998), and they do so in a variety of forms. This has been particularly so since the early 1980s when large-scale temporary migration became an integral part of the globalization of production and national economies (Wickramasekara 2000). With these women migrating either as single, independent workers at a stage in their lives when marriage is seen as appropriate, if not obligatory, or as wives (and mothers), the issue of marriage, or marital relationships, becomes closely intertwined with international migration. This connection—between work-related migration and marriage—has, however, been neglected by conventional migration studies. To some extent, this has to do with the lingering legacy of economistic types of studies having dominated migration theory for a long time (Kofman 1999). Recently, gender-sensitive, or feminist, perspectives of migration have begun to contribute new insights by pointing to noneconomic incentives to migration (Harzig 2001). In these studies, the family, or households, emerge as important units of analysis (see for instance Yeoh, Graham, and Boyle 2002), but migration's impact on marriage or marital relationships as such has not been explored in *their multiple dimensions and forms.*

Hence, this book attempts to combine analytically three fields of academic inquiry: marriage, work, and migration, analyzing marriage either as the result of labor- or work-related migration, and women's entry into the labor force after international marriage. There is a lack of theorizing and empirical studies that blends the three main strands—marriage, migration, and work—all addressed here in an international context and in ways sensitive to their gendered implications. In the little academic literature that does exist on marriage and migration, it is work by historians establishing a link between marriage and work migration. Such studies, however, have tended to look at monoethnic/monoracial couples in traditional settlement societies such as the United States (see e.g., Sharpe 2001). Often, the ways in which marriage and migration interacted were seen as related to imbalanced sex ratios, with female migrants "following" male pioneers (Sinke 1999). In the specific context of Asian women's experiences, works on the so-called "picture brides" fall into this category too (see e.g., Makabe 1995; Chai and Gabaccia 1992). Historically inclined studies on the phenomenon of "marriage migration" also include those discussing "war brides" (Nakano Glenn 1986; Kim 1977). Other studies focus on how these brides are represented by the host countries (Holt 1996; Robinson 1996; Saroca 1997). Yet in this discussion of marriage migration, little attention is paid to the women's subsequent entrance into the labor market. Other studies discussing marriage and migration are those typically by sociologists and geographers on "mail-order brides" (Cahill 1990; Chuah, Chuah, Reid-Smith, and Rice 1987; Cooke 1986; Cunneen and Stubbs 1997; Pendlebury 1990).

This book, however, investigates contemporary forms of international migratory movements consisting of various different types of mobility across borders, such as student migration, overseas contract work, and so on, to various destinations that are not all traditional places of permanent settlement (such as North America). We are interested in exploring the imbrication of work, marriage, motherhood, and migration in these various population movements. Scholars concerned with women's migratory patterns seem to be more comfortable discussing women as *either* migrants for marriage *or* as overseas contract workers (OCWs) (the woman as worker), especially women as unskilled laborers, domestic helpers, and carers in particular (see e.g., Ball 1997; Anderson 2000; Parreñas 2001a, 2001b, 2001c; Constable 1997). Here the image of the woman as migrant worker obscures her other roles as mother or wife (since husbands and/or children often remain in their country of origin). Since the women in these case studies are "contract workers," they are temporary sojourners rather than citizens. But what about the OCW who marries a "local" man or reunites with her husband in the country of her employment? Or what about the migrant for marriage who becomes employed? Is it wise to perpetuate the analytical framework that views migrant women as either migrants for marriage or overseas contract workers? Are women migrants best analyzed separately as migrant wives or migrant workers?

The chapters in this book aim at highlighting the diverse experience of Asian women migrants across class, educational backgrounds, location within their life-courses, ethnicity, and *types* of marriage (international and transnational). Our specific focus on Asian women serves to exemplify exactly this trend of increasing diversification of women migrants' experiences and the situations leading to, and arising out of, marriage. This is particularly important as far as Asian women are concerned because their proportion in worldwide migratory flows is growing, and yet they still tend to be stereotyped in popular writings as "mail-order brides," "domestic workers," or "sex workers."

Though there is a thriving literature on domestic workers abroad (especially Filipino domestic helpers), the scholarly focus has been closely aligned to four themes: exploitation, victimization, and problems of human rights epitomized by the hanging of Flor Contemplacion in Singapore (Hilsdon 2000; Tadiar 1997; Torrevillas 1996; May 1997); the "world" of domestic helpers including the "subtle forms of resistance" (like making jokes about employers) (Constable 1997); the "dislocation of nonbelonging" (where Filipino domestic helpers, whether in Rome or Los Angeles, occupy liminal spaces and are forced to negotiate even specific physical public "spaces" literally in the streets (Parreñas 2001a); and transnational motherhood (Hondagneu-Sotelo and Avila 1997; Alicea 1997; Parreñas 2001b). While the earlier studies dwelt on exploitation and victimization, the more recent literature has tried to make comparative studies (between workers in Rome, Italy, and Los Angeles, California, USA, for example, see Parreñas 2001a). In all these, women are still viewed primarily as "workers" even in the few excellent studies that discussed migrant women in their simultaneous roles as main income earner and transnational mother (Hondagneu-Sotelo and Avila 1997; Parreñas 2001a, 2001b; Constable 1999; Cohen 2000). Most studies discuss marriage only in the context of transnational relationships (i.e., in a monoethnic setting with, for instance, Mexican or Filipino women migrating abroad and leaving their same nationality husbands at home) or their case studies examine women's migration experience in the context of one specific type of job only.

Even when citizenship is factored into the equation, women are still perceived to be "negotiating citizenship," often achieving only "partial" citizenship because they are continually represented as female labor in the globalization process (Stasiulis and Bakan 1997; Parreñas 2001c). "Partial citizenship" becomes the norm because of the denial of the woman's reproductive role as "mother," since these women are forbidden from getting pregnant as part of their conditions of employment particularly for those employed in the Middle East and Asia (Parreñas 2001c).

Our approach problematizes the distinction between women as migrant workers (whether temporary or permanent) and women as migrants for marriage and unsettles these categories by providing studies from a variety of different contexts. In this way, we go beyond existing scholarly work on marriage and migration in which the "woman" is often locked into either the category of "bride" or "worker" and is oblivious of her transformation into other, or additional, roles such as "mother" and "citizen." By focusing on international migration as the main experience, the chapters in this book reveal that distinctions between these two analytical categories (wife or worker) are very much blurred. According to Penny and Khoo, international marriage[1] is one of the fundamental motives for migration "as people seek mates where they may" (1996, 29). Likewise, marriage might be the result of migration—unintended or deployed as a self-conscious strategy to, for example, escape from sex work or de-skilling (see Mix and Piper, chapter 3, and McKay, chapter 2).

In the context of marriage migration, it has to be noted that conventional migration studies (read labor migration) have typically ignored the phenomenon of marriage for, or as the result of, international labor migration. This is not so much related to a lack of gender-specific analyses of migration studies *per se*, but more so with a disregard of marriage as one issue of concern for migrants who are looking for work abroad. But even among single women professionals working overseas temporarily, "marriage" is still very much present in their minds, influencing major employment decisions of many. Willis and Yeoh argue that Singaporean women plan their careers expecting (or expected) to return home at a later date to get married (chapter 5). Though women are overseas workers, their mind-set is informed by the official Singaporean government's grand narrative of the Singaporean family (Willis and Yeoh, chapter 5). In this way, Willis and Yeoh not only look at marriage as an act or change of status but also at how its location within the life course may shape the nature of women's moves. Their chapter thus highlights the significance of migration in the life course even for those who are not (yet) married, including those who use migration to escape a more traditional type of marriage.

According to the historian Sinke (1999), marriage and migration have always affected one another, with marriage choices and job choices having developed in similar ways. The influence of an international "marriage market" has more often been a predominant factor in migration decisions of women who had fewer or other socioeconomic choices than men. In the case of a woman who migrates when already married, concerns for her marital relationship, or the family, are very much present at all times. Both of these scenarios, migration for marriage or migration of a married person, are experienced very differently by men and women. In some cases the category "married woman" is in itself problematic because some married women claim that they are single to facilitate the migration process (since it is easier to get certain jobs such as carer if one is single). Or they describe themselves as married prior to migration, but were not so in a strictly legal sense (civil law), but were cohabiting or involved in what one might want to describe as "common law marriage." This status has the advantage that a woman can get legally married to a "local" man in the destination country of her migration (see McKay, chapter 2, and Mix and Piper, chapter 3).

Taking a combination of interdisciplinary case studies and approaches (our contributors include scholars from history, psychology, sociology, anthropology, and human geography as well as one NGO practitioner), the authors use case studies of one or two countries to make interpretative arguments based on primary data gathered during fieldwork conducted within the last three years. The case studies cover a wide geographical spread: Filipinos in America, Canada, Australia, Japan, Spain, and Italy; Thais in Germany; Taiwanese in California; Singaporeans in China; East Asians in Japan; and Asian migrants in Malaysia among others. Though Filipinos appear as the main subjects in three of the chapters, this merely reflects the global statistical data on Filipino female marriage and migration more generally. There are larger percentages of Filipinos as domestic helpers in Spain, Italy, Greece (in one Greek dictionary the euphemism for "domestic help" is "Filipineza"), Singapore, Hong Kong, and Canada; and Filipinos as marriage migrants feature prominently in Japan, Switzerland, and Australia.

SHIFTING COUNTRIES, SHIFTING ROLES

In the context of international marriages, anthropologists and sociologists have to date tended to limit their research interests to the reasons why such marriages occur or the quality of the marriages (i.e., whether the marriages were successful or not). The problem with this perspective is that it remains one-dimensional: for instance, "mail-order brides" are forever labeled or categorized as "brides" and almost never become "women," still less do they become workers, or political actors and cultural mediators. Another neglected issue is women migrants' role as mothers. Although historically not a totally new phenomenon, as observed by Sharpe (2001), the contexts in which women migrate as mothers and how they deal with the implications of either split family life (Chee, chapter 7) or reunified families (Pe-Pua, chapter 8) seem to have widened and have so far received little attention by academics (except the literature on transnational motherhood (see Hondagneu-Sotelo and Avila 1997; Alicea 1997; Parreñas 2001a, 2001b). We, however, emphasize here that women who become international migrants through marriage move on to become mothers, workers, citizens, and cultural mediators. Performing voluntary work or civic work (for charity or for social and cultural activities) is linked to their role as cultural mediators. Filipino women married to Australian men in Mount Isa, Rockhampton, and Yeppoon, for example, perform folk dances during the town's festivals (see Roces, chapter 4; Roces 1996, 1998). Furthermore, they also do volunteer work for the Catholic Church and other civic organizations. While these activities could be interpreted as part of their strategies for coping in isolated towns and remote areas, such activities also have to be seen as positive contributions to the town's cultural and social life. At times, the volunteer work can have political implications; Filipino women campaigned actively for Mount Isa's former mayor and Member of Parliament for the state of Queensland (1999) Tony McGrady (he served concurrently as a member of the cabinet and as Minister for Mines and Energy [Queensland]). These "community engagements" in which migrants contribute to their host societies are an important aspect in the discussion revolving around citizenship (see below).

Unfortunately, the conflation of women domestic helpers and "carers" with the image of a good wife or mother prevents migrant women from reinventing themselves into something other than a woman who must do household work. There are contradictory discourses operating: women use international marriage as a way out of domestic work, but the men who marry them see them as marriageable material precisely because they perform domestic work. Deirdre McKay's study of Filipino women carers in Canada argues that these women suffer de-skilling where their overseas qualifications are not accredited and where domestic work as carers is the only niche for them (in the sense that once in Canada they cannot make use of their qualifications but are trapped in domestic work). Marriage becomes a strategy employed by women to escape from domestic work; but ironically, Canadian men see these women as marriageable precisely because of their association with domestic work. In fact, McKay's informants reveal that if they declare that they are Filipino-Canadian, the men who approach them initially lose interest because they prefer a newly arrived migrant domestic worker who then fits in with their orientalized visions of the woman/wife who will serve her husband (McKay, chapter 2). These orientalist imaginings (so prominent in the dynamics of the international marriage context) conflate the woman as wife with the woman as domestic worker, prompting contemporary Filipinos (in Manila) to label them *muchawa* (a Tagalog slang that combines the words *muchacha* or maid with *asawa* or spouse/wife) or a maid/wife. This definition of wife is not confined to cross-cultural marriages. In her chapter, Rogelia Pe-Pua poignantly reveals that those Filipino women who are domestic helpers feel that they are maids three times over because when they finally reunite with their Filipino husbands and children (Spain and Italy permit family reunions), they are still expected to perform their jobs as maids to their employers, while being at the beck and call of husbands and children. This expectation occurs despite the fact that the Filipino woman is often the primary breadwinner. The woman's job as a domestic helper is not separated from her role as wife and mother. And the migration experience is largely responsible for keeping her locked in this domestic niche. While the demand for domestic work gives her the opportunity to work overseas, cultural factors as well as the attitudes of the host country's society (enforced by, or resulting from, extremely narrow visa policies) do not allow her to break away from it. Thus, once she is a domestic helper, despite her attempts to escape from this type of work (through marriage for example), perceptions of "woman as domestic worker" continue to inform her relations as wife and mother. A similar trapped situation can arise for migrant sex workers wanting to escape this type of work by getting married, and yet by the nature of the men who choose to marry them, they often have to continue working in this sector (Mix and Piper, chapter 3).

It is this problematic blurring of the "Asian woman" as migrant worker and the "Asian migrant woman" as wife that is the main concern of this book. Using migration as the site where both intersect, we hope to contribute to the scholarship on gender, globalization, and migration by exploring how Asian women negotiate between their roles as workers, wives, mothers, and citizens. To us, migration is by and large a continuing process where women negotiate several roles or swap the priority of roles (albeit set within different degrees of constraints). While the process does begin when the woman decides to explore migration (and yes, we see women as agents in this process), it is more difficult to assign a moment when the process ends. Thus, "mail-order brides" become wives, mothers, workers, and citizens. Women overseas workers become wives, mothers, and citizens. There is also the case where women migrate to extend their role as mothers; Maria Chee discusses Taiwanese women who go to California to accompany their children who are studying there (see Chee, chapter 7). And then there are women who use migration to escape or postpone marriage (Willis and Yeoh, chapter 5).

In focusing on international migration, marriage, and work, we also look at *both* skilled and unskilled women workers. In doing so, we point to an emerging heterogeneity of gendered migration and breadth of class positions—a development that, according to Kofman (1999), has not been subject to sufficient analysis. The migration experience of highly educated or professional Asian women is explored in three of our chapters (Lee and Piper, Willis and Yeoh, and, to some extent, Chee). The highly skilled migrant woman has been largely neglected in the literature on women and migration. In the one truly gendered chapter of this book, Katie Willis and Brenda Yeoh disclose how male and female professional Singaporean expatriates in Shanghai (and it is interesting that unskilled or semiskilled workers are called "overseas workers" or migrant labor while professional migrants are called "expatriates") prioritize marriage in their professional migration plans. Among those posted overseas (here: China), Singaporean men may marry local women while Singaporean professional women are less likely to do so (as women tend to marry socially up). While Singaporean men consider staying abroad after marriage, most women single expatriates will go back to Singapore at a certain age in order to make marriage to a Singaporean national more likely. The expatriate experience is, thus, a temporary sojourn until women are ready to become wives and mothers. At the same time, some might use migration to escape the social pressure to get married altogether (Willis and Yeoh, chapter 5).

In their "think piece," Michelle Lee and Nicola Piper explore the career implications for highly educated women from a number of Asian countries who have met Malaysian men overseas as students and move with their husbands to Malaysia. Often these women seek paid employment (which is not always commensurate with their original career pattern) in their new country while some become transformed into full-time wives and mothers. The authors explore the notion of "transnational life-course perspective" (also touched upon by Willis and Yeoh, chapter 5) in more detail. Maria W. L. Chee's study on transnationally split families (more on transnationalism below) presents a fascinating chapter where Taiwanese women who were professionals in Taiwan migrate to California and give up their professions so their children can have a good education— the key to a high social status in Taiwan. Separated from their husbands who remain in Taiwan and remit money to California, these former professional women become migrants to stress their role as mothers and thus may be labeled transnational wives but not transnational mothers (a phenomenon hitherto still unexplored in the scholarship on gender and migration) because they sacrifice their wifely role (since they are separated from husbands) until their children finish their education and they can reunite with husbands in Taiwan.

WOMEN'S AGENCY, WOMEN'S STRATEGIES

Our approach is also to see these women as exercising agency, albeit more or less constrained; women decide to marry foreigners, women see marriage as a way out of domestic work or sex work (even if not always, or completely, successfully), women choose to work overseas to support the family back home or for their own sake, women opt to become citizens of the new country of residence. The analysis of Asian women's experiences as migrant workers or wives in international or transnational marriages is, thus, not simply a description of suffering. There are two axes of analysis involved: one is of women as "victims" of sociolegal and economic processes and the other is the potential for women as "subjects" or "agents," that is, as a social force capable of acting in their own interest. This notion—of the woman as agent and as potential contributor not only to the economy but also to the social and cultural life of the host country—has not been explored sufficiently enough by social scientists, and this volume therefore contributes to filling another nascent vacuum in this area.

While women are discussed in this volume as agents, and in many instances they use migration to expand their opportunities, it cannot be denied that their active decision to migrate can subject them to different types of victimization. As migrants for marriage they could be asked to relinquish control of the purse strings to husbands or in-laws, or they could be victims of a husband's "slave mentality" where wives are expected to be their personal maids (see Roces 1998; McKay, chapter 2). Migrants could also be subject to racial discrimination (see Roces, chapter 4, and Nakamatsu, chapter 9). Although the overall message in the chapters is that the women under discussion should not be viewed as mere victims and that they are agents in certain respects, this has to be qualified by contextualizing their specific experiences. This is, for instance, so in the case of the chapter discussing Thai women in Germany. Here, the decision to escape from social or economic victimization in Thailand is to go abroad, but unfortunately this can only happen in very limited types of jobs, with sex work being the most readily available option for many. Migrant sex workers who are foreign, and often with insecure residential statuses, are particularly pressurized to accept marriages to local men organized by others.

Long (1992) well summarizes the various levels and extents of agency: "The notion of agency attributes to the individual actor the capacity to process social experience and to devise ways of coping with life, even under the most extreme forms of coercion. Within the limits of information, uncertainty and other constraints that exist, social actors are 'knowledgeable' and 'capable'" (quoted in Moser and Clark 2001, 4). Following Long, we need to contextualize women migrants' experience to show to what extent they are victims and agents. Related to this is the observation by Moser and Clark (2001) that there is no universal interpretation of agency across cultures. Differences in determining agency and identity are linked to the importance of place and location in the constitution of multiple realities. Stereotypical essentializing of women as victims on the assumption of universal, simplistic definitions is what the contributions to this book attempt to avoid.

Instead we problematize these distinctions, highlighting the many instances where "victim" and "agency" are blurred. From the perspective of the women themselves, those who have become breadwinners are proud that their remittances have helped the financial status of their families in the homeland. In this very fundamental sense they cannot be labeled victims (see Roces, chapter 4). On the other hand, there is no doubt that in some cases the exercise of agency has resulted in further victimization. The story of former-prostitute-turned-migrant-for-marriage Ruthie Paredes (pseudonym) epitomized this blurring. Although international marriage to an Australian freed her from a life of prostitution in the Philippines, she became a victim of domestic violence and was hospitalized because she was six months pregnant and badly beaten. At this point, with assistance from the social services and a Filipina welfare worker, she left her husband to live on her own with a little help from the Housing Commission. She refused to take out a restraining order against him, convinced that he still loved her ("I'm his dreaming girl," she insisted). A few months after she gave birth to their daughter, her husband expressed a wish to reunite. When asked what she would do she replied: "Kakapit nalang ako sa patalim" (I will just hold on to the blade). The woman's choice to grasp the blade is an act of courage and agency. The fact that the blade cuts her proves that her agency does not necessarily mean an escape from victimization. Her motives are to gain a husband and fulfill Filipino womanhood (since in the Philippines women are defined as wife and mother), a poignant example of the gendered valence of symbolic capital (Roces 1998).

Another way in which migrant women are often portrayed as victims is the reference to them as "trailing wives," giving up their professional advancement to follow their husbands. In the chapter by Lee and Piper, the notion of "transnational life-course perspective" is used to show that in fact women pass through several stages or phases during their lives. While they may be independent migrants in one phase, they can be "trailing wives" in the next.

Another area in which the different levels of constraint and choice become clear is the "institution of marriage." Western radical feminists have critiqued the institution of marriage as one that discriminates against women legally and socioeconomically (Pateman 1988; Delphi and Leonard 1992). As there are typically stronger economic and social constraints on women than men, women often find themselves pressurized into marriage. Thus, as Walby (1990) argues, women's domesticity is often a result of gender inequalities in waged work. In other words, that marriage binds many women into unequal relationships with men is not intrinsic to the personal relations *per se,* but is linked to wider socioeconomic structures, sanctioned by the power of the state. While women are not usually wholly dependent on men, their work is generally lower paid and less secure than men's work, and many women work part time. Hence, women are likely to be at least partly financially dependent for most of their married lives (Jackson 1993). Because women are marginalized in the labor market, entering into marriage may offer them a better chance of economic security than remaining single.

These types of critiques, however, largely derive from monoethnic marriages and often from the pen of well-educated, Western, middle-class feminists. The picture of the disadvantaged, exploited wife might look rather different in the context of certain international marriages. Foreign wives can benefit from international marriages in a way in which same-nationality wives do not. This is to a large extent related to the socioeconomic situation in these women's countries of origin, which is often at the root of the decision to migrate abroad. It is hardly ever outright poverty that makes these women opt for labor and/or marriage migration, but more often deadlock work experience or the stigma of being separated or divorced from a previous husband. There are, therefore, additional elements that need to be considered when discussing marital relationships in an international context, particularly between spouses from countries at different socioeconomic developmental levels. Although it is often said that women from lower-income countries marry men from higher-income countries purely or mainly for economic reasons, there are also plenty of women who marry for noneconomic reasons, such as out of a sense of adventure, the desire to escape narrow family relations, because of a failed relationship back home, and purely love (see also Nakamatsu, chapter 9, and McKay, chapter 2).

How have women migrants expressed their agency? One way is through an improved economic positioning. Those who originally migrated as contract workers, be they in skilled or unskilled labor, have become breadwinners. Rogelia Pe-Pua's study of Filipino women domestic helpers in Spain and Italy show them becoming the main earners of not just their nuclear family but their extended families (which remain in the homeland). Although the more liberal laws of Spain and Italy allow domestic helpers to reunite with their families, it is difficult for husbands to find work, and thus, women become *the* breadwinners, eventually challenging cultural definitions of masculinity (which define men as breadwinners). This has dramatic implications for the marriage if the husband fails to adjust to his new status as "house-band" (Pe-Pua, chapter 8). Pe-Pua has also unraveled the migrant woman as instigator of extramarital affairs—lonely women who, when separated from their husbands, develop liaisons with other Filipino men in Europe (Pe-Pua, chapter 8). This is an interesting new variation from the usual stories and studies of men left behind in the Philippines who keep mistresses (who sometimes act as surrogate mother to the children) and sustain them with remittances sent by the wife.

Another form of expressing agency is by using international marriage as a conscious strategy to allow women to move away from particular forms of work—sex work and domestic work in particular. Pat Mix and Nicola Piper discuss how international marriage has been a strategy deployed by Thai sex workers in Germany to escape from this type of work. This, however, becomes more complicated as they tend to find themselves stuck in the quagmire of sex work–marriage–sex work, because the German men they marry often pressure them to continue sex work or else are unable to support them financially. Because with minimum knowledge of the German language these women (who have low levels of education in Thailand to begin with) have few employment options, marriage to a German national/citizen becomes their primary strategy even though they often have to get involved with several men until they find the "right" one who will finally "liberate" them from sex work.

Deirdre McKay on the other hand focuses on how Filipino women who have experienced de-skilling in Canada use marriage to a Canadian national as a means of moving out of domestic work. Most of these women have professional degrees from the Philippines—qualifications that are not recognized in Canada, where they find few opportunities in the broader workforce. Unfortunately for them, the Canadian men who want to marry them find them desirable because they are perceived to be good housekeepers, so marriage becomes both a salvation (from contract domestic work) and a form of entrapment because they are expected to be "domesticated" (see McKay, chapter 2).

In her chapter on Asian women who marry Japanese men through the introduction agencies, Tomoko Nakamatsu argues that these women were proactive in the decision making that ultimately culminated in marriage and migration. Furthermore, once married, wives were able to negotiate gender roles in the household, often able to eventually control the household finances. Though they were not pressured to find a job, some of these women were able to find work (although the work was unable to provide occupational upward mobility). Interestingly, these women become well placed to work in the very introduction agencies that facilitated their marriage and migration in the first place. This then problematizes their own subject position: "Are these women participating in the 'commodification' of other women who were lured into the marriage-migration market? Or are they helping these new migrants settle in Japanese society? Or does the job in an introduction agency merely highlight their ambivalence—they are both clients and marriage agents at the same time. In any case, the women's work at a marriage agency could be interpreted as part of their attempt to find a worthwhile career in Japan" (Nakamatsu, chapter 9, 194).

Women can also exercise agency as a group. Mina Roces's study of Filipino women migrants for marriage in the remote town of Mount Isa in North

Queensland, Australia, concludes that they coped with life in an isolated town and contributed to Mount Isa society through the nexus of an almost exclusively female world. Their engagement with the new environment is explicitly gendered: work and socials are often "women-only" affairs where husbands are marginalized or excluded. While some socials are reserved for husbands and family, women look forward to these women-only activities. Women get jobs together as a group, and their social life centers on female bonding from gambling, singing *karaoke* at the Irish Club, and rehearsing dance numbers for festivals and socials to regular lunch and afternoon *merienda* gatherings. It is the network of Filipino women, a "sisterhood" that facilitates the transition from bride to woman, from wife to worker, and from migrant to new Australian (see Roces, chapter 4). Since the sisterhood networks for job opportunities for its exclusive group and provides peer relationships with fellow women, it is possible that some sort of feminist consciousness could develop in the future.

TRANSNATIONALISM AND MULTIPLE MIGRATIONS

Since we have taken the perspective that migration is a continuing "process," we also take the view that there can be multiple migrations and/or transnational dimensions to these migrations. Michelle Lee and Nicola Piper write an intriguing chapter about both multiple migration and the transnational life cycle. Using a small number of preliminary case studies of men and women who meet away from their home countries, Lee and Piper show that migration is indeed a complex and multiple process with no definite end. In the specific context of highly educated women who met their husbands when both were students overseas, but who later chose to reside in Malaysia (country of origin of the men), the chapter shows that migration is not necessarily an end in the minds of these professional couples. Though the couples now live in Malaysia and currently have children, some of them envision another migration at some point in the future. The various migrations of these highly educated women are thus linked to the specific stage in their life courses. This means that a subsequent migration could accompany the next life course.

Lee and Piper extend the concept of "transnationalism" to that of the "transnational life cycle" (as opposed to the "trailing wife syndrome," which depicts these women as passive). Transnationalism is usually understood as involving migrants who "build ties that transcend geographical distance and political boundaries, and develop multiple relationships that may be familial, economic, social, cultural, religious, and political" (Chee, chapter 7, 138–39). The "transnational life cycle" implodes the processes of multiple migrations and women's life cycles (transstagional or transgressing life stages, Lee and

Piper, chapter 6). Stage 1 occurred when women met prospective husbands in a country that was not either of the couple's country of origin. In stage 2 the women migrated to Malaysia, sometimes compromising their own career advancement. Any future stage 3 migration may be influenced also by concerns for the children's well-being (Lee and Piper, chapter 6).

The transnational mother, on the other hand, is typified by the overseas contract worker or migrant (usually a domestic helper) who leaves her children behind (Hondagneu-Sotelo and Avila 1997; Alicea 1997; Parreñas 2001a, 2001b). The transnational mother in this sense epitomizes the contradiction of many women negotiating modernities (see Roces and Edwards 2000, chapter 1; Roces 2000). She could also be described as epitomizing the globalization of certain types of work, such as domestic service (Parreñas 2001a). Though extending the idea of women working outside the home to its maximum potential by working overseas, the migrant woman is still often locked into traditionally defined feminized tasks of domestic work and looking after children. This is well known as far as Filipinas are concerned, but there are other nationalities moving into these types of work in ever-increasing numbers as well (e.g., Indonesians, Sri Lankan, Vietnamese, Cambodians).

Hondagneu-Sotelo and Avila hesitate to claim that Latina transnational mothers forfeit their own motherhood, arguing that these mothers are "building alternative constructions of motherhood" (1997, 549) that contradict U.S., white middle-class models of motherhood. The phrase "I'm here but I'm there" encapsulates these women's unusual perceptions of motherhood. These transnational mothers (who interestingly criticize their employers for neglectful parenting), therefore, "advocate more elastic definitions of motherhood, including forms that may include long spatial and temporal separations of mother and children" (Hondagneu-Sotelo and Avila 1997, 566). Support networks provided by female members of the extended family in the country of origin make such transnational arrangements possible. And yet, this new form of motherhood comes at great emotional costs, prompting Parreñas to label the experiences as "the pain of mothering from a distance" and "the pain of growing up in transnational families" (Parreñas 2001b, 370, 375).

These arguments about transnational motherhood could be transposed to Maria Chee's Taiwanese women involved in transnationally split families who are of different class backgrounds than the transnational mothers discussed by Hondagneu-Sotelo and Avila (1997) and Parreñas (2001a, 2001b). Prioritizing "motherhood" over "wife," these Taiwanese women care for their children in California, relying on their husband's remittances from Taiwan for financial support. Much like the Latina transnational mothers, Taiwanese transnational wives redefine the parameters of "wife." These redefinitions of motherhood and wife, however, usually come at great costs: Transnational mothers worry about children's welfare, and even if reunited they can encounter great difficulty in reinstating their authority as a parent (Pe-Pua, chapter 8). Transnational wives, moreover, can be particularly vulnerable to the breakdown of their marriage (Chee, chapter 7).

CITIZENSHIP: THE "END" OF MIGRATION?

The importance of the role of states and immigration/citizenship policies on women's choices cannot be underestimated. Being a noncitizen, either married to a citizen or not, puts any migrant in a vulnerable relation to the state. The receiving state treats immigration matters as a system of laws, regulations, and practices by which it is decided who can live within a territory under what kind of conditions, as documented or undocumented (Anderson 2000). Immigration regulations are gendered in that they often do not accord female immigrants with their own legal status but assume them to be dependents of men (Espiritu 1997; Bhaba, Klug, and Shutter 1985). But immigration legislature is not just gendered, it is also based upon certain notions of the family, especially within the institutional setting of marriage. Marriage and migration are thus linked to citizenship and to relations of power created and sustained by the law. As well illustrated by Willis and Yeoh (chapter 5), concepts in which the law expresses the normative principles of marriage as an institution are part of a common language that reflects and shapes a society's collective values and perceptions (Vogel 1994, 78).

Migration theorists have pointed to the temporary nature of today's migration flows (see e.g., Castles and Miller 1993), with some going as far as claiming that citizenship rights are irrelevant and labor rights take precedence (Harris 1995). But much of women migrants' experience does not comply with such claims. Through marriage—for whichever reason—they do become potentially long-term settlers and citizenship does matter. Unfortunately, procedures pertaining to immigration and residence permits have become more rigid all over the world, even in more traditional immigration countries such as the United States (Parreñas 2001a; Piper 1998). Migration to receiving countries in East and Southeast Asia does not usually lead to permanent settlement, because of receiving governments' harsh policies that do not allow settlement of what is commonly defined as "unskilled" labor. Sending countries in this region (notably the Philippines)—being dependent on remittances—do not want to lose their nationals permanently, while receiving governments strongly object to granting immigrants permanent residency. In the context of rigid immigration and visa policies, marriage to a local man may constitute an important strategy for women to achieve economic and legal security (see McKay and Mix and

Piper, chapters 2 and 3). Regardless of whether a migrant is internationally or transnationally married, another issue that demonstrates the importance of citizenship is the absence of family reunification policies in many countries following the European model (which is also restrictive in that it does not permit wider family entry but is limited to nuclear families). In Singapore, for instance, citizenship via marriage to a local man is not possible as such marriages are prohibited. According to Castles (2000), the notion of turning immigrants into citizens seems thus unthinkable in much of Asia. What happens, however, is that through marriage (which is apart from a few exceptions usually possible), migrant women aim at achieving secure residential permits before embarking on the still bumpy road to gain full citizenship rights. At the same time, migrants who have enjoyed more liberal countries as far as the legal and social accommodation of newcomers is concerned, might intend to remigrate on the basis of the present country of residence being too rigid (see Lee and Piper, chapter 6). Precisely because of these barriers, the few scholars who explore this topic perceive these women as receiving only "partial citizenship" (Stasiulis and Bakan 1997; Parreñas 2001c).

Does the continuing process of migration end with securing residency and citizenship? Because we are arguing that migration is a process, women's negotiations with that process are continuous. This points to the distinction made by Piper (1998) between formal and substantive citizenship rights, which is of particular relevance to women in general, ethnic minorities, and migrants. "Formal" thereby refers to legal matters (such as residential, civil, political, and labor rights), with "substantive" covering social aspects (such as discrimination). Feminists have highlighted in general women's history as dependents and subordinates constituting "second-class citizens" as opposed to male citizens (Vogel 1994; Lister 1998; Pateman 1988). For migrant women, the picture becomes more complicated. Often without formal citizenship (at least initially), they find themselves in a much more precarious situation. Marriage does not pose an immediate remedy: In most countries, international couples have to be married for a certain number of years until the foreign spouse gains full residential rights independent from the local marriage partner. In many countries, such as Germany, the required length of marriage used to be five years. If problems such as domestic violence occur prior to the end of this period and the foreign woman seeks divorce, she risks deportation to her country of origin. Foreign women as wives, thus, lack some basic attributes of autonomous legal agency, but this can be improved when they gain proper formal citizenship rights. Changes in receiving countries' regulations in this regard often occur via NGO advocacy work and/or self-organization of the migrant women. According to Mix, nongovernment organization (NGO) activities in Germany, for instance, have succeeded in making the German government lower the required length of marriage from five to three years to allow foreign wives to remain in Germany after relatively early divorce. This, however, still leaves the issue of substantive citizenship, and there is plenty of evidence for discrimination and stigmatization of immigrants in general and Asian women specifically.

In cases like Japan, for instance, women migrants are prohibited from ever becoming part of the Japanese household (*koseki*) unless they become naturalized citizens, a lengthy and difficult process that hardly ever happens (Nakamatsu, chapter 9). Even with secure residential permits, the language barriers and lack of accreditation often ensure that migrant women remain ossified in specific niches such as domestic work (Canada, Spain, and Italy; McKay, chapter 2, and Pe-Pua, chapter 8) or sex work (Germany; Mix and Piper, chapter 3). On the other hand, citizenship enfranchises these women, allowing them to participate in the electoral system and therefore receive attention by vote-seeking politicians (see Roces, chapter 4).

So, although literature on migration claims that national citizenship has lost its importance in the present era of globalization (Soysal 1994; Sassen 1996), evidence from much of women's migratory experience shows that this is not correct (e.g., Parreñas 2001a). Soysal's theory of postnational citizenship is derived from the European Union context and based on the acquisition of economic and social rights linked to long-term residence as well as the emergence of an international regime of rights for migrants. The importance of world-level pressures in securing rights for immigrants appears overemphasized in these works, as remarked upon by Castles and Davidson (2000). In practice, in fact, this international regime of rights is weak and nonexistent outside of Europe (where migrants' rights are also limited) (Ghai 1999).

What does become clear in many of the chapters in this volume is the centrality of citizenship. Apart from acting as mothers, wives, and workers, these women also act as citizens—although not yet acknowledged in much of the public discourse about them. Despite language and cultural differences posing a major obstacle toward integration as new citizens (see Mix and Piper, chapter 3, and Pe-Pua, chapter 4), women's participation in civic work can in fact be a way of performing citizenship (Roces, chapter 4). As the chapters in this book show, citizenship potentially increases women's agency and broadens their choices. However, many migrant-receiving countries do not grant foreign women citizenship in their own right, but mediate their rights through their status of wife. Moreover, the acquisition of citizenship itself does not necessarily mean that these women would cease to be "other," because citizenship does not magically eliminate discrimination (see Roces, chapter 4, and Nakamatsu, chapter 9).

By including the issue of citizenship in the discussion revolving around work-related migration and marriage (or marital relationships), this book shows the diversification of Asian women's experiences as migrants in various regions of the world. Since we aim to present a multidimensional view of women migrants who experience multiple or divergent modernities (to borrow from Maila Stivens), our focus highlights the imbrication of woman as wife, worker, mother, and citizen in the context of migration.

NOTE

1. They use the term *intermarriage*.

REFERENCES

Adkins, L. *Gendered Work—Sexuality Family and the Labor Market*. Buckingham: Open University Press, 1995.

Alicea, M. "A Chambered Nautilus: The Contradictory Nature of Puerto Rican Women's Role in the Social Construction of a Transnational Community." *Gender and Society* vol. 11, no. 5 (October 1997): 597–626.

Anderson, B. *Doing the Dirty Work? The Global Politics of Domestic Labor*. London: Zed Books, 2000.

Ball, R. "The Role of the State in Globalisation of Labor Markets: The Case of the Philippines." *Environment and Planning A*, no. 29 (1997): 1603–62.

Bhabha, J., F. Klug, and S. Shutter. *Worlds Apart: Women under Immigration and Nationality Law*. London: Pluto Press, 1985.

Bulbeck, C. *Re-Orienting Western Feminisms—Women's Diversity in a Postcolonial World*. Cambridge: Cambridge University Press, 1998.

Cahill, D. *Intermarriages in International Contexts. A Study of Filipina Women Married to Australian, Japanese and Swiss Men*. Quezon City: Scalabrini Migration Center, 1990.

Castles, S. "Migration as a Factor in Social Transformation in East Asia." Unpublished paper. CAPSTRANS: Wollongong, 2000.

Castles, S., and A. Davidson. *Citizenship and Migration—Globalization and the politics of belonging*. Basingstoke: Macmillan, 2000.

Castles, S., and M. Miller. *The Age of Migration*. Basingstoke: Macmillan, 1993.

Chai, A. Y., and D. Gabaccia (Eds.). *Picture Brides—Feminist Analysis of Life Histories of Hawaii's Early Immigrant Women from Japan, Okinawa and Korea*. Westport, Conn.: Praeger, 1992.

Chuah, F., T. D. Chuah, C. L. Reid-Smith, and A. Rice. "Does Australia Have a Filipina Bride Problem?" *Australian Journal of Social Issues* vol. 22, no. 4 (1987): 573–83.

Cohen, R. "'Mom is a Stranger': The Negative Impact of Immigration Policies on the Family Life of Filipina Domestic Workers," *Canadian Ethnic Studies Journal* vol. 32, no. 13 (2000): 76–88.

———. "At Home But Not at Home: Filipina Narratives of Ambivalent Returns." *Cultural Anthropology* vol. 14, no. 2 (May 1999): 203–28.

Constable, N. *Maid to Order in Hongkong: Stories of Filipina Workers.* Ithaca: Cornell University Press, 1997.

Cooke, F. M. *Australian-Filipino Marriages in the 1980s: The Myth and the Reality.* Brisbane: Griffith University School of Modern Asian Studies, Center for the Study of Australian-Asian Relations, Research Paper 37, 1986.

Cunneen, C., and J. Stubbs. *Gender, 'Race' and International Relations. Violence Against Filipino Women in Australia.* Sydney: Institute of Criminology Monograph Series No. 9, 1997.

Delphy, C., and D. Leonard. *Familiar Exploitation—A New Analysis of Marriage in Contemporary Western Societies.* Cambridge: Polity Press, 1992.

Espiritu, Y. L. *Asian American Women and Men—Labor, Laws, and Love.* London: Sage, 1997.

Ghai, Y. "Rights, Social Justice, and Globalization in East Asia." Pp. 241–63 in *The East Asian Challenge for Human Rights,* edited by J. Bauer and D. Bell. Cambridge: Cambridge University Press, 1999.

Harris, N. *The New Untouchables.* London: Penguin, 1995.

Harzig, C. "Women Migrants as Global and Local Agents: New Research Strategies on Gender and Migration." Pp. 15–28 in *Women, Gender and Labor Migration—Historical and Global Perspectives,* edited by P. Sharpe. London: Routledge, 2001.

Hilsdon, A. M. "The Contemplacion Fiasco: The Hanging of a Filipino Domestic Worker in Singapore." Pp. 172–92 in *Human Rights and Gender Politics: Asia-Pacific Perspectives,* edited by A. M. Hilsdon, Martha Macintyre, Vera Mackie, and Maila Stivens. London: Routledge, 2000.

Holt, E. M. "Writing Filipina-Australian Brides: The Discourse on Filipina Brides." *Philippine Sociological Review* vol. 44, nos. 1–4 (1996): 58–78.

Hondagneu-Sotelo, P., and E. Avila. "I'm Here, But I'm There: The Meaning of Latina Transnational Motherhood." *Gender and Society* vol. 11, no. 5 (1997): 548–71.

Jackson, S. "Women and the Family." Pp. 177–200 in *Introducing Women's Studies: Feminist Theory and Practice,* edited by Diane Richardson and Victoria Robinson. Basingstoke: Macmillan, 1993.

Kim, B-L. C. "Asian Wives of U.S. Servicemen: Women in Shadows." *Amerasia* vol. 4 (1977): 91–115.

Kofman, E. "Female 'Birds of Passage' a Decade Later: Gender and Immigration in the European Union." *International Migration Review* vol. 33, no. 2 (1999): 269–99.

Lim, L. L. (Ed). *The Sex Sector—The Economic and Social Bases of Prostitution in Southeast Asia.* Geneva: International Labor Office, 1998.

Lister, R. *Citizenship—Feminist Perspectives.* Basingstoke: Macmillan, 1998.

Makabe, T. *Picture Brides—Japanese Women in Canada.* Ontario: Multicultural History Society of Ontario, 1995.

May, R. J. "The Domestic in Foreign Policy: The Flor Contemplacion Case and Philippine-Singapore Relations." *Pilipinas,* no. 29 (1997): 63–76.

Moser, C., and F. Clark (Eds.). *Victims, Perpetrators or Actors? Gender, Armed Conflict and Political Violence.* London: Zed Books, 2001.

Nakano Glenn, E. *Issei, Nisei, War Bride—Three Generations of Japanese American Women in Domestic Service.* Philadelphia: Temple University Press, 1986.

OECD. *Trends in International Migration.* Paris: OECD, 1998.

Parreñas, R. S. *Servants of Globalization—Women, Migration and Domestic Work.* Stanford, Calif.: Stanford University Press, 2001a.

———. "Mothering from a Distance: Emotions, Gender, and Inter-Generational Relations in Filipino Transnational Families." *Feminist Studies* vol. 27, no. 2 (2001b): 361–90.

———. "Transgressing the Nation-State: The Partial Citizenship and 'Imagined Global Community' of Migrant Filipina Domestic Workers." *Signs* vol. 26, no. 4 (Spring 2001c): 1129–54.

Pateman, C. *The Sexual Contract.* Cambridge: Polity Press, 1988.

Pendlebury, J. *Filipino Brides in Remote Areas.* Darwin NT: North Australia Development Unit, Department of Social Security, NADU Occasional Paper, no. 5, 1990.

Penny, J., and S. E. Khoo. *Intermarriage—A Study of Migration and Integration.* Canberra: Australian Government Publishing Service, 1996.

Piper, N. "Labor Migration, Trafficking and International Marriage: Female Cross-Border Movements into Japan." *Asian Journal of Women's Studies* vol. 5, no. 2 (1999): 69–99.

———. *Racism, Nationalism and Citizenship.* Avebury: Ashgate, 1998.

Piper N., and R. Ball. "Globalization of Asian Migrant Labor: The Philippine-Japan Connection." *Journal of Contemporary Asia* vol. 31, no. 4 (2001): 533–54.

Raghuram, P. "Gendering Skilled Migratory Streams: Implications for Conceptualizations of Migration." *APMJ* vol. 9, no. 4 (2000): 429–57.

Richardson, D., and V. Robinson (Eds.). *Introducing Women's Studies: Feminist Theory and Practice.* Basingstoke: Macmillan, 1993.

Robinson, Kathryn. "Of Mail-Order Brides and 'Boys' Own' Tales: Representations of Asian-Australian Marriages." *Feminist Review,* no. 52 (1996): 53–68.

Roces, M. "Negotiating Modernities: Filipino Women 1970–2000." Pp. 112–38 in *Women in Asia: Tradition, Modernity and Globalisation,* edited by Louise Edwards and Mina Roces. Ann Arbor: University of Michigan Press, 2000.

———. "*Kapit sa Patalim* (Hold on to the Blade): Victim and Agency in the Oral Narratives of Filipino Women Married to Australian Men in Central Queensland." *Lila. Asia Pacific Women's Studies Journal* vol. 7 (1998): 1–19.

———. "Filipino Brides in Central Queensland: Gender, Migration and Support Services." Pp. 145–52 in *Futures for Central Queensland,* edited by Denis Cryle, Graham Griffin, and Dani Stehlik. Rockhampton: Rural Social and Economic Research Center, Central Queensland University, 1996.

Roces, M., and L. Edwards. "Introduction: Contesting Gender Narratives." Pp. 1–15 in *Women in Asia: Tradition, Modernity and Globalisation,* edited by Louise Edwards and Mina Roces. Ann Arbor: University of Michigan Press, 2000.

Saroca, N. "Filipino Women, Sexual Politics, and the Gendered Discourse of the Mail-Order Bride." *JIGS (Journal of Interdisciplinary Gender Studies)* vol. 2, no. 2 (1997): 89–103.

Sassen, S. *Losing Control?* New York: Columbia University Press, 1996.

Sharpe, P. (Ed.). *Women, Gender and Labor Migration—Historical and Global Perspectives.* London: Routledge, 2001.

Sinke, S. M. "Migration for Labor, Migration for Love: Marriage and Family Formation across Borders." *Magazine of History*, Organizations of American Historians (Fall 1999): 17–21.

———. "The International Marriage Market." Pp. 227–48 in *People in Transit*, edited by D. Hoerder and J. Nagler. Cambridge: Cambridge University Press, 1995.

Soysal, Y. *Limits of Citizenship—Migrants and Post-national Membership in Europe*. London: University of Chicago Press, 1994.

Stasiulis, D., and Abigail B. Bakan. "Negotiating Citizenship: The Case of Foreign Domestic Workers in Canada." *Feminist Review*, no. 57 (Autumn 1997): 112–39.

Tadiar, Neferti Xina M. "Domestic Bodies of the Philippines." *Sojourn* vol. 12, no. 2 (1997): 153–91.

Torrevillas, D. N. "Violence against Filipina OCWs." Pp. 46–66 in *Filipino Women Migrant Workers: At the Crossroads and beyond Beijing*, edited by Ruby P. Beltran and Gloria F. Rodriguez. Quezon City: Giraffe Books, 1996.

Vogel, S. "Marriage and the Boundaries of Citizenship." Pp. 115–37 in *The Condition of Citizenship*, edited by B. van Steenbergen. London: Sage, 1994.

Walby, S. *Theorizing Patriarchy*. Oxford: Blackwell, 1990.

Wickramasekara, P. "Migrant Worker Issues in the ASEAN: Some Reflections." Unpublished Paper. Geneva: ILO, 2000.

Wijers, M., and L. Lap-Chew. *Trafficking in Women, Forced Labor and Slavery-like Practices in Marriage, Domestic Labor and Prostitution*. Utrecht: STV (Foundation Against Trafficking in Women), 1997.

Yeoh, B. S. A., E. Graham, and P. J. Boyle (Eds.). "Special Issue—Migrations and Family Relations in the Asia Pacific Region." *Asian and Pacific Migration Journal* vol. 11, no. 1 (2002).

Yeoh, B. S. A., and L. M. Khoo. "Home, Work and Community: Skilled International Migration and Expatriate Women in Singapore." *International Migration* vol. 36, no. 2 (1998): 159–84.

2

Filipinas in Canada—De-skilling as a Push toward Marriage

Deirdre McKay

FROM MIGRANT WORKER TO WIFE

Women migrate for many reasons, including offers of permanent jobs or labor contracts, anticipated improvements in their conditions of self-employment and trade, offers of marriage, and as participants in broader, household moves. This chapter complicates the distinctions between these different forms of migration in an exploration of the ways in which state policies, transnational economies, and migrant cultures play out in individual lives. Individual experiences show how the de-skilling experienced by migrant women as workers may push them toward international marriages. This argument is developed through an ethnographic analysis of the life stories of Filipina contract migrants in Canada.

This quote, taken from transcripts of an interview in October 1999 with Luz, a Filipina migrant in her forties, is indicative of the experiential connections between de-skilling and marriage.

> Because I don't want to be just a nanny anymore, I went for evaluation and my degree wasn't even recognized. And I became realistic about it. Even though we have a good education, it doesn't matter to them. Because we're Filipino we are only a domestic helper. . . . So then I got married . . . to my employer.

Like Luz, many female immigrants from the Philippines to Canada initially arrive as migrants under the Live-in-Caregiver-Program (LCP). The LCP was introduced by the Canadian government in 1992 as a response to calls for state-subsidized childcare. LCP migrants provide in-home care for children, elderly, and disabled people, thus freeing Canadian women to participate in the formal labor market.[1] By placing entrants in contract jobs as domestic workers, this program creates a specific immigration category.

Selection for the LCP is based on professional training (nursing, midwifery, or teaching) or equivalent experience. Despite this, the program places women in jobs within the domestic sphere of the home, a type of employment that does not count as "proper" labor market experience in Canada. When domestic workers are assessed for employment in other fields, LCP work is considered to be "just babysitting." Because their only Canadian references are from domestic positions, most of these women find few opportunities to use the skills and training they bring with them to Canada in the broader workforce. Though their Philippine qualifications and experience have been recognized as appropriate for entry-level jobs had they arrived directly into the Canadian labor market, two or three years of "babysitting" means they need re-skilling. Because most LCP women are remitting money back to the Philippines and saving to support their families, they cannot afford to enroll for skills-training courses. Instead, they tend to remain in domestic work and other, related, service occupations. In interviews, Filipina nurses, teachers, accountants, and journalists migrating under the LCP described their long-term reidentification as "housekeeper," "nanny," or what they glossed as a unitary category: DH—domestic helper.[2]

International marriage is one option open to women trying to escape the DH identity and segregation into domestic work. In the context of their experiences of de-skilling, attitudes to international marriage are ambivalent. Marriage is understood as both a kind of salvation from contract domestic work and a form of entrapment due to a process of "domestication" expected from both their Canadian husbands and the wider cultural environment.

To connect de-skilling and marriage, I offer an analysis of life histories that places the option of international marriage at the intersection of a racial political economy created by the Canadian state and a narrative of international romance attached to overseas work by domestic placement agencies and transnational Filipino culture.

DATA AND METHODOLOGY

The population of contract migrants who arrive in Canada to take up domestic work under the LCP is fairly well characterized. However, there are no statistics publicly available on international marriages to Canadian citizens contracted specifically by women arriving under the LCP. Hence, data on women's migration experiences and international marriage were collected in cooperation with the Philippine Women Centre (PWC), a nongovernmental organization based in Vancouver, Canada. Interviews were conducted with sixty

Filipinas from across Canada, representing women who had arrived through the LCP, the independent immigration stream, and second-generation Fil-Canadians. The interviewers were members of the PWC research team, a group of Fil-Canadians and recent immigrants to Canada who volunteer and/ or work with the Center's community programs and the author. The chapter also draws on the findings of another research project conducted by the PWC on Filipino "mail-order brides" in Canada (PWC 2000).

To contextualize the primary life history data, the author interviewed representatives of nine social service agencies with Filipina clients who had migrated under the LCP. These NGO and government workers reflected on the issues faced by their Filipina clients. By drawing on their breadth of experience within the Filipino and LCP migrant communities, they were able to suggest explanations for the trends emerging within the Filipinas' life histories. Interviews with Canadian government officials who administer the LCP and materials collected during fieldwork in the Philippines and Singapore are used to augment this data.

The methodological approach here thus relies largely on qualitative data and ethnographic analysis, supported, where possible, with social statistics. A database on LCP immigrants ordered from the Canadian government and other statistics on the Filipino community in Canada are used to contextualize the ethnographic data. As far as possible, I wish to let the voices of the migrant women and NGO workers describe the situation of LCP migrants in Canada.

Given the paucity of statistical data on international marriage for LCP migrants, this chapter builds an ethnographic description of the context of such marriages, exploring both dreams of transnational romance and stories of de-skilling.[3] My goal in linking de-skilling to international marriage is to highlight the diverse ways that women may renegotiate their options within particular forms of migration, blurring the boundaries usually applied to categorize forms of migration as "family strategy," "reunification," "marriage," or "contract work." Describing international marriages here, the focus is on the factors that push women toward them, rather than the legitimacy or success of the resulting relationships. The theoretical contribution of this chapter is to demonstrate how discursive constructions of femininity and ethnicities overdetermine migrants' circumstances and blur boundaries set by official immigration categories.

WORKER, WIFE, OR SISTER? BLURRED BOUNDARIES IN MIGRATION EXPERIENCES

LCP migrants are understood by Canadian immigration authorities to be labor migrants, yet many are simultaneously following romantic or family reunification strategies. This plurality of migration strategies arises from the personal histories of these women and the broader socioeconomic context of Filipino labor migration.

Considering these women as workers, their applications to the Canadian LCP arise from within a much more globalized flow of workers. Most Filipino LCP entrants who participated in our focus groups came to Canada after several years of domestic experience in other countries. Although their experience facilitates entry into Canada through the LCP, it marks the beginning of longer periods of professional de-skilling. In this regard, Canada is becoming a "graduate school" for domestics where the goal of migration is not economic benefits but citizenship. The long-term intention of LCP applicants, supported by the program itself, is to migrate permanently and have access to the broader labor market. New arrivals under the LCP rarely mention marriage as a goal of their migration. However, once women experience the restrictive nature of the program and find that it does not provide entry to other jobs, they become disillusioned with contract labor migration as a path to permanency. Since marriage to a Canadian citizen also permits a woman to achieve permanent residency status, often in circumstances that might seem less onerous than the LCP requirements, marriage becomes identified as an option for women at that point.

As a special immigration category, the LCP brings migrants to Canada as contract workers, giving them eligibility for landed immigrant status on the completion of a period of contract work as a live-in employee in a Canadian home. In 1992, the government reworked the existing Foreign Domestic Movement program and changed the name to the LCP. The purpose of the program remained to provide in-home care for Canadian families. Caregivers enter the country not as immigrants, but with pre-immigrant status. The success of their eventual application for landed immigrant status depends on their meeting the requirements of the program: they must work for a total of twenty-four months as a live-in employee in a Canadian home. They can change employers, but they can only work for one employer at a time and the twenty-four months of live-in work must be completed within thirty-six months of arrival. The bureaucratic complications of transferring from employer to employer discourages frequent changes of employer when work conditions are not satisfactory. Most LCPers simply want to finish the program and "graduate" to living independently from an employer's home.

Compared to the other countries that host migrant workers, the wages of such work are relatively low. The compensation for this is the apparent opportunity to become a permanent resident and leave domestic work. Entrants must have a two-year postsecondary qualification in a caregiving field—nursing, midwifery, or education—or equivalent experience either through work or "study" as a domestic.[4] Very few women who do not have a college education are accepted for the program. Many applicants feel there is an implied promise that, given their training, jobs appropriate to their qualifications, i.e., outside domestic work, will be available for them after they have completed the program. This is, however, not the case. If it were, "points" would be given for their qualifications.

Because the program requires them to demonstrate either these college level qualifications in midwifery, nursing, or education or equivalent work experience, many of these women come after several years in the labor force, often in Hong Kong, Singapore, or Saudi Arabia. For women who do not have appropriate college education, it makes better economic sense to take a first contract in another country, then apply for Canada on the basis of that work experience. This strategy of doing overseas contract work in other countries first, then "transferring" to Canada is called "deploying cross-country."

Because deploying cross-country is seen as the strategy most likely to succeed by would-be LCP migrants, Hong Kong and Singapore are, for them, stopover points on their route to Canada. It is easier and cheaper to find contract work in Singapore, Hong Kong, or Saudi (the Arabian Gulf) first, and then apply for the Canadian program. Officials at the Canadian Embassy in Manila corroborated this assessment, explaining that verifiable records of employment experience from Hong Kong and Singapore would get women through the approval process much more quickly. In the experience of immigration assessors, documentation of employment and education in the Philippines was often very difficult to verify and frequently false.

As one official explained:

> People in Singapore and Hong Kong are usually working as nannies and have been working as nannies and can produce independently verifiable references to that point. We get everything . . . here and our refusal rate is very high. Everyone knows about the LCP . . . it's advertised in the newspapers [by local recruiting agencies].

Given their several years of work experience, women arriving in Canada cross-country are usually somewhat older than Filipinas migrating to work on contract in Japan, Hong Kong, or Singapore. It was predominantly this group of women that we interviewed in our research in Canada. They had applied for entry into Canada via the LCP after they had already completed a stint of contract domestic work in another country. Many had thus already left children, relationships, and households they supported behind in the Philippines several years before their application. Their choices to apply for Canada rather than return to the Philippines were made for a variety of reasons. The rationale they gave usually entailed both personal factors and economic concerns that combined to make permanent residency outside the Philippines their preferred option. Relationship breakdown and social isolation due to their status as single mothers was cited by some respondents as a reason to remain abroad. Economic dependence on the part of their family in the Philippines was also common concern for migrants already overseas—they worried that their family could no longer make ends meet without a secure foreign currency income stream. These women claimed that the insecurity of contract work in Hong Kong and Singapore and the lack of opportunity to apply for jobs outside domestic work made contract migration in Asia a dead end. From their perspective, the idea of permanent status and nondomestic work in Canada looked like an appealing way to combine remitting money with personal security and career development.

For others, their time in Hong Kong or Singapore meant that their professional skills set would no longer be current in the Filipino labor market. Though they had left jobs as nurses, teachers, bank clerks, and accountants to take contracts abroad, their jobs at home were not waiting for them. After two or three contracts as domestic workers, they had made more money, but undermined their professional qualifications. Having not practiced their professions in years, they could only look forward to similar "domestic-type," low-skilled, low-paid work at home.

Reservations about reentry on the part of migrant women are well founded. Migrants who choose to return to the Philippines have limited possibilities for productive investments that generate a return on their savings, rather than exhausting the capital they have put aside while overseas (Gibson, Law, and McKay, 2001). The personal savings accumulated by migrant women are usually not of the magnitude to support large-scale entrepreneurial activities. Rather, returned overseas workers frequently open small "sari-sari" stores, selling basic grocery items and sweets, usually on credit. Another popular option is to invest in local transport networks, putting capital into small passenger vans or motorcycles with sidecars. Neither investment offers the same possibility for generating income for the household, nor the same social status as working overseas, even as a contract domestic. Thus, for Filipina migrants, once abroad, the pressures to remain overseas and find another contract are strong.

On completing a contract in Hong Kong or Singapore, for example, and not wanting to return to the Philippines, a migrant woman can explore several options. The strategies deployed to remain abroad extend well beyond "labor market" opportunities in the narrow sense. Networks of friends in Singapore or Hong Kong might suggest one or more of the following to a migrant: finding a new contract as a maid for an expatriate family; remaining with their current employer but negotiating better terms; working "freelance" for several households; and/or applying for work in a third country. The same friendship networks trade information on opportunities to date expatriates and apply to overseas marriage agencies. Women thus often contemplate international marriage while simultaneously planning to migrate to a new host nation and attempting to renegotiate their local labor conditions.

This plurality of strategies is illustrated in the story of Perlita, a Filipina interviewed by the PWC for their Mail-Order Bride project in 1999 (the transcript appears in its entirety in PWC 2000, 27).

> Perlita started but never completed a business administration degree in the Philippines. She ended up working as a secretary for one year in Manila, before leaving for Hong Kong where she was able to secure employment as a domestic worker through her aunt. She ended up working in Hong Kong for 10 years. . . .
>
> In Hong Kong, she was encouraged by her sister, a domestic worker in Canada, to submit her name to a "friendship" office in British Columbia. She was given the name of a man, Keith. They began corresponding. . . .
>
> Perlita's application to come to Canada under the LCP was successful and she arrived in Canada. Perlita hoped she could eventually obtain Canadian citizenship.
>
> Immediately she found employment . . . [and] worked for them for 21 months, falling three months short of the mandatory 24-month live-in requirement. . . .
> The reason . . . was because Perlita was already eight months pregnant by Keith. In fact, after her first year with her employer, she had moved in with Keith. . . .
> One month after the birth of her daughter, Perlita and Keith were married. Perlita never returned to work because Keith would not let her work outside the home.

Renarrating these sections of Perlita's story exemplifies they way that an application to migrate as a contract worker may be linked to both family reunification strategies (joining a sister already in Canada) and marriage-migration strategies (following up on her correspondence with Keith). It's not clear from the interview data who Keith was, other than that he had registered with a "friendship office" in hopes of meeting Asian women who might want to come to Canada. While official Canadian statistics would simply record Perlita as another LCP arrival, her decision to migrate for contract work was undoubtedly influenced by visions of a future of possibilities suggested both by the presence of her sister in Canada and the potential of a romantic relationship with a Caucasian Canadian man.

Though Perlita's experience is not necessarily typical for a Filipina domestic worker in Hong Kong, it illustrates the fluidity between the status of worker and wife. The ease with which a migrant may shift between self-understandings as wife or worker in Canada is already anticipated by the play of possibilities offered up for the migrant's imagination in Hong Kong.

A GOOD WIFE IS A GOOD WORKER: INTERNATIONAL
MARRIAGE FOR CONTRACT DOMESTICS

Domestic workers in international marriages are a familiar phenomenon in the Philippines. In the Philippines, rising rates of international marriage are popularly attributed to increasing flows of female contract migrants. Philippine-based academics have demonstrated the tendency for overseas contract work, in particular women's domestic labor, to produce increasing rates of international marriage (Paredes-Maceda 1995).[5]

Reporting on this trend seems almost to pose it as problematic, yet there is no evidence that such matches are somehow less founded in love and desire than unions between persons of the same citizenship. While most marital relationships have an economic as well as an emotional aspect, it is the evidence of feeling between the couple, rather than an economic calculus, that is supposedly the sign of the "real" nature of an international marriage. Yet, in any cross-cultural encounter, desire has its cultural logics (Stoler 1996). The crucial point to consider in understanding international marriage is the way in which colonial histories contextualize personal desires, creating narratives of transnational romance. Filipina women form their own identities within colonial histories that privilege a particular form of Americanized modernity and imaginary of romantic love. "American" men (a category that includes Canadians and all Caucasians who are not Spanish or South Asian) are seen to be good providers, romantic lovers, and unlike Filipino men, not given to keeping mistresses. The logics that might support the other side of the attraction, the desire of Caucasian men for Asian women, are likewise a product of colonial histories. As exemplars of "Asian" femininities, Filipinas are described as "traditional" women, supposedly uncorrupted by the feminism of "the West."

The specific character of domestic work itself may be seen to contribute to this form of intercultural desire. Our interview data indicates that it is in the particular nature of domestic work and the de-skilling it implies for many migrant women that their desire for, or openness to, international marriages may, in part, be understood. De-skilling of contract domestic workers is also understandable as a type of re- or hyperfeminization. Because domestic work is seen as the exercise of a set of "naturally" feminine skills and dispositions, it has often been un- or underpaid, usually provided as a set of free services exchanged between spouses in marriage. Since a "good" wife is a good (domestic) worker, a hard-working yet feminine woman makes a "good" wife. Thus a woman taking up a job as a domestic is also displaying skills and attributes that might be considered marital. In contrast, a woman getting her ticket to operate a bulldozer, for instance, might make far more money than a maid, but the job itself would not portray her to potential suitors as "wife-and-mother-like."

The capacity of Filipina women, especially migrant domestics, to extend exemplary domestic service has been cited as one of the major motivations of their non-Filipino partners in pursuing the relationship (Paredes-Maceda 1995, 112). Moreover, gendered patterns of labor migration determine the spaces in which such international relationships occur. The extent of these international relationships and the networks that facilitate the marriages are enabled and limited by the nature of Filipina labor migration (Paredes-Maceda 1995, 110). Where women are domestic workers, their future partners can quickly come to identify them with domestic space and all the stereotypes that this identification might imply. Doing domestic work may appear to infantilize women, making part of their romantic appeal a perception of their "helplessness" in the public space of their receiving society. International marriages between Filipina contract migrants and nationals of their receiving nations often have significant age differences between the partners with Filipinas marrying older men who are typically divorced or separated. Research interviews with Filipina brides revealed that the women are aware of their stereotyping by their husbands. As the Filipina brides of "foreigners" they understand that they are "perceived by their partners as domesticated, subservient, and faithful" (Paredes-Maceda 1995, 112). If these women gave an accurate assessment of their husbands' perceptions, it appears that the foreign spouses of migrant domestic workers also conflate domestic skills with marital virtues.

The preceding section has linked marriage to de-skilling while the next section shows how Filipinas in Canada exemplify this phenomenon of worker-to-wife migration and establishes the social and political-economic context where de-skilling takes place.

THE LCP: FILIPINA = DH

In our interviews, Filipinas in Canada report that the distinctive aspect of their ethnic, gendered identity was the common assumption that they are domestic helpers, even when they are not. The origins of this stereotype lie in their visibility as an ethnic group and their overrepresentation in both the LCP immigration category and in the occupations classified as housekeeping and childcare.

Since the LCP was introduced as a special immigration category, the vast majority of LCP entrants have been Filipinas (source: a data order from The Longitudinal Immigration Database [IMDB], CIC).[6] According to immigration officials interviewed by the author, applicants for the LCP are predominantly Filipino, with over 90 percent of the applications coming from the Philippines.[7] The LCP immigration stream makes Filipinos a significant group of immigrants—in 1998, they comprised the third largest group of immigrants to arrive in Canada by nation of origin (CIC 2000). In that year, Filipino arrivals were a mix of independent immigrants, their spouses and dependents, and LCP applicants and their LCP spouses and dependents. Data from previous years would suggest that women from the Philippines were heavily overrepresented in the LCP class, giving substance to the DH stereotype.

In the period 1990–94, the last period for which comprehensive data breaking down all classes is available, 51,885 immigrants from the Philippines landed in Canada, representing 9.3 percent of total landings. 33,905 Filipino women landed in all immigration classes, versus 17,980 Filipino men. Of those landing from the LCP principal applicant group, 21,400 people (72.3 percent) listed their country of origin as the Philippines. Ninety-eight percent of these Filipinos were women. Thus Filipinas made up 71 percent of LCP principal applicants achieving landed immigrant status, while women from other national origins represented 27 percent of this class. On the streets of upper-middle-class Canadian suburbs, these immigration statistics translate into a visible presence: "brown" women pushing the prams of "blonde" babies.

Though they arrive to take up "unskilled" work, Filipino immigrants are generally well educated. Immigrant Filipinos, men and women, are more likely to have a university degree (29 percent do) than native-born Canadians. Despite the apparent parity in their educational attainment, Filipino immigrant women in Canada earn less, on the average, than Filipino men (CIC 2000). This suggests that Filipinas in Canada suffer discrimination on the basis of both their ethnicity and their gender. This discrimination may be related to the LCP as their point of (non)entry into the Canadian labor market.

Canadian immigration officials refer to the LCP as a "back door" for applicants whose skills, education, work experience, or family situation would not have qualified them for acceptance as independent immigrants through the regular immigration process. Selection for immigration to Canada has been based on a "points" system, with points being awarded for education, training, and work experience according to the anticipated demands of the Canadian labor market. Qualifications in nursing, teaching, and midwifery have not been awarded immigration points in the recent past on the basis that there is a sufficient supply of skilled workers in the Canadian labor market already. Thus the LCP opens a route for those without the skills or education assessed as desirable by Canadian government labor market analysis. On the part of the general Canadian population, then, this creates the impression that LCP migrants are "unskilled" and "uneducated." These impressions contradict the social statistics collected on the LCP migrants themselves, yet are widely believed, in part because immigrants are also known for misrepresenting their status.

THE MURKY QUESTION OF MARITAL STATUS

The most common form of "misrepresentation" for LCP migrants is that of their marital status. Filipinas arriving to do domestic work in Canada are typically in their thirties and forties. In the 1990–94 period, 15,090 women from the Philippines landed in Canada under the LCP. The largest group of these women were aged 25–44 (13,770), while only 365 were 15–24 and 955 were 45 years or older. The prevalence of the twenty-five to forty-four age group suggests that many of these women were or had been married. This is supported by research done with Filipina LCP migrants in Toronto where, of the women interviewed by Stasiulis and Bakan (1997, 131), twelve identified as married or partnered, two as separated, divorced or widowed, and eleven as never married. Migrating to Canada in the middle of their reproductive years, many of these women have been married and have dependent children in the Philippines. As caregivers, they may also be selected, by the nanny agencies and employers, to be older—more "responsible" and "experienced"—and to be constrained in their decision-making by responsibilities to family at home (see Pratt 1997).

Despite what women may report at any given point, the actual marital status of many Filipina contract migrants arriving in Canada is difficult to define. From our focus group interviews and life histories, we learned that abandonment or relationship breakdown is one of the reasons behind the decision to go overseas for many Filipino women. Divorce is not possible in the Philippines, but can be filed for abroad. Leaving the country also removes women from the social stigma attached to being a "single mom," while allowing them to provide for their families in the absence of a male breadwinner's contribution. Single moms are women who have children without a husband. Sometimes this occurs through abandonment of the family by the husband or the absence of a legal marriage and meaningful commitment to the relationship by the male partner in the first instance. Many women who are in relationships apply to go overseas as "single," either because their de facto partnerships were never legally formalized as marriages or because they have been advised to do so by migration agents.

Nongovernmental agencies are familiar with this fuzziness of marital status. One of the NGO workers I interviewed specialized in filing "quickie" divorces for LCP migrants. Another NGO worker, Carla, explained the strategy of concealing marital history as one of expediency:

A lot of these women come here as "single"—they come through the LCP and a lot of them are "single"—that's one of biggest groups here. They prefer single women as opposed to married, so a lot of the women, they have to lie and say they are single.

The "they" Carla refers to is a composite of employers, immigration officials, and nanny agents. Beyond its currency in gaining employment as a contract worker, being "single" is associated with the possibilities of a new life anticipated by the migrants themselves. For these women, being "single" means starting life anew and taking on new forms of decision making as "single women" rather than under their old, Philippine identifications as "wives of . . ." After years of (metaphorically) "following" their husband, they are happy to take on the breadwinner role and manage their families as single mothers, though at a distance. Following a husband often means moving around to different cities and rural areas in the Philippines as he looks for work, finding part-time and contract work as they go. Women talk of the stress of sending children back to relatives in rural areas when the husband's urban employment falls through and being told, yet again, that he has decided to transfer to another job. For many such women, after several years of marriage, their husband is a burden and they are happy to divest themselves of their responsibility to him, in order to focus on their children.

"Single" also means "single and available"—migration may offer these women a second chance in love.[8] In Carla's experience the idea of being "single" and independent reinforces the wish to marry internationally. Canadian men, in particular, are perceived as being more egalitarian in marital relations than Filipinos.

> I guess for a lot, the minute they land here, they start making their own decisions. Which means they build more confidence in themselves because they are starting to make decisions so the confidence builds up. . . . I'd like to add something else to this. That's where we see a lot of inter-racial marriages as well—where a lot of Filipino women they say "we're single, not wives." When they come that's what they say. "Oh now that I am independent and I'm competent to make my own decisions, I don't want to marry a Filipino man." . . . So they end up marrying out of the Filipino ethnic group—let's say a white person.

Carla goes on to explain that the relationship expectations of newly "single" Filipinas and Canadian men often do not coincide.

> But then the white person says, "I prefer a Filipina because they are very domesticated." And they both end up with different expectations. We get a lot of those! Interracial marriages where expectations were different. . . . A Filipina marrying a white man because he is not Filipino, thinking "I'll be independent" and expecting she'll be freer and a white man marrying a Filipina because he thinks she is domesticated; she'll cook me three meals a day, etc.

Here is an experiential example, where the image of Filipinas as domestic workers overdetermines the nature of their international marriage. The construction of Filipinas as amenable, dependent, and "domestic" is linked to the actual circumstances of migrants' employment experiences in Canada, rather than their personal dispositions or professional training. As opposed to the model of "dependent housewives," the women interviewed in our study discussed their desire for freedom and independence as an important part of entering into a transnational marriage. As female partners, Filipinas were not focussed on economic security. None of the women interviewed here had married Canadian men who were high-income earners and all of them kept working themselves after marriage. Perhaps this was, in part, to continue to support their families back in the Philippines.[9]

LABOR MARKET SEGREGATION AND DE-SKILLING

With such a large proportion of women entering the country under the LCP, many Filipinas in Canada come to understand themselves not as women or as Filipinos but as workers segregated on the basis of ethnicity. This segregation is a very real and demonstrable phenomenon. As workers, the disjuncture between their education and previous work in the Philippines and their current positions in Canada creates alienation and dissatisfaction. As migrant women, LCPers are in an anomalous situation—though contract migrants, they are unlikely to return home. Rather, they have the opportunity to become landed immigrants, an opportunity conditional on their acceptance of working conditions not applied to Canadian citizens (Stasiulis and Bakan 1997). Because they "accept" jobs that are unacceptable to citizens, Filipinas in Canada can be discursively constructed as being of lesser value than citizens and other European arrivals as employees and migrants (Pratt 1997). Discourses of racial inferiority and the "natural" domesticity of women intersect to create "popular" explanations for the prevalence of Filipinas in DH-type jobs.

The de-skilling of women who are already long-term overseas workers compounds and reinforces this stereotyping of Filipinas as DH. Just the DH job, on its own, is enough to marginalize a woman from the mainstream of Canadian society. Here is the work role of the LCP caregiver described by an NGO worker, herself an LCP entrant and former nanny describing how the broader public understands domestic workers:

> You're isolated . . . intellectual stimulation is very limited . . . and then the problem too when you are ready to go into the workforce. Most employers . . . will not recognize this as a Canadian work experience, being a live-in domestic worker. It is not considered as a job. It is not considered as a profession. The problem is domestic work is considered something anybody can do. In the general public, if you are a domestic worker you would be considered probably as

intellectually a little bit limited. You have limited education; so the job that is left over for you to do is maid work.

The racial aspect of Filipinas' experiences of segregation is very marked in Canadian urban centers. Social statistics suggest that this segregation is not only perceived but also the reality of the Canadian labor market. In Vancouver, for instance, statistics on labor market segmentation show that women of Philippine ethnic origin are found disproportionately in DH-type occupations. If all occupations were allocated without regard to ethnicity, the index of segregation would be 1.0. Looking at Vancouver, Dan Hiebert found that Filipinas had an index of segregation of 8.6 for the occupation labeled "housekeeper" and an index of segregation of 6.9 for "childcare worker" (Hiebert 1997, table 5). This means women from the Philippines were 8.6 and 6.9 times more likely, respectively, to be found in that occupation than if jobs were distributed irregardless of ethnicity. Women from the Philippines exhibit the highest degree of occupational segregation of any group (Hiebert 1997, 26). This phenomenon is likely a result of the influx of Filipina women under the LCP and the social situation described in the quote above.

Feelings of expectations denied, social denigration, and limitations in accessing nondomestic work were expressed by Filipinas in interviews in the present study:

Lydia (teacher): I worked in Hong Kong for four years. . . . If I compare like my salary in Hong Kong as domestic helper and the salary as a classroom teacher in the Philippines, is triple more than I get here. I arrived here in 1991 under LCP, for my 8 years here I had four employers and until now I am still doing domestic work or working as live-in caregiver.

Aida (accounting graduate): I already know that my work will be a nanny, a domestic helper. But what I knew, that is only for my stepping stone. That's only the start. Then I have hope that I could be able to upgrade myself. I can go to school, get my landed [immigrant status.] But now I feel I've screwed up because of the LCP, living and working with my employer. I've changed employers many times.

Maria (teacher): I worked in Singapore for almost 3 years and I work here for live-in-care for more than 2 years. So the de-skilling thing is also there, right? Like you have the hesitancy or . . . —do you know that you can do it?

Veronica (nurse): (M)oney-wise, we really are incapable of pursuing another career, we are helping family. We need to support our family in the Philippines leaving us very little amount for everyday living.

De-skilling is thus both a structural and a psychological phenomenon, created as much by the economic limitations of providing for dependents overseas as the undervaluing of Philippine work experience and qualifications in the Canadian labor market. Geraldine Pratt's (1999) exploration of the discursive construction of Filipina domestic workers shows how discourses on race and gender and economy intersect in their lives to produce de-skilling and labor market segregation in Canada. Pratt finds that "the effects of discourse emerge out of and further exploitative north/south international relations through the sedimentation of Filipina immigrants to Canada within a limited range of low-paid occupations" (Pratt 1999, 234).

While retraining and obtaining Canadian qualifications and experience would be the most practical option for many of these women, it is difficult for them to move beyond their identification as DH.

FACTORS CONTRIBUTING TO THE DH IDENTITY

LCP migrants face major obstacles in moving back to training and professions. As migrant workers, rather than "independent immigrants," they find great difficulty in saving money, accessing Canadian training and social welfare services, and creating networks of contacts beyond domestic worker friends.

Settlement services for immigrant women target stay-at-home mothers with small children who require language training (Lee 1999). Such services are only available after landing as an immigrant, which, for most LCPers, happens between two and three years after they arrive in Canada. Undertaking education and training while under the LCP is prohibited by the government (Pratt 1999, 222). This makes it very hard for LCP migrants to go back into the same profession they had or use the training they acquired in the Philippines.

Settlement services directed at basic language training and child-rearing are particularly poorly designed for Filipinas, since women from the Philippines are usually in the workforce. Eighty percent of Filipino immigrant women (15–64) participate in the workforce, a higher rate than all other immigrant (62 percent) and native-born Canadian women (67 percent) (CIC 2000). This figure is virtually identical to that for Filipino immigrant men (CIC 2000). Given their workforce commitments, finding time and money for refresher courses or re-training to upgrade skills acquired in the Philippines is particularly difficult. This may be the reason why, though 32 percent of all Philippine immigrant women have postsecondary qualifications in health-related fields, only 20 percent have employment in this area (CIC 2000). While it is likely that the 20 percent are independent immigrants, the 12 percent who have not reentered healthcare may well represent LCP arrivals who have moved into service sector jobs that are not classified as "health care" work such as live-out caregiver. For instance, LCP arrivals qualified as nurses but working as caregivers or nurse's aides simply do not have the time or capital to invest in refresher courses that would update their skills.

Using data from IMDB CIC, I identified the LCP immigrant Filipinas whose employment history over the ten years prior to landing classified them as nurses and examined their industry of employment at their 1995 tax return. The data suggests a definite de-skilling trend for nurses arriving under the LCP.

Based on those filing taxes in 1995, in the 1980–1984 period, only five Filipina nurses arrived under the LCP (then, the FDM). In 1995, all five of these women were employed in nursing. Of the 1995 immigrant taxfilers landing in the 1985–1989 period, 80 Filipinas were nurses, but only 25 percent or 20 of those women had nursing as industry of employment. For the 1990–1994 landings, a smaller proportion of Filipinas again, 24 percent (30/125), were working as nurses, but a relatively larger number of nurses had landed. Most of the nurses landing in this period were in caregiving or service sector jobs in 1995. The service sector work would include occupations such as nurse's aide, geriatric care worker, live-out nanny, sales clerk, food service worker, and the like. Many more women with nursing education and experience as nurses arrive under the LCP, however, than the few who are classified as nurses on the basis of their employment history at landing.

The LCP experience thus presents a major problem for those agencies providing social services to the Filipino community. The basic economics of this problem are described in the following, an excerpt from an interview between the author and a Filipina immigrant settlement worker who is a former LCP entrant.

> *Maria:* Well LCPers who are citizens here—some of them just stay in the service sector. LCPers—none of them have upgraded their profession.
> *Author:* Even after they have landed immigrant status they are still not upgrading?
> *Maria:* They can.
> *Author:* But are they—are they actually upgrading?
> *Maria:* That's the problem there. They can. But after you are landed now you are facing trying to leave a job like Marvelous Muffins, like Superstore, or a sort of secretary job. How much is the minimum wage? $7.15 per hour. If you have one regular job, you work 40 hours and they are only giving you $700 or $704 in a month. How much is your rent? How much is your food? Personal expenses? If you are planning to go to school, if you are planning to raise yourself, you have to either get a student loan or you have to borrow with your friends. Most LCPers have a family—taking their family here after they are landed. It's hard to survive. The transition phase is difficult. For most of them it leads to two jobs, three jobs—not even the time to spend for their children. Not enough sleep!

Lastly, the double isolation of Filipinas doing domestic work contributes to their segregation by limiting their job search and social networks, as described by another, non-Filipino, NGO worker.

Author: What about entering into the workforce after the caregiver contract ends?
Sasha: That's another big, big difficulty because you come by yourself, being sponsored by an employer or your family, you're coming by yourself then afterwards when you have finished with your live-in caregiver work then you need to network to go into the other work field. But it's so difficult. You probably know very few people who are in that other field that you may be looking at. Because you have been working in isolation, mostly you work with other domestic workers. And I see that even more in the Filipina community, where actually between the Filipino community which is already landed immigrant—or people who came directly as landed immigrants—they look down on the domestic workers. There's a very strong separation. "So you're only a nanny; we don't really communicate with you or we don't really deal with you." And so the Filipinas have a tendency to stick within their domestic workers group.

Filipina migrants to Canada are isolated in their workplaces, segregated in the labor market, and suffer from the social stigma of being DH both within their community and in mainstream Canadian society. While migrant women may try to be "altruistic mothers" and "dutiful daughters," as suggested in the quotes from Filipinas above, they also strategize to make choices that advance their own personal goals for a secure future in the face of segregation and stereotyping. Some of these women see that marriage, particularly to a non-Filipino Canadian, might offer a path out of their isolation and dead-end jobs. As the PWC describes it, "For the women, the restrictive conditions of the LCP . . . push them to enter . . . marriages. For the men, the LCP provides a ready pool of women and brings to life the stereotyped Filipino woman— fuelling their desire for a Filipino wife" (PWC 2000, 48).

To substantiate the PWC's claims that de-skilling under the LCP leads to marriage, here is Carla's comment on the marriages of her LCP friends to Canadian men:

Carla: A lot of them—like my friends for example—a lot of friends who came through LCP—the majority of them end up with Caucasian men because . . .
Author: I have yet to figure it out, but I know a large number of Caucasian men who prefer to date Asian women and are quite open about this. In terms of the stereotypes that they associate with Asian women—I wonder whether or not the women from Asia that they meet are living up to these stereotypes? What were their expectations around the relationships? It's something that is not spoken about much. . . . There's this stereotypical idea of Asian domestic femininity, that seems to then be projected on to women—like the women who are coming here under the LCP.
Carla: I guess it has a lot to do with the Canadian Government not recognizing their educational background. They don't give credit to education. While these LCPers are teachers and nurses and engineers. I even know one who is a lawyer back home and they come here as domestic workers and after working as

domestic workers they are not able to continue their professions—professions that they had back home. Some sort of de-skilling going on. A lot of de-skilling going on. . . . A lot of them end up as nursing aides, working in group homes for the elderly, a lot of them ending up in service jobs—like fast food, hotels, restaurants but similar to what they did as domestic workers.

Carla connects the marriages of her friends with their experiences of de-skilling, suggesting that such marriages are, at some level, a way out of stereotyping and segregation, a way of prying open the Canadian labor market. Where it appears that the LCP may lead to continued segregation into domestic work, international marriage becomes a competing strategy for a migrant woman to gain the right to settle permanently. While Carla does not deny the potential for love and affection in these relationships, she is troubled by the overdetermining nature of de-skilling.

Having outlined the racial political economy created by the Canadian State and described the segregation of migrant women in the labor market, I now turn to narratives of transnational romance attached to overseas work by domestic placement agencies and transnational Filipino culture.

FROM CAREGIVER TO WIFE IN CANADA

Employment agencies and employers both cite Filipinas' caring attitudes as one of their desirable features as a caregiver-employee (see Pratt 1997). Nongovernmental organizations working to support Filipina migrants make clear linkages between the LCP and international marriages: "Government policy that constructs an image of Filipino women as domestic workers fuels the growing demand among Canadian men for Filipino wives" (PWC 2000, 51). This section presents examples from the Canadian context that illustrate how the desirable qualities in a romantic partner overlap with the attributes of a good caregiver.

In the first instance, our respondents reported that it was notable how Canadian men seemed to be searching for Filipina wives of a particular sort. Simple Filipino ethnicity was not enough—Canadian men wanted to meet new arrivals or women still in the LCP. The Filipinas interviewed thought that the Canadian men were expecting such women to be "unspoiled" and to live up to the ideals of feminine domesticity out of gratitude for being "rescued" from the LCP. Marriage to a Filipina on the part of a Canadian man seems to be discursively constructed around expectations of gratitude and exoticism and connected to her ongoing association with labor in a "domestic" rather than "public" space (see PWC 2000).

Here is a quote from a young, second-generation Fil-Canadian woman, describing what it is like for her to "be Filipina" in Vancouver. Her story illustrates how ideas of gratitude and domesticity seem to be particularly attached to women who are recent arrivals or are still living in the Philippines, rather than "assimilated" Fil-Canadians like her (PWC 2000). That this kind of experience is reported by a second-generation Canadian Filipina shows up the fact that it is not her ethnicity, per se, but the assumed naiveté or domesticity of Filipinas who are "fresh off the boat" that attracts "older Canadian men."

> *May (healthcare worker):* When I was at the bus stop or at the mall, I would get stopped by older Canadian men, I would get asked if I was Filipino, if I said yes then they would want to continue the conversations, asking me what I did here, asking me how long I have been here. But if I said no I wasn't Filipino, they would not continue the conversation. They would leave. I think this might be one of the reasons why before I denied myself as Filipino, because of the stereotypes attached to being Filipino here in Canada.

In May's experience, she is frequently approached by non-Filipino, Canadian men and found lacking. It is not her Filipino ethnicity, per se, that is of interest to these (Anglo) Canadian men, but the extent to which she can fulfill their stereotypical expectations of innocence, naiveté, and servility. She reports that when she indicated that she was an assimilated Fil-Canadian, the men who had approached her lost interest. She understands this to mean that such men were only interested in "new arrivals" who could not "read" the Canadian cultural scene easily or were not settled into Canadian social networks.

May's understanding of the Filipina that these men were searching for, Asian brides, corresponds with the findings of the PWC's (PWC 2000, 39–40) study of "mail-order brides" in Canada. This research project describes a small sample of Filipino women who have entered into international marriages. Forty women participated in the PWC project, their ages ranging from twenty-three to fifty-two, with eleven being between thirty-six and forty. Of the forty, eight had come to Canada via the LCP and two of these women were still working under the LCP at the time of the interview. Seven of the forty had worked in other countries as domestics before coming to Canada. Thirty-two of the women had university degrees. Of the twenty-one women in the study who worked outside the home, they were in service-sector jobs such as store clerk, chambermaid, babysitter, or domestic worker. Though this sample may not be representative of all Filipina migrants, it does suggest that women involved in international marriages are well educated but employed in Canada in non-commensurate, "feminized" service-sector positions.

Many of the women interviewed in the project married Canadian partners fairly soon after their arrival in the country. They often found their partners during a period in which they felt vulnerable, unsupported, and financially insecure. This time of vulnerability marked their coming to terms with an ongoing but uncertain future as a domestic worker because they had experienced rejection of their skills in the mainstream Canadian labor market.

The PWC research team describes the typical experience of a respondent as:

> Out of economic necessity, she moved abroad to work as a migrant worker and ended up as a bride of a Canadian man. As she moved through the roles of domestic worker to wife and mother, her options constricted and her situation worsened. (PWC 2000, 35)

Their analysis suggests that experiences of racialization and de-skilling are pushing women into marriages that may further restrict their economic and personal options.

Ally's Story: *I Got Married with My Employer*

De-skilling works as a push factor for international marriages in Canada. This section builds on the preceding discussion of de-skilling and international marriage by presenting a single case of blurred boundaries to illustrate the ways in which state policies, transnational economies, and migrant cultures play out in a single life. Ally's experience of a failed marriage to her widowed employer reflects both her own strategies and desires and the broader set of legal constraints and social policies that construct her subject position as a contract domestic worker.

Author: How much is your salary and what year is that?

Ally: That was 1991. I'm receiving from my husband about $600 something and the minimum is $680. I worked long hours, too—hard to count.

Author: How many years did you work with him?

Ally: Two years but he paid me by cheque and I cashed it, used it in the house.

My salary from my husband is actually one thing that is really hard for me because I could hardly send money back home to the Philippines. Because he uses my salary to buy diapers, milk for my stepson.

I'm already landed after two years. I got my landed status and he wanted to get married because I'm planning to move to the city, to get a better job. Because I don't want to be just a nanny anymore, because I know I can make it. I thought I can practice my degree here—be a nutritionist or a dietitian. But then I went for evaluation and my degree wasn't even recognized, even though I've passed my board exam. I proved to myself that, even though I'm not going to upgrading, I can probably be capable in whatever jobs are around. And I became realistic about it. I'm not shy to become a domestic worker. That I'm a Filipino woman, I'm not ashamed to anybody. Everybody is the same. (B)eing a Filipino . . . they look at us like we're small. Even though we have a good education, it doesn't matter to them. Because we're Filipino we are only a domestic helper. They only can control us because they have the money and power, of course, here in Canada.

So then I got married. After a year of marriage, I got pregnant.

I have a daughter, but I find it hard, I feel like I was a maid—I don't have any power at all. I was isolated; I can't have a Filipino friend.

Then I started going to counseling and I had my self-esteem again. I'm a Filipina and I should leave my husband. I couldn't take it any more. I went to school and upgraded myself and I felt a lot better. It's not right that he says I'm good for nothing. I believe in myself—that I have skills, that I know I can do it without him.

In Ally's story we can see how the boundaries between the labor involved in domestic service and the economic relations of marriage are difficult to draw. As a domestic worker, she uses her salary to buy milk for the baby she is employed to care for. As a wife, she feels like a maid. Perhaps, for her husband, a good wife is a good worker, but Ally is not happy with her choices. She wants to have her skills and training recognized and to be able to access the broader Canadian labor market. She married her husband after realizing that she would not find the kind of work she wanted after leaving the LCP. Their relationship did not make the transition from employee-employer to marital partners and this weakened her self-esteem. After she went to retraining courses and counseling, Ally's confidence increased and she decided to leave her Canadian husband.

Again, Ally's story is not necessarily a typical experience, but a revealing one. Any job situation where people work in close proximity could potentially lead to romantic intimacy. Yet affairs between office coworkers or manager and subordinate, however, are not quite comparable to domestic worker/employer relationships. The rhetoric of domestic work as feminized and natural makes the boundaries between the professional and the intimate more fragile and easier to transgress. When Ally became romantically involved with her employer, she apparently forfeited the right to disburse her salary as she wanted. At this point, she was cohabiting premarriage but still working for her husband-to-be as an employee under her LCP authorization. One condition of this relationship was that she would continue to perform her domestic work, but her husband would now appropriate her surplus and redirect it into the domestic needs of the Canadian household unit. Such exploitation would likely not happen, nor be seen as acceptable, if Ally were working and dating her employer in a public-sector job.

By offering this singular story I do not want to suggest that it is the personal relations between Filipina migrants and Canadian men, per se, that necessarily lead to exploitation of Filipina women who marry Canadian men. It is the wider socioeconomic context in which the LCP places migrant women that contributes to their vulnerability and stereotyping. Recall the comments made by the NGO worker on the presumed intellectual limitations of female domestic workers. The Canadian context is one in which a particular group of women have been released from domestic work to participate in the formal labor market, only to be replaced by another group of ethnically distinct women as caregivers. The feminine nature of women's work and its unpaid status have not been effectively challenged by this change of workers. The message has simply been that some women can do "skilled" work, so long as other women can be found to do the housework. Because their employment is in private homes and "normally" performed by female household members for free, migrants easily become invisible as workers. As domestic labor, migrants can find their paid work subsumed into unpaid, "just helping out" through the rhetorics of "the household unit" or being "part of the family." This makes it very difficult for LCP migrants to limit their working hours, get paid for overtime, enforce the provisions of their contracts, and generally demand to be treated as employees (Pratt 1997). Ally's story shows just how easily her job was subsumed into her new position as partner and wife without her explicit consent. In no other industry would it seem acceptable to redirect an employee's salary to the corporation if she commenced a romantic relationship with her manager.

Why Ally as a Filipina might have been particularly open to international marriage is also of interest. Transnational romance and international marriage are part of the Filipino imaginary of life abroad. The following section explores how marriages with foreigners are promoted transnationally, examining data collected in sending areas in the Philippines and migrant employment agencies in Hong Kong.

DREAMS OF TRANSNATIONAL ROMANCE

Transnational romance is a familiar theme for migrant women, even before they leave home. Movies, radio programs, and comic books published in the Philippines tell the stories of overseas contract workers, making romantic versions of migration part of Philippine popular culture. These stories circulate, along with migrants themselves, even in remote, rural areas. While it is true that most Filipina migrants are well educated, this does not mean that they necessarily come from urban areas. Women from the provinces, rather than the cities—*probynsyanas*—supposedly make the most desirable contract workers because they are less sophisticated and more biddable than urban women (Tyner 1996).

Many Philippine villages have a surplus of young, university graduate women who can not find any work commensurate with their qualifications. Since their families have often struggled for years to provide the necessary resources to educate them, they are determined to escape agricultural work and practice their profession. As "dutiful daughters" they feel obliged to look for work abroad when they can find none at home (McKay 1999). During a year-long stint of field research in the mountains of the northern Philippines, I met several women who had returned after completing contracts overseas. Other women I met or heard about were "permanent" abroad, having married in their host countries. In the remote rural villages of the north, these female overseas contract workers (OCWs)-turned-international wives returned home as visitors, with luxury goods showing their enhanced status. In a context where overqualified women were returning to agricultural production, a "foreign" marriage seemed appealing.

Women who had been educated to do office jobs found themselves under-employed, doing temporary work, struggling in small business, or "already/again" stuck in the domestic agricultural economy. My friend the history teacher, for instance, planted short-term cash crops while saving money for agency fees and dreaming of a more glamorous lifestyle, secured by contract work in Taiwan. The first step in achieving her dream was to move from her rural village to take up factory work in an Export Processing Zone near Manila. This move, she thought, would bring her closer to the cosmopolitan woman, experienced in "modern" production, that overseas employers desired.

Other sorts of desire were also part of her imagined future. She had seen domestic worker migrants who had become the wives of apparently wealthy foreigners visiting her own village. Like other Filipinas migrating to take up domestic work overseas, my friend could envision marrying a national of her host country or another expatriate. She was not alone in holding this expectation, nor had she formulated it independently.

I also asked some of the returned migrants about their romantic connections abroad. From their stories, I found that relationships with boyfriends appear to be unbalanced but constituted reciprocal ties that could be mobilized to provide personal economic security for the migrant while abroad (McKay 1999). What was perhaps more interesting was the story of progress my respondents attached to the different subject positions a migrant woman might pass through. As an "ideal type" model, it seems as if a Filipina migrant begins as a domestic helper in a desirable receiving country, often having to go "cross-country" to get there, and then moves through other roles—geriatric care worker, cleaner, service worker are common—to the final goal of permanent residency. Marriage to a host national was understood by these women as one way to shorten the transition from contract worker to resident and hasten the achievement of personal economic security (McKay 1999).

International marriage is also promoted in much the same manner—as an enviable short cut to secure residency overseas—by domestic employment agencies in Singapore and Hong Kong. Thus women who learn about transnational marriage in their sending villages have their perceptions reinforced by migration agents overseas who use transnational romance as a recruiting strategy. In Singapore and Hong Kong, the transnational aspects of the context for imagining relationships with foreigners are circulated through the migrant workers' networks, along with information on life in Canada, the LCP program, and Canadian dating agencies. The LCP program is not advertised by the Canadian embassies in Asia, but information (and misinformation) on it spreads by word of mouth between recruiting agencies with ties to Canada, Canadian employers working in Asia, and the extended networks of their employees. The program is thus picked up on by employment agencies and these agencies advertise the possibility of international marriage as a positive feature of the Canadian program. Such relationships are touted as realistic options by agencies recruiting in Singapore and Hong Kong.

Some examples of the kinds of linkages made between the LCP and international marriage in Singapore are displayed by the photographs on the front windows of maid agencies in Lucy Plaza Mall, Orchard Road. These posters only portray marriage as the outcome of LCP migration so that citizenship and permanency are implicitly bound up in the marriage relationship, rather than associated with the LCP program itself. They come from an agency called Inter-Mares—Lucky Plaza, Orchard Road, Singapore, 23 April 2001. At the top of the agency's front window display was a banner that read "Canada is not closed!" Under the banner a sign read "Canada need(s) caregivers."

Posters that appear in the window include:

(1) Corazon Fuller of Vigan, Ilocos Sur [wedding photo from newspaper]

> Fairy tales can come true
> It can happen to you
> If you apply to Inter-Mares

> Cora came to Singapore in 1983 through (you guessed it) Inter-Mares. In 1986 she went to Vancouver. If you guessed that Inter-Mares sent her there, you guessed right, again! (Of course, she's no longer a Nanny!)

And (2) Erlinda Velosa Watson of Tarlac [wedding announcement card with message—Mr. Tom with our real appreciation, Bill and Linda Watson]

> Erlinda came from Tarlac in 1984. In 1986 she went to Toronto to work as a nanny. Bill said to her one day, "Why be a Nanny; marry me and my children will call you Mommy." Miss Velosa said yes, and she is now Mrs. Watson. Now Erlinda is the proud mother of three children of her own, and mother of six all in all. She now lives in her own home near the world-famous Niagara Falls.

What these photos and the accompanying captions illustrate is the way that middlemen in migration—the employment agents—pick up on the discourse of transnational romance as a marketing strategy. These narratives that circulate at the mesolevel influence women's perceptions of the options open to them—

of what may yet happen for them in a place like Canada. Women, like Perlita, may choose to pursue these options, not through an agency, but through independent or family contacts as well. Other women, like Ally, see, read, and familiarize themselves with these half-suggested stories as scripts of possibility. These narratives locate Caucasian men as the desirable partners who control the economic future and life aspirations of peripheral women. Domestic work, LCP migration, or nannying is constructed in these poster narratives as a diversion on the path to the true success to be had in marriage.

Reading the texts that accompany the photographs, it is evident that the idea of a transnationally mediated marriage is an outcome of the desirability of the Filipina as a partner. This desirability appears to rely on the same performative characteristics of a "domestic" femininity sought by employers: "Why be a Nanny; marry me and my children will call you Mommy." This quote suggests that the work itself won't change, only the woman's title and that this is somehow natural to her.

These stories of domestic work leading to marriage establish distinct discourse on femininity and progress: from DH one can move through the positions of virtuous migrant to wife. While, in many cases, women who enact these dreams, like Ally or Perlita, are motivated by their own aspirations for a better life, their aspirations are, in many ways, scripted by the popular culture of their home and transnational workplaces. Equally, their understandings of their subject positions as worker and migrant are influenced by the perceptions of opportunities abroad held by their families and networks of friends. Many of these people appear to be giving the message that, while domestic worker is good, "wife" is somehow better.

Frequently expectations of international romance are both developed and met through networks of women already abroad. The appearance of this narrative in recruiting agency ties women's experiences in Asia to the understandings of female migration and transnational gender that circulate in Canada because women in Asia, seeing such posters, will begin to ask their Canadian contacts about boyfriends, male friends, and dating. Those overseas are often happy to help out. In fact, sometimes it may be easier for a woman already abroad to find a potential partner through her transnational networks than to be accepted under the LCP.

In Canada, a few Filipino women who have settled after their own stint in the LCP place advertisements in the paper, looking for men interested in becoming pen-pals with their sisters and friends in the Philippines, Hong Kong, and Singapore (PWC 2000). After the LCP, they address their isolation and homesickness by building their own social networks through intermarriages they facilitate. For some people, the LCP itself is facilitating a new round of marriage migration.

Here is a story collected by the PWC that shows how an LCP migrant became a marriage broker:

> Emma became a domestic worker seven years ago. She also wanted to bring her two sisters to Canada. However, despite Emma's efforts, her sisters could not meet the LCP qualifications. As they could not come through the LCP, the sisters got married to Canadian men. (PWC 2000, 49)

Where the family of the original LCP migrant could not gain entry to Canada through the LCP, they entered by means of marriage. Emma set her sisters up with Canadian pen-pals through a network created through connections of her Canadian husband. This shows how transnational marriage for LCP women might be, at first, about gaining permanent residency and maybe better jobs, but then it can also begin to facilitate entry by marriage for female friends and relatives. Other Filipino migrants have created businesses built around this possibility (PWC 2000)—specialized dating agencies based in Canada recruit from among LCP women, as well as handling files from Filipino women in other countries and in the Philippines.

> Nina, a former live-in caregiver, sees herself as assisting Filipino women when she sets them up in her dating service. She firmly believes that when she marries off one of her women to a Canadian man, she has done her duty to help Filipino women by giving them stability and a better future. (PWC 2000, 49)

In this example, the LCP migrant thinks of herself as "saving" other women from the degrading work, economic struggle, and social marginalization of domestic work. She is offering them the solution she found for herself: stability in the form of permanent residency gained through marriage. She can also potentially find work for these migrant wives in ethnic enterprises—businesses owned by other Filipino immigrants. While it isn't always the case that Filipino women are set up with Canadian men by friends and family or through dating agencies, many find that social structures and economic conditions place them in a position where such relationships become more attractive. And thus we return full circle—from labor migration under the LCP that then becomes marriage, yielding marriages facilitated to bring family members to Canada as labor.

CONCLUSION

The stories of Filipina contract migrants to Canada told here illustrate the ways mobile women blur the boundaries between the categories of voluntary migration recognized by the state: labor, marriage, and family reunification. A single migrant woman's life story might crisscross among all three categories. We could imagine a woman who moves "domestically" for work in the transnational public space of an export-processing factory in the Philippines, then takes up domestic work in the private space of an employer's home, overseas—in Singapore. She then may marry a foreign national, say, a Canadian citizen, and relocate again, this time working in a migrant enclave with coethnics in her receiving nation. Eventually she might herself sponsor female family members to join her work team and marry conationals. This imagined every-migrant was not interviewed, but, if she were found, her story might be quite subversive.

Stories of women's experiences of migration in the region expose the politics that demarcate the fluid boundaries between public/private and domestic/transnational spaces. And such stories also show up the political-economic use that receiving states may make of such divides. Here I have shown that blurring boundaries results in female migrants falling through the cracks of state policies and services. Because women's lives and migration experiences are marginal to the discourses that describe "proper" migration and thus "appropriate" citizenship, migrant women are disadvantaged as laborers. State agencies posit women as wives and families, not workers, yet migrant women are almost always involved in some form of the cash economy. Thus migration moves women to the margins—the margins of state services, policies, and protection.

Migrant women's stories show up the boundary projects of states for the heteronormative power relations they impose on their populations. Through de-skilling female migrants, receiving nations such as Canada can develop "domestic" industries that rely on enclaves of immigrant women who do not benefit from even the most minimal regulation of working conditions, hours, or pay; do not vote; and have no presence in civil society—in other words, women who are functionally noncitizens. Individual women in this situation are stereotyped and denied a sense of "appropriate belonging" as a citizen of the receiving country. These women are ashamed of doing a "low" job, of not fitting in, of being identified with unruly, irresponsible, "problematic" migrants. This is the situation in which marriage to a host national emerges as a viable option for migrant women—a way of addressing the "shame" of domestic work and affiliating herself to her host society, while distancing herself from some of the stereotypes of her ethnic group. Thus the employment and Canadian labor market circumstances of Filipina contract migrants, combined with colonial logics of desire and transnational postcolonial Filipino culture, come to produce their international marriages.

NOTES

This chapter discusses the results of a larger project: "Filipinas in Canada: Geographies of Social Integration/Exclusion in the Canadian Metropolis." This co-operative project between Dr. McKay and the Philippine Women Centre was funded by a grant from the Vancouver Centre of the RIIM (Research on Immigration and Integration in the Metropolis) Project (www.riim.metropolis.net). Thanks to Professor David Ley of RIIM at the University of British Columbia and Luningning Alcuitas-Imperial of the PWC for their contributions to the project. Dr. McKay was supported by an SSHRC Postdoctoral Fellowship. She thanks Sandra Davenport at The Australian National University for her research assistance in producing the chapter.

1. Single parents and sole caregivers of elderly and disabled people also benefit from caregivers arriving under the program.

2. Diocson-Sayo, Cecilia. Philippine Women Centre, Vancouver, British Columbia, Canada. Personal Comment. 4 December 1998.

3. See Louise Langevin and Marie-Claire Belleau, "Trafficking in Women in Canada: A Critical Analysis of the Legal Framework Governing Immigrant Live-in Caregivers and Mail-Order Brides." Status of Women Canada, October 2000, www.swc-cfc.gc.ca/publish/research/020215-066231252X-e.html (February 2002).

4. These program requirements also ensure that the successful applicants for the LCP are 90 percent female. Though a few men work as caregivers in Canada under the LCP, they are usually expected to do private duty nursing, or work as drivers or handymen, rather than the household chores and babysitting expected of women.

5. This same observation would also apply to sex work, but Paredes-Maceda's research was done with domestic workers.

6. Statistics on immigrants with the Philippines as place of birth and LCP as category were specially ordered for this study.

7. Interview with immigration officials, Canadian Embassy, Manila, 12 December 1999.

8. Love is unspecified here and lesbian relationships are not unknown, but don't predominate. The important aspect is love, rather than gender. But, since none of our interviewees identified as lesbian and those who spoke of their relationships spoke of relationships with men, lesbian relationships won't be discussed.

9. The continued transnational economic ties between internationally married migrants and their families in the Philippines are undoubtedly a source of tension in their marriages. However, no data was collected on this issue, perhaps marking its sensitivity.

REFERENCES

Citizenship and Immigration Canada. "A Profile of Immigrants from The Philippines to Canada." 2000. http://cicnet.ci.gc.ca/english/pub/profile/philippines-e.html (accessed in 2000).
———. "Facts and Figures 2000: Immigration Overview." www.cic.gc.ca/english/pub/facts2000/1imm-05.html (accessed 27 January 2002).
———. "The Longitudinal Immigration Database (IMDB): An Introduction." IMDB Technical Paper for presentation at the CERF—CIC Conference on Immigration, Employment and the Economy, Richmond, British Columbia, October 1997.

Gibson, Katherine, Lisa Law, and Deirdre McKay. "Beyond Heroes and Victims: Filipina Contract Migrants, Economic Activism and Class Transformations." *International Feminist Journal of Politics* vol. 3, no. 3 (2001): 365–86.

Hiebert, Daniel. "The Color of Work: Labor Market Segmentation in Montreal, Toronto and Vancouver, 1991." RIIM Working Paper Series, no. 97–02. Vancouver: Vancouver Centre of Excellence, 1997.

Langevin, Louise, and Marie-Claire Belleau. "Trafficking in Women in Canada: A Critical Analysis of the Legal Framework Governing Immigrant Live-in Caregivers and Mail-Order Brides." Status of Women Canada, October 2000. www.swc-cfc.gc.ca/publish/research/020215-066231252X-e.html (accessed February 2002).

Lee, Jo-Anne. "Immigrant Settlement and Multiculturalism Programs for Immigrant, Refugee and Visible Minority Women: A Study of Outcomes, Best Practices and Issues." Victoria: B.C. Ministry Responsible for Multiculturalism, June 1999.

McKay, Deirdre. "Migration and Masquerade: Gender and Habitus in The Philippines." *Geography Research Forum* vol. 21 (2001): 44–56.

———. "Imagining Igorots: Performing Gender and Ethnicity on the Philippine Cordillera Central." Ph.D. thesis, University of British Columbia, 1999.

Paredes-Maceda, Catherine. "Filipino Women and Intermarriages." *Asian Migrant* vol. 8, no. 4 (1995): 109–13.

Philippine Women Center of B.C. *Canada: The New Frontier for Filipino Mail-Order Brides.* Research Directorate, Ottawa: Status of Women Canada, 2000.

Piper, Nicola. "Wife or Worker? International Marriage in the Context of Labor Migration—The Case of Asian Women in Japan." Paper presented at the Conference Migration and the Asian Family in a Globalizing World, National University of Singapore, April 2001.

Pratt, Geraldine. "From Registered Nurse to Registered Nanny: Discursive Geographies of Filipina Domestic Workers in Vancouver, B.C." *Economic Geography* vol. 75, no. 3 (1999): 215–36.

———. "Stereotypes and Ambivalence: The Construction of Domestic Workers in Vancouver, B.C." *Gender, Place and Culture* vol. 4, no. 2 (1997): 159–77.

Stasiulis, Daiva, and Abigail Bakan. "Negotiating Citizenship: The Case of Foreign Domestic Workers in Canada." *Feminist Review* vol. 57 (Autumn 1997): 112–39.

Stoler, Ann. *Race and the Education of Desire: Foucault's History of Sexuality and the Colonial Order of Things.* Durham, N.C.: Duke University Press, 1996.

Tyner, James A. "The Gendering of Philippine International Labor Migration." *Professional Geographer* vol. 48, no. 4 (1996): 405–16.

3

Does Marriage "Liberate" Women from Sex Work?—Thai Women in Germany

Prapairat R. Mix and Nicola Piper

Migration is a road many take to seek other opportunities and to break away from oppressive local conditions including those caused, or enhanced, by globalization processes (Gills and Piper 2002; Pettman 1996). In the case of migration of Thais, the first post-WWII wave consisted mainly of the middle class—people such as doctors, engineers, and nurses—who went to the United States in the late sixties. The largest group of Thais living abroad today is still in the United States where, according to the U.S. Bureau of the Census, in 1990, 91,626 permanent Thai settlers resided, of whom 32,064 were based in California alone (Stern 1998, 54). In the late seventies and eighties, a large number of skilled and unskilled workers were recruited for work in the Middle East, involving tens of thousands of predominantly male Thai workers.[1] Since then, intra-Asian migration has been most prominent with large numbers of Thai workers going to countries such as Taiwan, Malaysia, and Singapore (Chantanavich, Nittayananatta, Mix, Ruenkaew, and Khemkrut 1999). Migration of Thais to Europe, on the other hand, has been very low in numerical terms.

Women have participated in these gendered migratory flows from Thailand in increasing numbers, in jobs such as factory workers, domestic helpers, and sex workers, and as "mail-order brides." Thai women are also represented in cross-border flows in the context of what has been termed "trafficking" from economically less-developed to more advanced countries (Williams 1999; Piper 1999).[2] Significant in this context, as argued by a number of feminist commentators, is the link between local sex tourism and sex work abroad (Truong 1990; Chant 1997). Hence, much of these migration flows involve relatively high risks and often result in insecure immigration statuses. Moreover, association with the "mail-order bride" business or sex work has a strong stigmatizing effect upon these women in both receiving and sending countries. We are here, however, not so much concerned with the debate on definitions of trafficking per se. Our purpose is to discuss the availablility and consequences of certain methods that allow legal entry or residence for women from low-income countries like Thailand into high-income countries like Germany.

Although the number of Thais constitutes a small fraction of all foreigners in Germany, the overwhelming majority of Thai women migrate either as sex workers or as wives. Since 1975, increasing numbers of Thai women have migrated to Germany with their German husbands—a trend that parallels Thailand's popularity as a German tourist destination. By August 1998, figures show 26,443 women out of a total of 31,405 Thais in Germany (Amnesty for Women 1998). This gender imbalance is due to the increasing number of Thais, especially women, who have traveled to Germany to work or to marry German men from the 1980s onward (Chantavanich et al. 1999). Many Thai women came to Germany with the help of agencies, hoping to earn high incomes through sex work or in the entertainment sector (where Thai transsexual and transvestite dancers also came to work). By 1994, there were 18,995 Thai women married to German men residing in Germany (Chantavanich et al. 1999).

The migration of Thai women to Germany provides a classic case study of unskilled or low-skilled women's attempts to migrate in the context of rigid and stringent immigration or visa policies. This chapter explores Thai women's experiences as unskilled migrants and the process of gaining entry and a secure residential status in Germany. We argue that women's strategies as intending migrants and as migrants have focused primarily on marriage to a German national in order to start a new life that has to be seen against the backdrop of limited choices.

PROFILE OF THE THAI FEMALE MIGRANTS IN GERMANY

Many of the women who end up in Germany were at some point in their lives involved in the sex and entertainment business in Thailand. Thailand is known for its flourishing sex industry (Lim 1998) whose expansion has largely been related to U.S. military presence (at its height in the late 1960s) and gendered forms of development strategies of which the promotion of tourism has been a crucial part. In the early 1970s, areas like Pat-Pong, a small red-light district in Bangkok, became a venue for American soldiers and later for Western and Asian male tourists to Bangkok. Increasing German tourism to Thailand resulted in some German men taking Thai women back to Germany as wives, either with the intention of making them continue to work in the sex trade or not (Seabrook 1996). Work in German bars and brothels for independent Thai sex workers (i.e., those who came without "sponsorship" by a German man) began in the mid-1970s. In this initial phase, these women were able to make good money, rendering this type of work very attractive.

Many Thai women who work in the German sex trade come from provinces in Thailand's central northern, northeastern, and northern regions. In the mid-1990s, women from southern Thailand also started coming to Germany to work in the sex trade (Daily News Newspaper 1998). The average Thai female sex worker in Germany has completed compulsory primary school education or less. Some are illiterate. Most Thai women who migrate to Germany are from the lower to middle classes. Many have encountered financial problems in Thailand due to separation/divorce, widowhood, or collapsed family businesses. One third of them have debts of between 500–750 Euro (20,000–30,000 Baht), with some having run into even higher debts of up to 2,500 Euro (100,000 Baht) (Chantavanich et al. 1999, 62). Knowing that they can earn 4–5 times, or even 10 times, more in Germany than they could in Bangkok constitutes a big attraction for seeking work overseas (Chantavanich et al. 1999, 64).

The information in the four detailed case studies presented here has been collected over a six-year period and is based on interviews, observation, and interaction with the women in the course of Pat Mix's day-to-day work for Amnesty for Women.[3] Mix has provided assistance to each of the women for a period of two to six years. The names of the women have been changed in order to protect their identity.

These four case studies do not represent the whole range of Thai women's experience in Germany, but they illustrate very well the linkages between migration, sex work, and marriage. These cases have been selected by Mix based on the many years she has been working for Amnesty for Women as a social worker. Being a Thai national herself, Mix is in a special position to establish good relations with the Thai women in need and to offer assistance by way of counseling in their native language.

"SOUTH-NORTH MARRIAGE"

The phenomenon of women from lower-income countries seeking spouses from wealthier countries has been the subject of a large number of studies. Symbolic referents like "mail-order brides," mainly used by Western commentators, have acquired pejorative meanings. The tendency to characterize this phenomenon as a "marriage market" in which the women are classified as commodities has been criticized by Robinson, who comments that "the 'market' metaphor ignores the role of states in regulating particular forms of migration" (2001, 5). Other migration scholars, by contrast, have done exactly that: emphasize the crucial role of the state as regulator, at the sending as well as receiving end of migration (Piper and Ball 2001; Tyner 2000). What remains the case in much of the literature on women migrating as brides, however, is an overwhelming depiction of the women as victims. Sarsenov and Svedberg (2001) have argued in the context of Russian "mail-order brides" that to assume a clear south-north division between "southern-woman-victim" and "northern-man-offender" is far too simplistic. Rather, there are a variety of scenarios under which women migrate for marriage. Although women from lower-income countries may marry men from higher-income countries mainly for economic reasons, there are also other, noneconomic reasons for which "southern" women seek "northern" men, including a sense of adventure, the desire to escape narrow family relations, because of a failed relationship back home, and purely love (interview results by Piper; see also Nakamatsu 2001). A far less dramatic reason for wanting to migrate is the simple desire to travel abroad and experience a different world. Many Thais are said to idolize the developed world and nurture the dream of going abroad (Reunkeaw 1999).

Considering the overwhelming presence of Thai migrant women in the sex trade in Germany, it becomes vital to distinguish different types of sex work and also between different historical stages or phases of the migration process, as proposed by Skrobanek, Boonpakdi, and Janthakeero (1997, chapter 5). This notion of different phases or "waves" has been very well expressed by Marjon Wijers, an expert on forced prostitution, who comments upon the reality of sex work in the context of her native country, the Netherlands, in the following words:

> Some of the first women to come from abroad . . . were clearly disadvantaged, recruited in cruel ways, forced into terrible conditions—all the clichés. But when you have spent some period of time in a country, you start to make contacts and to organise. Soon these women were sending for their aunt or their sister—they were organising the migration of female friends and relatives. Within a few "generations" of migration, this group of women learned Dutch and became more independent. (Sex Work Migration Newsletter 2001, digest no. 30, p. 7)

Likewise Mix found that the "first wave" of Thai sex workers in Germany involved more extreme cases of bondage or slavery than today. In addition, it has mostly been relatives and friends in recent years who take on the role as recruiters or migration facilitators than total strangers.

Two serious issues, however, remain part of the migration pattern of most Thai women: indebtedness and a certain level of deception (and there are cases, albeit few, where the men are being deceived too). Many of the women whom

Amnesty for Women assists have been forced to pay levels of fees to agents, friends, or relatives for their assistance in organizing visas, marriages, employment, and travel that seem totally out of proportion. Also, there are matchmaking agencies that charge the women *and* men fees for services that they do not provide. For the women, a situation that comes close to prostitution (albeit unpaid and thus even more exploitative) is represented by one common scenario in which an agency arranges for various men to "try a number of women out" before agreeing to marry one of them. A woman might end up having to sleep with a number of men before being finally "chosen" for marriage. Hence, there are a number of situations that involve sex work of a different kind. What all of these situations have in common, however, is that they are the result of wider economic and sociocultural inequalities rendering sex work as an important source of income for women. We, therefore, agree with Kempadoo who argues that "sex work is another resource that women rely on to support and shelter themselves and families . . . to more generally improve the quality of life for themselves and kin. The amount they can potentially earn in the sex trade on a temporary short-term basis can be an initial pull and can be a retaining force" (1998, 128). To avoid temporary sex work becoming long term, some Thai women opt for marriage with foreign men.

Migration in the search for employment and migration for other goals (marriage) are in fact blurred in the women's own understanding as marriage is foremost about economic security. Women seek to marry German men to improve their livelihoods and to be able to send money home to relatives. This obligation to send remittances is a paramount concern for many women migrants. These women often consider first their family back home or children from previous relationships and their education when they decide to migrate abroad. Women's stories about previous relationships include their experience of being relegated to the status of "minor" wives in their country of origin. None of these women would aspire to the status of "minor wife," but circumstances and socioeconomic pressures pushed them in that direction. Others were deserted by their husband or partners, who subsequently did not support them financially. Most women who migrate to Germany have been in relationships before and have experienced problems with their partners, such as alcohol abuse, domestic violence, gambling, infidelity, and the like. In many ways, these women's approach to marriage with Western men is rooted in the same concerns that they have for marriage in general—with the only difference that the decision to marry a Western man derives from the hope for a real improvement of their relatively weak economic and social position. These women often do not realize the totally different power asymmetry between them and their foreign husbands, which is clearly in favor of the latter, particularly when the couple resides in the husband's country of origin. In addition, immigration

and visa regulations can have the effect of pushing migrant women into marriages with men whom they would have otherwise not married had there not
been specific pressures.

WIFE OR SEX WORKER? METHODS OF MIGRATION TO GERMANY

The number of Thai women who were married and lived in Germany increased from 36 in 1975 to 388 in 1985. In 1993, there were 1,468 new
marriages between Thai women and German men closely followed by
Filipino–German marriages (they total 1,042). Before 1990, a minority of Thai
women who traveled to Germany independently as Thai citizens were not required to have a visa to enter Germany, which was one of the factors that drew
many Thais specifically to Germany. Since 1990, however, they have had to obtain a "visitor's" visa and this means they need assistance particularly from
someone residing in Germany who is willing to write a letter of invitation. We
argue, therefore, that the continued rise in the number of Thais legally married
to German citizens is significantly related to the new requirement for Thai citizens to obtain visas. The argument that Thai women marry German men in
order to obtain legal status in Germany could be read as implying that these
marriages are purely "paper marriages." But this is too simplistic a picture.
There are various scenarios in which this marriage migration takes place. Some
enter as sex workers and subsequently marry (i.e., meeting German men in
Germany). Others enter as "fiancées," to become wives through matchmaking
agencies, or help by relatives or friends. A third scenario is to arrive as legally
married wives to men whom they had met in Thailand (in the men's capacity
as either tourists or business people). Hence, these women have either met
German men in Thailand while working in the sex and entertainment industry, or they are to be introduced to German men after arrival in Germany. The
latter scenario can be divided into two subscenarios: These men are genuinely
interested in a Thai woman as a wife, or they are pimps who intend to make
these women work as prostitutes. Unfortunately, even the first subscenario does
not always result in total avoidance of sex work: men who seek foreign wives
through introduction agencies often are the type who do not find wives otherwise, i.e., they are disabled or unemployed. In Mix's experience, there have
been a number of Thai women whose husbands' income was not sufficient and
because of lack of other skills, the women ended up working in the sex
and entertainment industry.

Before the immigration regulations were changed in 1990, the typical scenario was of Thai women entering Germany as sex workers on a tourist visa
with or without the help of an agent; they worked in Germany as sex work-

ers and often subsequently married a German client. Since 1990, Thai women have to enter Germany by invitation, and those who do enter have no network of relatives, friends, or acquaintances in Germany and cannot obtain a German visa without assistance from a broker. Subsequently, the cost of references and brokerage fees went up (Skrobanek et al. 1997). By the 1990s, a network of Thais residing in Germany had emerged, and thus many women were able to enter on visitor's visas. Those women who arrive in Germany as invited tourists nonetheless have to get married by the time their three-month visitor's visa expires if they want to stay on and/or work legally. These issues deserve more detailed scrutiny.

Immigration Visas

A tourist or visitor's visa to Germany for residents from what are classified as developing countries can be acquired in several different ways (German Embassy, Bangkok, 1996). Most Thai women who travel to Germany to work in the sex industry or to marry German men use these types of visas.

Tourist visas are granted to applicants who can convince the German embassy that their trips will be self-financed and that they intend to return to Thailand at the end of the visa period, i.e., that they have steady jobs with "reasonable" incomes and sufficient assets. In 1996, 15.34 percent of the total visas granted were to applicants in this category. Anyone who travels with a Schengen visa (which allows free travel between Germany, France, the Netherlands, Belgium, Luxembourg, Spain, Portugal, Italy, and Austria and recently Denmark and Sweden)[4] can stay in the country for three months when sponsored by a resident in Germany (or another Schengen country) who is financially responsible for the applicant. Most sponsors are friends, relatives, or German partners of the visitor.

A *visitor's visa* is granted to applicants who can convince the German embassy, in a similar way, that their trips are going to be sponsored by a German citizen or any other permanent resident holder in Germany. In 1996, 19.87 percent of the total visas granted were to applicants in this category. Thus one in every five Thais who receives a visa from the German embassy in Bangkok is sponsored. This type of visa is issued to people who want to visit their family and relatives in Germany. Again, the sponsor is financially responsible for the visitor's stay in Germany. The visa expires after three months and can be extended.

Another visa category open to Thai women is the so-called *artist's visa*. This type of visa is used for visiting artists, such as musicians or dancers.[5] The visa allows the migrant to stay for a period of three years, but it can be renewed on a yearly basis thereafter, at which time agents usually ask for service fees from the artist. In the late 1980s, many Thai women traveled to Germany using the artist's visa, a trip that was arranged by bar or club owners. The women usually had to pay for this arrangement, a price that included the airline fare and visa fees, as well as food and lodging in Germany. The visa's validity is restricted to the duration of the job contract. When the job contract is cancelled or expires, the artist loses the right to stay in Germany (Amnesty for Women 1998).

The actual immigration paths also vary from case to case. Some Thai women arrange for a tourist visa on their own or travel unaccompanied to Germany. Many of them have some experiences of traveling abroad but some are traveling for the first time. They pay all their own travel costs and are met at the destination by friends and relatives who act as sponsors. This network of sponsors is essential because many women cannot apply for tourist visas without the help of friends or relatives. There are no payments, other than gifts, for such arrangements. In another scenario, the women are accompanied by friends or relatives who arrange the trip. In this case, the trip to Germany is completely sponsored and organized (including work places, marriages, and so on) by friends or relatives. Many Thai women who come to Germany using this method have already worked as sex workers in Thailand and understand that they will have to pay back all of the costs to their sponsors. Women who travel accompanied by friends or relatives nearly always travel with tourist or visitor visas.

Women can also be accompanied by an agent. There are two types of agents: (1) a representative of a formal agency that provides jobs abroad and (2) a representative of a private agency that is run by local Thai women and Thai women who live in Germany. Because the German immigration laws are so complicated, some Thai women feel unable to arrange the journey themselves and hence seek assistance from agents who produce an invitation from German residents for Thai women to apply for a tourist visa. Some agents find someone who will marry a Thai woman so that she enters Germany as a wife—which points to the clear existence of "sham marriages" (see below). Alternatively, the agents have a job on offer in a bar, cabaret, or brothel. Those who travel to Germany accompanied by agents usually travel with an artist's or tourist visa. Women have to pay relatively high fees (from 4000–7500 Euro) for these arrangements.

"Sham Marriages"

Many Thai women decide to marry German men to secure their residential status and/or work permits either prior to or after entering the country. It is impossible to express in percentages how many "paper marriages" there are, but they do exist. There are a number of terms referring to similar incidences, including "paper marriage," "sham marriage," or "marriage of convenience," and it is not clear whether they are supposed to indicate differences. We use the terms here interchangeably to refer to scenarios where the women had no prior contact at all to their "husband" and clearly marry purely to secure a legal immigrant status. Such "marriages of convenience" can cost anywhere between 4000 and 10,000 Euro.

Before 1990, some of the women who worked illegally in the sex trade decided to obtain a legal resident visa by paying German men to marry them. There seem to be plenty of German men taking advantage of the situation and who were willing to marry the women for a price. It is wrong to assume that all the men who agree to such arrangements are brothel owners who "marry" to recruit sex workers for their establishments. Among the case studies here, there is a Thai woman who paid a German student to marry her. One woman from among our cases not only paid for a sham marriage, but was also asked by her "husband" to pay him to agree to a divorce so that she could marry another German man she really wanted to live with.

From Sex Worker to Wife to Citizen?

Germany's residency and naturalization laws pose a reasonably high obstacle to these foreign spouses who wish to become citizens in their own right. Until recently, migrants who married German citizens had to be married for four years before achieving full individual rights (independent of their status as spouse). The law enabled a man to threaten to send his wife back home to her country if she did not do his bidding as authorities would deport her if a divorce occurred before the end of the four-year period. Amnesty for Women and other women's organizations in Germany campaigned against this law for many years, achieving a victory in June 2000, when finally a new immigration law was passed that enables migrants to obtain their own independent status after only two years of marriage to a German spouse.

Some women leave the sex trade after marrying, while others continue to be sex workers or become sex workers because their husbands are unemployed and they have no other options. Finding work other than sex work is not easy for Thai women who usually do not speak German or English well enough. Thai women with resident visas are allowed to work legally in the entertainment sector as well as in any other job. In reality, their choices are limited if they lack good German or English. In this respect, they are inferior to their Filipino counterparts who usually speak very good English and have achieved higher educational levels (and thus find learning a new language less troublesome). The women among our sample made little effort to learn German, and their definition of leading a successful life was typically measured by the achievement of economic security. They did not consider integration into German society a priority. Instead, they tend to concentrate on the education of their children who are left behind in Thailand and/or are the offspring from marriages with Germans.

CASE STUDIES

The following four cases illustrate the complex nature of the linkages between sex work, marriage, and migration.

Case Study 1

Manida was thirty-five years old at the time of the interview, she was born in Central Thailand, and has four years of primary school education. Her family, large by Thai standards, was very poor. Her mother had a small food stand in the market near her home; and as her father did not have a regular job, he would help his wife cook when he had no other work to go to. All four sisters left school after only four years in order to help their mother. Her mother died of cancer when Manida was six years old. Her sisters raised her and when she finished four years of primary school, she also quit school to help out around the house and look after her younger brother when her sisters were busy with the food stand they ran. Her father died when she was nine. One of her sisters moved out with her boyfriend, leaving the other sisters to run the food stand. Later on they all found jobs working in a factory. One of her sisters had an English boyfriend who was working as a supervisor at the factory. When his contract ran out, he had to return to England. At this point he asked her sister to marry him. They got married and went to England. Manida said that her sister was fine in England but was unable to send money home because her husband had gone back to university to further his studies. As they had to budget their expenses, there was no extra money to send home as he had promised before they married. Three years later, a second sister married an Englishman, a friend of Manida's husband, and she moved with him to Dubai. So Manida was left with her unmarried sister and younger brother. Manida was nineteen years old then.

Manida married a Thai Chinese and moved in with her husband's family as is usual in the Chinese tradition. They had a small grocery store in the market. She did not get along very well with her mother-in-law. After a year she had a baby girl. When her daughter was two years old she left her husband. She said that she thought of her two sisters who had married European men and hoped to do the same. So she did not go back home to her sister and brother. Instead, she went to Pattaya, hoping to find a job in a restaurant, but she ended up working in a go-go bar. Manida never told her sisters about her jobs in Pattaya. She sent money to support her brother's education, but while in Pattaya, she never contacted her daughter or her husband's family.

Eventually she found a German boyfriend who asked her to come to Germany with him to work for a period of three months. She informed her sisters about her journey to Europe and went to Germany, hoping to earn some money during the three-month period so that she could quit her job on her return to Thailand. Her boyfriend took her to Frankfurt where she worked in a brothel. He asked her to help him pay for the expenses of the journey and arrangements. She agreed. After two months, her boyfriend suggested that she marry him in order to get a permit to stay in Germany. Manida said that at first she was not sure, but that she was tempted by the amount of money she earned every day. She knew that she would also have to pay him if she married him, but in the end she agreed, and so they married and moved to Hamburg.

In Hamburg, her husband rented an apartment for her to work with other Thai women. Manida said that she had saved a lot of money to send home for her brother and sisters. She planned to work for another year or so, after which she would go back to Thailand. During this time, she had one regular client who came to meet her very often. She told him her story. He told her that he wanted to help her and marry her. Her husband threatened to kill her when he learned about the affair. But Manida carried on working for another year and still stayed in contact with her German boyfriend. Finally, she told her husband that she wanted a divorce or else she would go to the police. Her husband accepted it in order to avoid problems and also because he had two other Thai women working for him.

Manida decided to get married again, and although she does not love this man very much, she considers him "a nice man." He has a steady job, even though he is not the rich man she had hoped to marry. He agreed to give her 400 DM every month. Now Manida has a three-year-old son and works as a maid in a hotel. She said she is happy now and never looks back at the past. All her sisters are now living in Hamburg, Germany. Two of them came to work as sex workers after their divorces and later married German men. The other two sisters came for arranged marriages, which Manida arranged herself, while her youngest brother still lives and works in Bangkok.

Case Study 2

Noi was thirty-two years old when interviewed, she was born in northeast Thailand (Isarn), and has four years of primary school education. Her mother inherited a lot of land from her parents, but preferred to run a small business.

She did not want to work as a rice farmer, and so rented her inheritance out to other farmers. Her father worked as a bus driver. Noi said that she had a wonderful life as a young child. However, her father's gambling gave the family financial problems. Her father wanted to go to work in the Middle East, so they had to mortgage some of their land in order to pay for the traveling expenses. Because he was cheated in the deal he never made it to the Middle East. He went back to gambling again. Later, he lost everything. They had to move to another province, and Noi had to quit school. Noi said that the nightmare began when she had to start working in a rice field at the age of 12, earning only 25 Baht (US$0.50) per day.

Her neighbor came back from Bangkok and asked whether she wanted to come to work in Bangkok as a housemaid. She agreed because she felt she did not have another alternative. She worked for a couple who had one young child. The husband was a government employee. She had to work every day and earned 1,500 Baht (30.00 Euro) a month, sending most of the money home. She worked there for two years when her boss asked whether she would like to come to Japan with them to look after their daughter because he had been posted to work there for four years. She was very excited about traveling abroad. In Tokyo, Noi only had to look after the girl, while her employer's wife looked after the household. She was paid only 3,000 Baht (75.00 Euro) per month to work in Japan with the family. Later, she was introduced to a Japanese man by her elderly Japanese neighbor who thought that Noi was treated unfairly. Noi left the Thai family after staying with them for two years and moved in with her Japanese boyfriend. He was still living with his parents, 300 kilometers to the south of Tokyo. She thought that Japanese people would be like Thai people because they are also Asian. She was mistaken. His parents hated her because they thought she was a sex worker like many other Thai women who live and work in Japan.

Noi tried her best to help out in the household. She said "I helped them with everything, washing their clothes, ironing and cleaning but they never showed me any love." She tried to tell her boyfriend about this problem but he always ignored her. She loved him because in some ways he was a good, responsible man. He gave her money to send home every month. Later on she found out that he went to a bar where Thai sex workers were employed. This upset her, causing them to have many arguments. Finally she left him after he beat her badly. She went to work in the bar. Her boyfriend (the one who beat her) was a *yakuza* (mafioso). She worked as a prostitute and later became manager of the bar (a mama san). When the police came to the bar to arrest the *Yakuza* gang, she was also arrested and sent back to Thailand. But by that time, Noi had saved a lot of money.

She went home to visit her parents and gave them most of the money she had, and then went to Pattaya to look for a job. She worked at a bar there for three months before she was asked by a Thai woman if she wanted to go to work in Germany. She came to Germany with an artist's visa arranged by the same Thai woman, who was married to a German man. She was told that after she started working she would have to repay a large sum of money for the visa, traveling costs, and so on. Within six months of arriving, Noi was free of debts. She worked in a bar in a red-light district in Hamburg. The artist's visa lasted for three years and could not be extended. Noi said she wanted to quit and look for another job, but her limited ability of German prevented her from acquiring other means of employment. Her visa had nearly run out when she met a German student who came to the bar with his friends. They met outside on her day off and she told him about her problems. The bar owner did not want to have her in the bar anymore, because she did not make enough money for the bar, as she did not accept clients very often. The student agreed to marry her in order to help her stay in Germany.

They got married, but he found a job in the south of Germany and moved there after his graduation. She lived in Hamburg alone and quit the job. She joined a two-year program in a textile workshop, a program that is subsidized by the government to help women who are drug addicts or those who wanted to leave the sex trade and needed to acquire new skills in order to do so. Noi joined her husband in the south of Germany after she finished the program. It became a real marriage when she became pregnant. Now Noi is very happy with her life. She said that she cannot send money to Thailand anymore because she has her own family. "They have had enough money from me," she said. "I need to have my own life."

Case Study 3

Angsana (twenty-eight years) was also born in Isarn (northeast Thailand), enjoyed five years of primary school, and also comes from a large family. Her mother opened a small food stand at home in order to help her father, who could not support the family with his income as a rickshaw driver. Later, her two brothers left school and also became rickshaw drivers. She left school after five years when her two older sisters went to work in Bangkok. Her mother wanted her to help out at home. She was eleven years old. She did not know what kind of work her sisters did, but they sent money home regularly. Her father died two years later. Angsana stayed home with her mother and brothers. One of her brothers married but continued to stay at home with Angsana, her younger sisters, other brother and mother. He stopped working, simply waiting for his sisters to send money home every month. One of her sisters came home with a German boyfriend and said that she was going to live in Germany with him. She promised to try to find a job and send money home. They did not hear from her for a long time. Another brother decided to go to work in Saudi Arabia, and her mother gave him all the money she had. Angsana was very upset about this situation, saying that it was unfair because the money was from her sisters' savings. She was sixteen years old when she met her husband.[6]

She left home and stayed with him in a small village nearby. Her husband was a truck driver. When Angsana already had three children, her sister came back from Germany. Her sister gave her mother some money and said that she had been unable to send money home earlier because she did not work and her husband never gave her any extra money. She had divorced her husband and was now working again. Angsana told her sister that her own husband was hardly at home and that when he was at home, he beat her and the children. Her sister told her that she used to work as a sex worker in Bangkok before she went to Germany and had hoped to retire from this type of job. But because her husband did not support her, she went back to sex work. When the husband came to know this, he was angry and demanded that she quit her job or else he would divorce her. She agreed to the divorce and carried on working. She asked Angsana whether she wanted to come with her and work in Germany, but Angsana hesitated because it entailed leaving her children with her mother. But her sister argued, "You have nothing to lose." Finally, Angsana went to Germany in 1993 on a tourist visa (with the help of her sister's German boyfriend).

But when she arrived in Berlin and realized what she had to do, she changed her mind and did not want to work. But her sister said that she had to work, otherwise there would be no money for her children at home. Because she only had a tourist visa, Angsana had to work in an apartment brothel, not in a bar like her sister. Her sister helped to pay for everything from the beginning. Before her visa ran out, her sister said that she could extend it for another three months but that after that she had to go back to Thailand or find someone to marry her. Within six months, Angsana managed to save some money and remit it to her mother. She said that it was very hard, but that once she started to earn money, everything became easier. She did not want to pay anyone to get married, so she decided to stay in Germany illegally. She moved to Hamburg and worked in an apartment brothel. Many other Thai sex workers worked in the same building without any trouble from the immigration police. She met a German man who wanted to marry her but her illegal status made it very complicated to do so. Unfortunately, she was arrested by the immigration police when they raided her apartment building. She was jailed for three weeks before being charged with illegal immigration, not prostitution. In court she pleaded not guilty claiming that she was waiting to get married. She was set free but fined. She finally got married but carried on working, as her husband was unemployed at that time.

Angsana stopped working when her husband found a job. She has not been back to Thailand since she went to Germany six years ago. She said she missed her children very much and would like to bring them here. She still has to wait for legal documents that are not yet ready. She will ask her other sister to come here too. The other sister who brought Angsana to Hamburg is still working in the sex trade.

Case Study 4

Maleewan is the oldest among the interviewed women (forty-three) and also originally comes from Isarn (northeast Thailand). Both of her parents died in a road accident when she was four years old. Her sisters raised her and later, they all moved from Isarn to Bangkok. Two of her sisters worked in a factory and the other two opened a small food stand, selling Isarn food. Maleewan did not go to school until she was nine years old, because her sisters had no house registration to show the authorities. She left school after two years because she was embarrassed that she was so much older than the other pupils in her class and started helping her sisters at the food stall. They rented a small house near Klongthoey, the biggest slum in Bangkok. Two of her older sisters married and moved out, leaving her with her sister and younger brother. She met her first husband when she was seventeen years old. He was a taxi driver and came from the same province as Maleewan.

He moved into her house because she wanted to work with her sister. She had one daughter with him and the marriage went well during the first two years. Then one day his first wife came to her house. He was already married and had three children at home in the northeast. She was very disappointed and angry, and they split up. Then her sister returned to the northeast and Maleewan managed the stall with the help of her brother who could only work after school and on weekends. Maleewan met another man who came to eat at the stall every day. Later he also moved into her house and helped in the stall. Maleewan got pregnant but continued to work until the day she went to the hospital. She said her husband was very good until she was pregnant with her third child, when she found out that he had started seeing other women. They fought every day and before she gave birth to the third child, he took all the money she had saved and disappeared.

Maleewan recalls that terrible time. Her eldest daughter helped her a lot with the household work and looked after the baby even though she was only six years old. Her sister came back from the northeast after she heard the news. Maleewan borrowed money to start her business again. One day, she met a neighbor who came to eat at her stall. She looked very rich with her thick gold chain. She said that she had just come back from Germany where she worked. She asked whether Maleewan wanted to come to work with her in a Thai restaurant there. She would pay Maleewan's traveling costs and Maleewan would have to pay her back within the first three months in Germany. Her sister warned Maleewan that going to Germany could be dangerous and that they might force her to work in the sex industry, because she had seen a lot of reports in the newspapers and on TV. Maleewan said "I have to take a risk." She added that she had had two husbands, slept with them without ever earning any money, and still they deceived her. Maleewan borrowed a large sum of money at a high rate of interest and gave it to her sister to look after her children and carry on the food stall business.

On the way to Germany, her neighbor told her, as she had expected, that she would work in a bar not a restaurant. Maleewan worked in a go-go bar in a red-light district of Hamburg. Her neighbor told her that she owed her 8,000 DM for the arrangements but that this amount would be deducted from her salary later. Maleewan said that she was shocked by the high amount of the debts. She started to work after one week. She said that the Thai women she worked with were very friendly and taught her a lot of things. Maleewan worked for seven months before she was able to pay back all her debts, both in Thailand and Germany. Maleewan did not want to return to Thailand as she had thought she would before she paid off her debts. She wanted to earn more money for her children. She knew that she could never earn as much as she did in her current job. Maleewan worked in the go-go bar for two years before one of her regular clients asked her to marry him. She decided to marry him but continued working. She said she needed someone to be with her and look after her, but he did not earn enough to support her family in Thailand. She told him that she would work for another two or three years. She was already thirty-six years old.

Her husband acted as her chauffeur. He would drop her off in the evening and pick her up after work. Later, he quit his job. Maleewan said that she was forced to pay for expenses at home. Maleewan left her job one year later and refused to support her husband. She also stopped sending money back home, believing she had sent enough remittances over the years. She found a cleaning job, from which she earned 15 DM per hour. Her husband was very angry about it, but he could not do anything. The marriage went downhill. She and her husband went to Thailand for the first time after three years. She thought of bringing her children back to Germany, but her husband did not want them to come. They quarrelled very often about money. Finally, he told her to leave the apartment because he had fallen in love with another Thai woman whom he met during the holiday in Thailand. Maleewan went to stay with a Thai friend. During that time she met her friend's brother-in-law and fell in love with him. She divorced her husband one year later and now has a permanent resident's visa and stays with her boyfriend. Maleewan said that she does not have to marry again. She cleans three times a week for a company and cleans a private home as well. She earns enough to get by in Germany. She said she might go back to Thailand but not just yet.

CONCLUSION

Many Thai women have used some kind of sex-affective method to migrate to Germany in the search of a better life—either as legal wives or as "sex workers-to-be-wives." Marriage is often the goal and outcome of sex workers' migration as it offers an important, if not the only, means to obtain a secure residence permit—i.e., as a ticket to immigration. This "marriage migration" is one crucial step in these women's strategy employed to escape from poverty or misfortune and to begin a new life outside of sex work. Unfortunately, the strategy of using marriage to escape sex work and find economic security has not worked in the long run for many of these women. First of all, as is apparent from the case studies, few women have escaped from sex work, including those who married German men. True, some entered a marriage of convenience to be able to work in the sex trade in the first place but the ultimate goal was to marry someone who could support them financially and allow them to send remittances. This strategy was supposed to free them from sex work. In the majority of cases, however, they were still compelled to work in the sex trade even after marrying Germans. They discovered that either their German husbands would not/could not support them (and provide cash for remittances), or that their husbands were pimps who profited by their continued participation in the sex industry. Interestingly, when confronted with this disappointment, many of the women looked for yet another German husband who they hoped would make their dreams come true this time. Hence, there is the pattern of Thai women sex workers embroiled in multiple marriages, until at last they find the "right" husband—a true provider. They can then leave sex work to be housewives or else to move to less lucrative but socially more acceptable low-skilled jobs such as cleaners or domestic helpers. Female Thai sex workers in Germany thus tend to be interlocked in two types of cycles: 1) sex work–marriage–sex work or 2) marriage–sex work–marriage, whereby many go through a series of "husbands" and disappointments. Some eventually free themselves from sex work, send remittances, and enjoy a good marital relationship.

NOTES

1. In 1988, there were 92,175 Thai workers in the Middle East (Chantavanich, Nittayanantta, Mix, Ruenkaew, and Khemkrut 1999).

2. We are fully aware of the problematic notion of trafficking and its analytical (albeit in practice often blurred) distinction from smuggling. For a more detailed discussion see Piper and Uhlin (2002).

3. Amnesty for Women was established in 1986 in Hamburg, Germany. It is not related to Amnesty International, but is a migrant center set up to assist primarily Southeast Asian, Latin American, and Eastern European migrants. The group engages in campaigning against trafficking in women and forced prostitution.

4. This visa category is the result of the Schengen group set up in 1985 as the result of an agreement among certain European countries to abolish their internal borders.

5. This type of visa is not a uniquely German phenomenon. It also exists in Japan and Korea, where it is commonly known as "entertainer's visa." However, the legal periods of duration vary. In Japan, this visa is only valid for six months at a time.

6. "Husband" does not necessarily refer to a legal marriage (civil law marriage), but can mean a common law relationship. In the interviews, the women used the term husband, but the real situation might be such that these men were not civil law spouses.

REFERENCES

Amnesty for Women (AfW). *Germany: A Paradise for Women?* Hamburg, Germany: AfW, 1999.

———. *Yearly Report.* Hamburg, Germany: AfW, 1998.

Chant, S. "Gender and Tourism Employment in Mexico and the Philippines." Pp. 120–79 in *Gender, Work and Tourism*, edited by T. M. Sinclair. London: Routledge, 1997.

Chantawanich, S., S. Nittayanantta, P. Mix, P. Ruenkaew, and A. Khemkrut. *The Migration of Thai Women to Germany: Causes, Living Conditions and Impacts for Thailand and Germany.* Bangkok: Asian Research Center for Migration, Institute of Asian Studies, Chulalongkorn University (in Thai language), 1999.

Daily News Newspaper (Bangkok, Thailand). February 13, 1998 (in Thai language).

German Embassy, Visa Department, Bangkok. *Visa Statistics.* Bangkok: German Embassy, 1996.

Gills, D.-S. S., and N. Piper (Eds.). *Women and Work in Globalising Asia.* London: Routledge, 2002.

Kempadoo, K., and J. Doezema (Eds.). *Global Sex Workers, Rights, Resistance, and Redefinition.* New York: Routledge, 1998.

Lim, L. L. (Ed). *The Sex Sector—The Economic and Social Bases of Prostitution in Southeast Asia.* Geneva: ILO, 1998.

Nakamatsu, T. "Marriage by Introduction: Social and Legal Realities of 'Asian' Wives of Japanese Men." Paper presented at the Annual Meeting of the Association of Asian Studies, Chicago, March 22–25, 2001.

Pettman, J. J. *Worlding Women: A Feminist International Politics.* St. Leonards, N. S. W.: Allen & Unwin, 1996.

Piper, N. "Labor Migration, Trafficking and International Marriage: Female Cross-Border Movements into Japan." *Asian Journal of Women's Studies* vol. 5, no. 2 (1999): 69–99.

Piper, N., and R. Ball. "Globalisation of Asian Migrant Labour: The Philippine-Japan Connection." *Journal of Contemporary Asia* vol. 31, no. 4 (2001): 533–54.

Piper, N., and A. Uhlin. "Transnational Advocacy Networks and the Issue of Female Labour Migration and Trafficking in East and Southeast Asia. A Gendered Analysis of Opportunities and Obstacles." *Asia Pacific Migration Journal* vol. 11, no. 2 (2002): 171–96.

Reunkeaw, P. "Marriage Migration of Thai Women in Germany." Paper presented at the 7th International Conference on Thai Studies, Amsterdam, the Netherlands, July 4–8, 1999.

Robinson, K. "Marriage Migration, Family Values and the 'Global Ecumene.'" Paper presented at the International Workshop on Migration and the "Asian Family" in a Globalising World, Asian MetaCentre, National University of Singapore, Singapore, April 16–18, 2001.

Sarsenov, K., and E. Svedberg. "Mail-order bride migration from the former Soviet Union to Scandinavia." Paper presented at the Political Studies Association, Manchester University/U.K., April 10–12, 2001.

Seabrook, J. *Travels in the Skin Trade—Tourism and the Sex Industry.* London: Pluto Press, 1996.

Sexworkmigration network. *Digest Number 30,* e-mail newsletter: sexworkmigration @yahoogroups.com. Accessed June 27, 2001.

Skrobanek, S., N. Boonpakdi, and C. Janthakeero. *The Traffic in Women—Human Realities of the International Sex Trade.* London: Zed Books, 1997.

Stern, A. *Thailand's Migration Situation and Its Relations with APEC Members and Other Countries in Southeast Asia.* Research Paper no. 011. Bangkok: Asian Research Center for Migration, Institute of Asian Studies, Chulalongkorn University, 1998.

TAMPEP (Transnational AIDS/STD Prevention among Migrant Prostitutes in Europe/ Project). *TAMPEP Final Report.* Amsterdam, the Netherlands: TAMPEP, 1997/1998.

———. *TAMPEP Final Report.* Amsterdam, the Netherlands: TAMPEP, 1996/1997.

———. *TAMPEP Final Report.* Amsterdam, the Netherlands: TAMPEP, 1995/1996.

Truong, T.-D. *Sex, Money and Morality: Prostitution and Tourism in South-East Asia.* London: Zed Books, 1990.

Tyner, J. A. "Migrant Labour and the Politics of Scale: Gendering the Philippine State." *Asia Pacific Viewpoint* vol. 41, no. 2 (2000): 131–54.

Williams, P. (Ed). *Illegal Immigration and Commercial Sex—The New Slave Trade.* London: Frank Cass, 1999.

Wongchai, Y., N. Chitsawang, S. Singhasene, S. L. Sombat, and S. Yodpet. *Economic and Social Factors Affecting Thai Women, Determination Practicing Prostitution Abroad.* Research Paper, Faculty of Sociology, Thammasat University, Thailand, 1991.

4

Sisterhood Is Local: Filipino Women in Mount Isa

Mina Roces

Filipinos are the fastest growing new migrant population in Mount Isa, the small, remote mining town in northern Queensland. Arriving in more significant numbers since the 1980s, they are mostly women migrants for marriage—brides intending to become miner's wives in the isolated town with a population of 22,863 (Australian Bureau of Statistics 1996). But although the predominant popular perception is that these women remain somewhat ossified in the status of "bride," in reality they quickly enter the workforce and are literally visible in the service and hospitality industries. Workers in K-Mart or Woolworths, and housekeepers in the Mercure Hotel and other hotels, waitresses in the Irish Club (the hub of the town's social life), chefs in restaurants, nurses' aides in nursing homes, day care mothers, museum assistants, and secretaries in offices, these women participate quite actively in the town's working life. The town has hired a Filipino woman as a migrant helper to advise the incoming migrants of the services available to them. The town's airport manager, Mariane, is also a Filipina who came to Mount Isa as a bride. Hence although the primary reason for migration is marriage (they come as either brides or fiancés), these women quickly become mothers, workers, and citizens.

While a job gives them the economic wherewithal to send much needed money back to the Philippines (many women see it as their duty to send money back to relatives) and financial independence, a job also helps them cope with life in an isolated area deprived of the support of their kinship group. Women interviewed speak of wanting to work "or else they will go crazy." But women's contributions to the small town go beyond paid work. Women also volunteer for civic activities such as singing in the church choir; dancing for multicultural events, at nursing homes, or for charitable causes; fund-raising for the church; and other civic activities. Most eventually apply for Australian citizenship, and many participate in the town's political life. They campaigned for Member of Parliament (MP) Tony McGrady for example, distributing leaflets, making rosettes (small corsages made up of ribbons like boutonnieres), and putting up posters. Tony McGrady himself is aware of their voting potential and perhaps that partially explains why he attends most of the social events of the Filipino community. In this sense, contrary to common Australian perceptions that these Filipino "mail-order brides"[1] only come to Australia to get a better life and then exploit Australian social services (particularly those less fortunate who become victims of domestic violence), in reality, many of these women make diverse contributions to their new country. The primary contributions are in the area of the town's labor force and civic life. The folk dance group for example is very popular in the town and is often asked to perform for town festivals and events. As participants in the workforce and the community's social, cultural, and religious life, these women negotiate for themselves a public space despite their double marginalized status as miner's wives (miners are perceived to be members of the working class who are also geographically marginalized because they live in remote, isolated rural areas) and as women of color (often subject to daily discrimination).

Their engagement with Mount Isa is gendered: work and socials are often "women-only" affairs where husbands are the ones marginalized or excluded. While some socializing is done with husbands and family, women look forward to these "women-only" activities (and by this is usually meant Filipino women exclusively, see below). They help each other obtain employment as a group, and their social life reveals tight female bonding from an all-female gambling group to women's *karaoke* night on Wednesday at the Irish Club, women's rehearsal for the dance groups, and women's lunches and gossip gatherings. In this sense Filipino women migrants have created communities that helped them to both cope with life in Mount Isa and contribute to the town's life through the nexus of an almost exclusively female migrant world. Deprived of their kinship group so crucial to survival in the Philippines, women's networks have facilitated the transition from bride to woman, from wife to worker, and from migrant to new Australian. The "sisterhood" of Filipino women replaces the kinship group and it acts in the interests of these women in the midst of an otherwise hostile environment.[2]

FILIPINO BRIDES IN AUSTRALIA

The topic of Filipino brides in Australia has been a popular one for social scientists in both countries since the mid-1980s. The literature, most of it excellent, has privileged studies profiling the Filipina wife or Australian husband

(Cooke 1986a, 1986b; Scaramella 1988), the reasons for the proliferation of Australian-Filipino marriages and the politics of migration (Cooke 1986a, 1986b; Cabigon 1994; Smith and Kaminskas 1992; Jackson 1993), or an analysis of the happiness or success factor in Australian-Filipino marriages (Cahill 1990; Pendlebury 1990; Vogels 1987; Chuah, Chuah, Reid-Smith, and Rice 1987; Smith and Kaminskas 1990; Smith and Boileau 1994; Brown 1994). On the other hand, feminist scholars see this migrants-for-marriage phenomenon in terms of the commodification of women, as a form of prostitution or trafficking in women (De Stoop 1994; Boer 1988). From this feminist perspective, the paramount image of the Filipina migrant is that of the woman as victim. Two prevailing perceptions of the Filipina migrant in Australia are the woman as victim of domestic violence or homicide or, ironically, the woman as manipulative and scheming who marries only for the purpose of exploiting Australian men. This aggressive, materialistic woman is also represented as a willing "sex slave." The latter image is encapsulated by the character of Cynthia in the film *Priscilla Queen of the Desert*, an obviously orientalized former bar girl who tricked her Australian husband into marrying her. Australian feminist scholars have tackled these contradictory orientalist images of the Filipina "mail-order bride" held by the Australian public and the Australian men who marry these women, as well as the media that on the surface appears to empathize with the women but that reinforces such orientalist imaginings (Simons 1998; Holt 1996; Saroca 1997; Robinson 1996; Cunneen and Stubbs 1997, esp. 114). The image of women as victims of domestic violence is substantiated by the statistics, which reveal that Filipino women in Australia may be overrepresented as victims of homicide with Filipino-born women aged between twenty to thirty-nine holding a homicide victimization rate that is 5.6 times that of other Australian women in the same age group (Cunneen and Stubbs 1997, 30–31 and 122). There is no doubt that the victim label has evidence to support it, particularly if one extended the definition of victimization to include not just domestic violence but also the lack of financial independence (women hold the purse strings in the Philippines), and the "slave mentality" wherein wives are expected to be a "maid," cooking three hot meals a day, cleaning and serving their husbands who also expect them to fulfill every sexual fantasy in bed (see Roces 1998a). Such a view, though in some cases accurate, is still one-dimensional, obscuring the possibility of the blurring of distinction between victim and agency (Roces 1998a), neglecting other aspects of the Filipino woman's role as wife and mother, or of their success in assimilating and participating in multicultural Australia (as laborers in the workforce or as citizens), as well as the woman's engagement with issues of identity. After all, many women married Australian men in order to fulfill roles of wife and mother denied to them in the Philippines as *solteras* (bachelor women) past marriageable age (Roces 1998a). At the same time, as married women in Australia they enhance their roles as dutiful daughters or sisters remitting money back home to the extended kinship group in the Philippines.

The literature on migrant women and the use of support services in Australia is limited to empirical studies in the areas of demography, labor, employment/unemployment, and health care.[3] Most studies are interested in the phenomenon of the marriage for migration and the quality of the marriage. In this perspective the women remain fixed as "brides" but not women, as incoming migrants who need support services rather than as women who contribute to Australian society (see though Roces 1996). Filipino women are defined as "wife and mother" but not as "worker." I would like to fill an important gap in the scholarship of the field by focusing on Filipino women's contribution to Mount Isa (read Australian) society through their new roles as workers and as civic workers because their contribution to other aspects of society that do not necessarily translate to paid work is also counted as an important facet of their new roles as migrant women and as Australian citizens. In addition, this chapter explores women's reactions to a harsh isolated environment and suggests that women's abilities to adapt to the small remote mining town deprived of their kinship support group is through interaction with a "female world," a local sisterhood. Since most Filipino women migrants eventually live in mining towns set in isolated rural areas like Mount Isa (Cunneen and Stubbs 1997, 17; Perdon 1998, 26), the experience of the Filipino women in Mount Isa is a case study for a significant portion of the migrants for marriage.

Filipino women have been coming to Australia as migrants for marriage since the 1970s but the steady increase began in the 1980s and continues at the turn of the century. In 1983 and 1984, for example, they increased by 164 percent with 1,729 visas given to fiancées (excluding those given tourist visas but who stayed and married Australians). In 1988–1989, 2,133 visas were issued making the Philippines the largest single source of spouses/fiancées entering Australia (Perdon 1998, 23). The Filipino immigrant population in Australia reflects this migrant-for-marriage phenomenon with the gender bias in favor of women (twice as many women born in the Philippines as men born in the Philippines). In 1991, for example, approximately 70 percent of Filipino women migrants in Australia were sponsored as fiancées of men who were Australian residents (Cunneen and Stubbs 1997, 13). Between 1999 and 2000 the largest number of spouses who came into Australia came from the UK (in the 1990s the numbers of Filipinos coming as spouses dropped proportionally compared to the 1980s) but the Philippines ranked third with 2,135 persons. In Queensland, the statistics for settler arrivals shows a definite gender bias with significantly more Filipino females (364 persons) coming compared

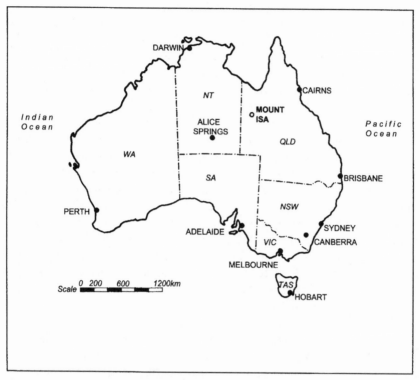

Figure 4.1. **Map of Australia Showing Mount Isa**

to 124 males (*Population Flows* 2000, 21, 78–79). The Filipino immigrant community in Australia, particularly outside the metropolitan centers such as Sydney, Melbourne, or Perth, is a remarkably gendered one: one could argue that a significant proportion of Filipino migrants in the Australian countryside is composed of migrants who came as brides.

MOUNT ISA

Mount Isa is an ideal site from which to study the interaction of race, gender, and class in the experience of Filipina migrants for marriage. A small remote mining town, the experiences of Filipinas are much highlighted: both their contributions and their visibility assume clear proportions. For instance, Filipino women visibly stand out as shop assistants in shopping centers, particularly at Woolworths, and as waitresses in the Irish Club. In a town that has been predominantly white, apart from Aboriginals, the only other women of color in any significant numbers are the Filipinas. Filipino women interviewed disclose that when they were new arrivals in Mount Isa, it was not difficult to make contact with fellow Filipinas because it was easy to spot them in public places such as the shops and in the Catholic Church. (Since Filipinos are predominantly Catholic, the best way to meet fellow Filipinos if you are a new migrant is at weekly mass. Because there is only one Catholic Church in Mount Isa, the church become the site for connecting with the Filipino population of the town.) At the same time, their physical presence in a predominantly white environment calls attention to them as targets for discrimination.

On the other hand, it is much easier to measure the impact of their contributions to the town precisely because of its small size. Filipinos in Sydney for example (the largest grouping of Filipinos is in NSW) are scattered and it is difficult to assess their contributions or impact on the city as a whole. In Mount Isa the fact that the local MP has recognized their potential as a voting group is evidence that they are perceived as a potential political force. In the cultural arena, their presence in multicultural events or even community events such as town fairs and show days is already institutionalized: the food stalls selling Filipino food and the folk dance group performing Filipino folk dances are becoming part of Mount Isa's invented traditions.

Mount Isa is a mining city on the Leichhardt River in northwestern Queensland, 1,867 kilometers by road northwest of Brisbane and 977 kilometers by rail west of Townsville (*The Australian Encyclopaedia* 1996, 2156). It is a mining town centered around the company MIM (Mount Isa Mines). The 1996 census notes that out of 265 persons born in the Philippines, there were 69 males and 196 females (Australian Bureau of Statistics 1996). Though these are the official figures, there is a perception among the Filipino and Australian community members that these numbers are far from accurate and quite conservative. They themselves estimate between 300–500 Filipinos (the Parish priest and the local MP Tony McGrady estimate 500–600 Filipino women). The Filipino Association of Mount Isa had 114 financial members in July 1999 and 117 financially paying members in 1998. Filipinos have also been identified by the MICDA (Migrant Office) and the town's Member of Parliament as the fastest growing immigrant community (interview Bohannan, interview Tony McGrady July 1999). Moreover, there is much movement of peoples—miners and their families move into the town and out again when they retire. Some stay only until they accumulate enough capital to buy a house and then move on. In addition, MIM makes a number of contract appointments that may last only a few months. The town's population figures reflect this fluidity (23,667 in 1991 and 22,863 in 1996) (Australian Bureau of Statistics 1996); despite the influx of new immigrants the town's population barely increased over the last decade. Thus, statistics on actual numbers of Filipinos in Mount Isa are not reliable. It is also difficult to procure statistics that break down Filipinos according to their means of employment. There is an unpublished survey of Filipino Women and Children (Developmental Years) in Mount Isa written by Maree Escreet of the Ethnic Childcare Resource Unit in 1990. Escreet, who based her work on a sample of 113 women, does give a breakdown of the women's employment in the town.

METHODOLOGY

This study is an ethnographic study in which Filipino women married to Australian men and a smaller number of Filipino women married to Filipino men were interviewed about employment, social life, and how they coped with life in an isolated town. In addition, I participated in their social activities for the brief time I spent in Mount Isa. A research assistant (pseudonym Kim Kiessling), who was also the migrant helper in Mount Isa, was hired in advance to arrange interviews and to introduce the researchers (my colleague Associate Professor Cheng Soo May and myself) to the women of the town. Interviews were conducted with twenty-three Filipino women wives, all of them employed in some way, including two who were still looking for permanent jobs and two who could only find part-time intermittent employment. All women have been given pseudonyms here. Interviews with eight employers (all white Australians) were also arranged (the Laura Johnson Garden Settlement, the Mercure Hotel, the Mount Isa Chamber of Commerce, the Irish Club, the Day Care Center). In addition, the local MP Mr. Tony McGrady and the only Catholic parish priest, Father Mick Lowcock, kindly agreed to talk to us. Unfortunately the management of Mount Isa Mines (MIM) refused to be interviewed (this after an appointment was already made).

It is important to recognize the limits of a study that relies on interviews or qualitative data drawn from a random group of women. The point is not to suggest that the experiences of these women reflect the experiences of all Filipino women in Mount Isa. Interviews are, of course, marvelous opportunities for the women to reinvent themselves presenting only what they want the researcher to see. Interviews with employers revealed little because they were invariably defensive; most were anxious to stress that they did not discriminate against Filipinos. Employers explicitly stated that they employed Filipino women, that the women were very hard-working, and not likely to complain.

On the other hand, socializing with the Filipino women and the interview experience itself revealed many useful insights about work and life in Mount Isa and offered the opportunity to check certain claims made in interviews. This method offers a valuable means to gather primary data to study women's

experiences in Mount Isa, especially women's agency in the context of a marginalized minority group in a remote mining town. There are no written
records of their experiences to date. Most Filipina women did not want to be
interviewed alone, and preferred to be interviewed in groups of two or three.
Also, in most cases, interviewees liked to turn the interview into a social event
where food was served and women laughed and socialized while they exchanged life stories. This was also a good interview format since a one-on-one
interview could be intimidating. If they felt they were not "alone" and that
others were happy to be part of the project, they were more relaxed and willing to share their experiences. At the same time the interview became less formal and was happily transformed into a social occasion. These interview cum
"social occasions" allowed women to become more forthcoming about their
own life situations. Furthermore the relationship between the researcher/
interviewee in terms of subject position assumes an interesting twist here. All
the women interviewed were married (or had been married) and because the
cultural construction of the feminine in the Philippines is "wife and mother,"[4]
I was assigned a lower status because I was single. The first question they usually asked me was "Do you have a spouse?" (*May asawa ka ba?*) and when I
replied in the negative, they would tease me about being single, suggesting that
I stay in Mount Isa longer to find a miner husband among the bachelors din-
ing in the Irish Club. From then on they felt comfortable revealing their life
stories to me even if they were recorded on tape.

Although initially the intention was to interview only those Filipino women
married to Australians, four women married to Filipino miners were also interviewed. A majority of women were married to miners (see table 4.1), though
not all Filipino women were married to miners. The Filipina airport manager
for example, is married to a cleaner (but who also worked for MIM); Kim, employed as the migrant worker is divorced (the ex-husband was a miner); and a
couple of husbands had retired. All the Filipino women who participated in the
study were enthusiastic respondents (some were already interviewed for a previous study conducted by the University of Queensland on Filipinos and mental health) who were proud to talk about their attempts to get jobs, their
experiences in getting their qualifications updated, and their new life as successful wives, mothers, and workers in Australia. Almost all women did not want
to use pseudonyms. They wanted to see their names in a book! They saw themselves as successful women who have made happy marriages and who are
financially independent (even sending remittances back home). In this very fundamental sense these women cannot be categorized as victims (though one was
a former victim of domestic violence but she remarried—the offending husband is now in a mental institution). And though a marginalized group in a predominantly white racist town, they have made a visible social impact and are in

the process of empowering themselves through the sisterhood. I see these women as marginalized because not only are their educational credentials not recognized (most women have university degrees, see table 4.1., and see also chapter 2 for a comparison with Filipino women in Canada), but also because they suffer from overt racial discrimination. The women interviewed spoke constantly of being subjected to blatant forms of discrimination that included strangers accosting them and asking them to "speak English" because "this is an English-speaking country" (interviews with Tina, Lisa, Merlita, Narelle, Jennifer Langley, Libra, Em, Mariane, and Myra Soriano 1999). These same interviewees also observed other more subtle forms of discrimination such as extremely patronizing behavior (interviews with Tina, Lisa, Merlita, Narelle, Jennifer Langley, Libra, Em, Mariane, and Myra Soriano 1999), part of it due to the perception held by Australians in rural towns that all Filipinas come from very poor backgrounds and come to Australia for "a better life." Narelle observed: "Just like I said, in reality, we may be Australian citizens, but when people look at us, they don't see Australians do they? . . . You know the saying goes like: to be considered half as good as men you have to be considered twice as good to be considered half as good. Well, it goes double than that again for us" (interview 1999). These women are also geographically marginalized because they live in isolated, remote areas. Although as wives of miners these Filipino women may be quite well off, (since MIM salaries are high and a job in MIM holds some status and prestige), they experience marginalization in the many ways they are reminded publicly that they are "other."

FILIPINO WOMEN IN MOUNT ISA AND REDEFINING "WORK"

Interested specifically in the transition from wife to worker, this study deliberately chose working women and ignored the full-time mothers or full-time housewives (though "work" was defined very broadly: it included women earning an income by selling jewelry at home, and nonpaid work such as civic and community or church work—we interviewed one Deaconess involved heavily in civic work who described herself as a housewife). Almost everyone interviewed disclosed that a job was necessary not just for the financial remuneration and self-esteem but also as an essential coping strategy for life in the isolated town. A job also gave them financial independence and the chance to send remittances back to the Philippines to their needy relatives. Almost all women interviewed sent remittances to the Philippines. Mariane, the town's airport manager and a member of the Mount Isa Chamber of Commerce, proudly announced that her remittances helped build a concrete house for her family back in the Philippines.

From the moment they arrived in Australia as "brides" or immigrants these women were determined to earn a living motivated primarily by a desire to send money back but also because they discovered that a job was fulfilling and essential to combat strong feelings of loneliness. The main obstacle to employment is the nonrecognition of their overseas qualifications. In most cases, these women had college degrees that were not recognized in Australia. In other cases, women had difficulty with English. The town itself could only boast of few employment opportunities. Given the limited choices many women have opted to take the office skills course at TAFE, obtaining jobs as receptionists, secretaries, or clerks. Others have joined the day care moms training program (in 1999 there were nine Filipina day care moms working for one day care center). Others are self-employed: they design and sew dresses, or they accept orders for cakes and baked goods. So although a section of Filipino women in Mount Isa combined the roles of wife and worker, most are in jobs that are associated with traditional definitions of the feminine as "mother," "housewife," or "carer." In many cases this involves work in the so-called traditional "domestic spheres." For instance, there are eight Filipino waitresses/kitchen hands in the Irish Club, nine Filipino day care mothers for the Mount Isa Family Day Care, and three Filipino chefs/cooks in the Maestro restaurant. There are five Filipino housekeepers in the Mercure Hotel. The supervisors at the local McDonalds were Filipinas (in 1999). There is a Filipina cleaner and a Filipina nurse's aide (who has nursing qualifications in the Philippines that are not recognized in Australia so she can only work as a nurse's aide) in the Laura Johnson Garden Settlement home. Dressmaking is another occupation, while the others who have taken the office skills courses at TAFE college are secretaries/administrative assistants and receptionists. Filipinas are also shop assistants at Woolworths and K-Mart. A number of them work at the local McDonalds. Apart from Mariane (the airport manager), the migrant helper (Kim—who has a B.A. in sociology from the University of Queensland—she came with a degree in fine arts from the University of the Philippines, but completed an Australian degree here), and Narelle (an MIM onstream analyst who was formerly an electrician), most women worked in traditional female occupations: cleaning, caring for children or the sick and aged, cooking, sewing, serving food, or as secretaries and receptionists. Table 4.1 breaks down those interviewed according to occupation and their husband's occupation.

Interviews with employers in the Mercure Hotel, Laura Johnson home, the lead chef of the Irish Club, the Mount Isa Family Day Care, and Migrant Center all attest that their Filipino employees are quiet achievers who work hard and rarely complain. But many perform jobs well below their educational attainment. Those who balked at the thought of taking a few years (where they would not earn an income) to get a university qualification opted to take the

Table 4.1 Summary of the Educational Qualifications, Employment, and Husband's Employment of the Filipino Women Interviewed in Mount Isa in 1999

Pseudonym	Educational Qualifications	Occupation	Husband's Occupation
Luisa	Bachelor of Arts (English), University of Iloilo Master of Arts in Psychology from University of Santo Tomas (Philippines) Master of Arts, University of Queensland Ph.D. student University of Queensland	Regional Licensing Officer/National Food Authority/Municipal Customer Service Officer, Queensland Transport	Filipino husband trained as an engineer. Project manager/ private contracting company
Carmita	Secretarial student in the Philippines	Waitress, Supervisor (Irish Club)	Divorced, new partner is (?)
Angelita	Registered nurse (RN) in the Philippines Pre-nursing, De La Salle University, Bacolod CL, Montelibano Memorial Hospital School of Nursing	Assistant nurse, Laura Johnson Garden Settlement	Inspection Officer for Health and Safety in the Department of Mines and Energy
Rosarita	Bachelor of Arts, Foreign Correspondence from Far Eastern University, Philippines	Sold jewelry/civic work Committee Member—Ethnic Resource Centre	Miner MIM, now retired
Lisa	Two years Industrial Engineering in the Philippines (did not graduate)	Casual, grocery assistant Pack & Save, nurse's aide in a rest home, food steward Harrash Hotel, relief cleaner, filling shelves at Woolworth's	Mining engineer MIM Filipino
Pacita	Third-year high school	In between jobs	Fitter MIM
Tina	Two years accounting at the Philippine College of Commerce	Chef	Miner MIM
Merlita	Bachelor of Science and Commerce Accounting major, Claudia Maris College, Morong, Rizal	Data transcriber—airport, Roadhouse cook, rental manager real estate front desk, Mount Isa Hotel	Miner MIM

(continued)

Table 4.1 (continued)

Pseudonym	Educational Qualifications	Occupation	Husband's Occupation
Narelle	Australian credentials: electrician	Electrician MIM, onstream analyst in the MIM lab	MIM above ground
Nida	Three years at the University of the Philippines, Baguio (did not finish degree)	Stocktaking supervisor Woolworth's	Divorced (husband used to own a shop and a Mr. Whippy ice cream van)
Jennifer Langley	Bachelor of Science in Elementary Education, Philippine Normal College	Administrative assistant Mount Isa TAFE	Filipino miner MIM
Kim Kiessling	Bachelor of Arts major in Fine Arts from The University of the Philippines Bachelor of Arts/Sociology from The University of Queensland	Was a registered nurse, now a migrant resource worker	Divorced/ husband was a miner MIM German immigrant
Melanie McGraw	Finished Hotel and Restaurant Management a two-year course from Olivares College, Parañaque, Manila	Part-time receptionist to a doctor	Australian miner MIM
Ruthie	A degree in education from Far Eastern University, Philippines	Admin/Resource Officer for Queensland Health	Miner MIM (timberman or check officer MIM)
Editha Casiano	University Graduate, Adamson's University, Manila	Day care mom	Filipino miner MIM

Table 4.1 *(continued)*

Jessah	Bachelor of Arts and Bachelor in Development and Education (Philippines)	Looking for permanent job Casual Woolworth's	construction
Teresa	Medical technologist graduate, South Western University, Cebu City, Philippines	Deacon, Church of the Living Water, presenter Christian Radio	Miner MIM
Anita	Bachelor of Science in Commerce, major in management, St. Ferdinand College, Baguio	Assistant manager/museum	MIM miner, Spanish
Larissa Yulo	Accountant graduate, Divine Word University, Tacloban Leyte, Philippines	Bookeeper/then data entry MIM, clerk at the dealership motors	Filipino miner MIM
Libra	?	Bakes cakes	(?)
Em	?	Kitchen hand, cleans houses	Pensioner/formerly controller MIM
Myra Suriano	?	Dressmaker	Truck driver for MIM, Miner
Mariane	Bachelor of Science in Commerce University of San Agustin, Manila	Airport General manager Mount Isa Airport	Cleaner MIM

Note: Names are pseudonyms. Those women with Filipino husbands are identified; otherwise all other husbands are white Australian unless otherwise specified (though there are a number of immigrants from Germany, Spain, and the United Kingdom). As illustrated, most of the women have tertiary qualifications some of which were not recognized in Australia.

office skills course at TAFE. This short course gave them the opportunity to obtain clerical work immediately. In a small town such as Mount Isa this seemed to be the popular option because there are fewer opportunities for professionals with university qualifications.

It was quite obvious that the women interviewed were clearly determined to work—any particular job "as long as its honest work." Some preferred self-employment like dressmaking or baking cakes or selling jewelry to their friends. Jessah arrived in Mount Isa only six months before the interview. She has been looking for a full-time job but only succeeded so far in obtaining part-time employment. She has a bachelor of arts degree and a bachelor in development and education from the Philippines. She worked as a receptionist in a restaurant in Malaysia where she met her Australian husband (who worked contract jobs in construction and painting). In Mount Isa she has worked as a cleaner, as a stocktaker at Woolworth's, and even did volunteer work (unpaid) as a data processor in an office. She is happy to stay in Mount Isa but would desperately like full-time employment for something to do (interview July 1999).

Nida has tried a multitude of jobs, including self-employment. She went to university in the Philippines (Baguio) but came to Australia as a bride, first living with her husband in a caravan (a mobile home attached to a car) in Bundaberg (1982). Her first job was to manage the family's fish and chip shop where she also sold embroidery items imported from the Philippines. From shopkeeper she turned vendor selling vegetables and fruits, some of which she grew herself. Eventually both husband and wife decided to purchase a Mr. Whippy ice cream van and sell ice cream around Queensland (a business they thought would be lucrative because of the hot weather there). It was not. They moved to Mount Isa in 1989 but the peripatetic nature of the job (where they had to follow the show circuit around the state for several months of the year) began to tire them both. Nida is now separated from her husband and works as a section manager of the variety department at Woolworth's where she is in charge of the stocktaking (interview July 1999). Nida is very proud of her job where she is much appreciated by her manager because of her dedication, efficiency, enthusiasm, and commitment. She is also the choreographer of the main folk dance group in Mount Isa.

Tina was a short-order cook who then became a chef simply through a series of cooking jobs in the various restaurants in Mount Isa. Her credentials, however, included two years of accounting at the Philippine College of Commerce and work experience as an assistant accountant in the Philippines. When she arrived in Australia in 1979 as a bride, she worked as a kitchen hand in the Irish Club. From there she became a cook at the Sherwood House restaurant, and later a hamburger cook at the Roadhouse restaurant (where six other Fil-

ipino women friends also worked). She claims because there were a good number of Filipino women who worked there, they became easy targets for verbal
abuses such as "go back to your own country" (interview 1999). When the
Roadhouse restaurant closed down, the Filipino employees there moved collectively to the Verona Hotel and some of the cooks became housekeepers.
Tina also worked in the kitchen of the Verona Hotel. Eventually three Filipino
women who had jobs in the kitchen of the Verona Hotel were invited to work
as chefs in the nearby Maestro restaurant (also owned at that time by the owners of the Verona Hotel). Tina claims: "The 'owner' prefer Filipina because
doesn't matter how hard we work but we don't whine, we don't complain, we
complain to ourselves but we don't complain to them" (interview 1999).

Kim Kiessling was probably one of the earliest Filipinos to go to Mount Isa,
immigrating with her German Australian husband in 1968. She held a Bachelor of Arts degree from the University of the Philippines and was already working in Manila as an art teacher for the American school there. Her first job in
Mount Isa was as a teacher's aide but she then moved to the Ethnic Child Care
Resource Unit and then the Migrant Access Project Scheme. She opted to become a registered nurse (trained in Australia) and worked in the hospital at the
Laura Johnson until 1991. In 1990 larger numbers of Filipino women began to
arrive in Mount Isa so the Catholic parish priest Father Mick (Kelly) recommended her for a job at the Catholic Welfare Services (renamed Centacare),
which required her to assist in migrant settlement. She then completed a bachelor of arts degree in sociology from the University of Queensland, and at the
time of the interview worked as a Community Settlement Service Officer part
time with Centacare (interview July 1999). Kim was one of two Filipino
women interviewed who, although arriving with a degree from a Philippine
university recognized in Australia, still opted to go to university again to obtain Australian qualifications. Luisa, who already held a master's in education
from the University of Santo Tomas in the Philippines, went back to university
and gained a master's in sociology from the University of Queensland. She is
now working on a Ph.D. in linguistics also with the University of Queensland.

Mariane, the town's airport manager, holds a bachelor of science in commerce
from the University of San Agustin. In this case, she is a clear example of a woman
working in a male-dominated field where she is the "boss" to male employees.
A strong, confident, and competent woman, she has to endure male employees calling her the "Filipino Hitler." Both Mariane and Kim are well known in
the Mount Isa community, often appearing in the local newspapers and other
community newsletters. On November 11, 2000, the Philippine ambassador to
Australia Her Excellency Delia Domingo-Albert honored Mariane with a
Filipino-Australia Women Achievement Award "in recognition and celebration of
her outstanding contributions to enhance the professional and personal status

of Filipino women in Queensland in the context of multiculturalism, raising awareness of the community about Filipino women's significant contributions and strong commitment to Australia and its future, thereby raising the status of Filipino women in Queensland and in the wider Australian society." She was one of the seven Filipino women achievers in Queensland given this award.

Work is also a gendered experience. Filipino women work together as a group or help each other get jobs with the same employer. Perhaps working together as a group or in the same place makes the job less lonely or threatening. In distinct groups, they present a visible reminder that Filipino women do contribute to the working culture of the small town.

The Filipino women's contribution to the Mount Isa "work" culture is further heightened if one extended the definition of what constitutes "work" to include civic work or unpaid work that benefited the community in some way. Redefining work would make "workers" out of women who are commonly labeled "housewives." Since women do not receive "pay," women's enthusiastic participation in civic work reveals them as proactive agents, volunteering their services to the community (see also Yeoh and Khoo's study of expatriate wives in Singapore who get involved in civic work, 1998). Rosarita's husband discouraged her from seeking paid employment because he would lose his benefits. A bachelor of arts graduate in foreign correspondence from Far Eastern University, Rosarita then decided to do volunteer work with the Ethnic Resource and ICAN, which handles children with additional needs. Teresa, who describes herself as a "housewife," is the Deaconess for the Church of the Living Water (a Pentecostal Church). She is in charge of the Filipino section of the Christian radio program (105FM between 12:30 and 1:30 on Fridays). She is a participant in Women's AGLOW, a Christian organization of women. As Deaconess she is also required to lead Bible Study groups and prayer. Her only free day is Monday. Hence, though she does not get paid for it, Teresa "works" from Tuesday to Sunday (interview July 1999).

Most of the Filipino women interviewed are involved in civic work. Ruthie, who is an administrative officer at the Community Health Service Center, sings for the Catholic Church choir (interview July 1999). An active member of the Filipino Association, she is also editor of their newsletter. Mariane is the church lector and reader who served as past president and past vice-president of the Filipino Association. Kim is youth leader for the Uniting Church and vice-president of the pottery group. She also volunteers for the Zonta women's group and does illustrations for the publications (short stories) of the writer's workshop. A member of the Women's Consultative Council, she is also very active in the Filipino Association. Narelle is vice-president of the Filipino Association and Jennifer Langley is public relations officer of the Filipino Association. A public relations officer with the Toastmasters, Jennifer is also part of the P & C, the Parents Association at school (interviews 1999).

Father Mick Kelly, who is the town's only Catholic priest, disclosed that many Filipino women volunteer to help the parish—from singing in the choir and leading mass as lectors or readers to helping in the parish office and cleaning the church. In particular they were active in selling raffle tickets and fundraising for church charities. They had the reputation of raising the most money for the church (Kelly, interview July 1999) largely from the popular food stalls at charity functions. Filipino women also campaigned for the local MP, Tony McGrady. They made rosettes, handed out fliers, put up posters and raised funds by organizing cake stalls (McGrady, interview July 1999). In return McGrady gave them personal assistance in the process of sponsoring relatives to come to Mount Isa as immigrants.

THE CONCEPT OF THE "SISTERHOOD"

The notion of a universal sisterhood has already been challenged by feminist scholars. Women of color criticized the idea that all women could have common interests, particularly if they are divided by class and other differences. Ien Ang has argued that the "homogenizing idea of sisterhood" has been attacked by contemporary feminisms because: "After all, not all women share the same experience of 'being a woman', nor is gender enough to guarantee a commonality in social positioning" (1995, 58). Ang also casts doubt on the compromise (suggested by Pettman) that differences among women could "unproblematically be turned into a 'unity in diversity' once they are 'recognized' properly" (Ang 1995, 49). Furthermore, the idea of a multicultural overarching framework that contains these women's "differences" could imply that they all must comply with feminism's "essentializing frame" (Ang 1995, 60). Hence, there are definite limits to the "very idea of sisterhood (and thus the category 'women') and on the necessary *partiality* of the project of feminism as such" (Ang 1995, 61). Indeed, the Filipino women in Mount Isa who must rely on their female networks are first to concede that there are many innate jealousies, enmities, and cliques among themselves and that they have to be choosy about which female groups they join. In fact, quite predictably, the women's friendship groups are broken up along ethnic lines: Tagalog speakers are one group, Cebuano speakers another, for instance. Those from particular regions in the Philippines are more likely to support each other as a group and experience some rivalry with other groups from different regions (replicating the rivalry of kinship alliance groups in the Philippines). Hence, even among the Filipino women, the concept of an overall sisterhood of Filipino women in Mount Isa is not without its limitations. Just as an overarching feminist grand narrative would be pernicious because it implies that to include everyone one must accept the "master discourse" that speaks from a decidedly white feminist perspective, the notion of the sisterhood of Filipino women in Mount Isa must not insist on a unity of all Filipino women. But the idea of a "sisterhood" as an analytical category within a specific positioning of marginalized women vis-à-vis white persons is useful particularly in a small remote town and in the context of the category of miner's wives.

While the male miner has been represented as an exploited victim of capitalist class structure but as oppressor of women within the patriarchal structure of gender, the miner's wife (read white wife) is reinvented as "supportive, obedient, rather conservative and apolitical, family centered, parochial and oppressed" (Gibson-Graham 1995, 173). The miner's wife in contrast to the male miner experiences the "double dose of exploitation and oppression" because she is structurally positioned as lower class as well as a subordinated woman (Gibson-Graham 1995). Gibson-Graham challenged this essentializing image created out of the paradigm of structural Marxist analysis, suggesting that the poststructural perspective that redefines power (i.e., not just emanating from class) allows for an interpretation that gives women political subjectivity enabling them to enact social change (Gibson-Graham 1995, 175). Wives of miners therefore also have political agency and respond to changes from above in terms of their own personal interests for advancement.

A literal application of the Marxist model would read the Filipina miner's wife as subject to a triple mode of oppression: she is oppressed by class, gender, and ethnicity. She is subject to racial discrimination outside the family domain and subject to patriarchal power in the domestic sphere. At home whether married to an Australian or a Filipino husband the women are also subject to patriarchal relationships.[5] In one interview situation, for example, the woman's husband insisted on being present at the interview and intervened periodically to answer questions directed specifically at his wife. Since the interviewee had a few other Filipina friends present (who were also willing to be interviewed) she (pseudonym Tina) mumbled (in Filipino) to the Filipinos in the group: "Gago talaga ito: babatukan ko ito mamaya eh" (He is stupid/crazy, I'll deal (literally hit him) with him later.). This did not stop her husband, who continued to interrupt during the entire evening interview. In the beginning she would remind him that "Hello, its not you [that these questions are addressed to]." But the husband continued to interrupt and answer questions directed at her and about her. Finally the exasperated Tina told him to "Shut up! Go and watch TV there!" In truth, the husband was actually very proud of her work achievements and praised her in his responses, but the point was that he wanted to "speak" for her at all times—a clear manifestation of his attempt at patriarchal control. After being told to "Shut up!" the husband then responded with "She'd be shouting, if she shouts at me I don't like it." Although Tina excused her husband's interference with the statement "He loves me too much," she showed her own form of "everyday resistance"[6] by speaking out in a language he could not understand and then later standing up for herself and telling him to leave.

Another Filipina (Editha Casiano) married a Filipino miner who was the possessive and jealous sort and thus did not approve of her going out of the house without him (even to socialize with the other women). The sisterhood of Filipino women encouraged her to step out and socialize with them despite his objections, giving her moral support. Her husband has finally relented to "allowing" her to socialize with other Filipino women because she told him without their social networks she would "go crazy in this town." After all, even her work as a day care mother kept her at home.

In both cases the women who were subjected to the husband's strong patriarchal authority received support from the sisterhood of Filipino women. I argue that the appeal of the sisterhood lies in the fact that it is only with other Filipino women that they can form relationships based on equality. Like the women in eighteenth- and nineteenth-century New England who were subordinate and dependent on men, these Filipino women "would find truly reciprocal interpersonal relationships only with other women" (Cott 1977, 168). Nancy Cott, writing of the experiences of the New England women in another century, discussed the friendships women formed with other women; friendships that contrasted with their unequal relationships with husbands: "This closest of relations between a man and a woman made the woman subordinate. . . . Friendships between women, on the contrary, required no such subordination or disparagement of women's capacities" (Cott 1977, 172–73). In the diaries kept by these women Cott discovered that female friendship was necessary for emotional expression and security (Cott 1977, 173). Since women were not regarded as peers of men, they sought peer relationships with other women (Cott 1977, 188). Moreover, since from the women's perspective nineteenth-century mores offered no other appealing alternative to marriage, despite women's subordination in the partnership, female friends became the best way to balance their lives (Cott 1977, 193).

In Mount Isa, the female friendships were crucial in coping with racial discrimination, a patriarchal marriage, and/or life in an isolated mining town. Women socialize with each other without their husbands and give each other emotional support. While interviewing Anita, a local museum manager at her workplace, we were interrupted by another Filipina who wanted emotional support and advice because she was "having problems" with her husband. Another woman interviewed (pseudonym Rosarita) said she welcomed into her home one Filipino woman who was fleeing an abusive husband. Female gatherings, which sometimes occurred almost daily, gave them companionship and a new "kinship group." At the same time it gave them an opportunity to plan activities in a small town where they all had to entertain themselves. While friendships were also formed with white women, perhaps the presence of racial discrimination meant that these friendships were less common. Furthermore, the shared language (evidenced by the breakdown of sisterhoods in terms of dialect and locality) and culture predisposed friendships between Filipinas exclusively. In general, the Filipino women feel more comfortable speaking in their own language and a small number had difficulty with English (so the interview was conducted in Tagalog—a problem, though, if Tagalog was her second language and Cebuano or Ilongo her first). In the Wednesday night *karaoke* session, my research associate (she was born in Singapore) opted to stay at the hotel. When the Filipinas learned that I attended without her, three of them immediately exclaimed that it was a good thing because we can all speak Tagalog.

The sisterhood also replaced the kinship group as the primary alliance group. In the Philippines it is the kinship alliance group that is the focus of an individual's identity and loyalty. In a country where there is almost no welfare support, it is the kinship alliance group that looks after the individuals, including the less fortunate. If a woman, for instance, marries someone incapable of supporting her financially, the kinship group helps out. At the same time if the woman at any point becomes subjected to physical violence or domestic abuse, it is the woman's kinship group who protects her and demands retribution from the man's kinship alliance group.

Deprived of their kinship alliance group in Australia, the sisterhood becomes a powerful substitute. It not only complements a patriarchal marriage, it empowers a group of marginalized women collectively. It networks to gain jobs or employment for its women members, it supports women who are victimized by abusive husbands, it organizes social affairs to combat loneliness, it provides emotional support to its members, and it has the potential to fight for these women's interests (women see the local MP for help in bringing relatives into Australia as new migrants in family reunion schemes, etc.). While individual Filipino women may be marginalized in the society of Mount Isa, the sisterhood/sisterhoods of Filipino women are in the process of empowering Filipinas as a group, challenging any portrayals of these women as mere "victims."

NEGOTIATING SPACE

Filipino women's contributions to Mount Isa society in both the economic and social sphere could be interpreted as the sisterhood's attempt to negotiate a space in the public sphere for a marginalized group who want to make an impact and a visible presence in a small town infamous for ubiquitous racist sentiments. Although the women seem to have no trouble acquiring jobs and employers interviewed praised the women's diligence as employees, interviewees still lament the overall atmosphere of discrimination they experience not so much from employers (with the exception of one interviewee) but from town residents in general. Their children are accosted by mothers who tell them to "go back home," or "go back to the boat," or "speak English because this is an English-speaking country," for example. Those married to Australian men are more apt to stand up for themselves in these situations because their husbands give them advice on how to deal with it while those Filipinos married to Filipino men tend to suffer in silence and are less confident about confronting overt racism directly. Why are the women so visible in church activities, charitable and civic work, multicultural fairs, and as political advocates of local politicians? As a marginalized group in a remote isolated area, these women become involved in the town's social, economic, and religious life in order to negotiate a public space for their group.

Are Filipinas able to negotiate a public space for their group because, despite the racism and sexism of the small mining town, Australian society is open to their participation in church activities (which are not exclusively Filipino) and cultural life? Though it is tempting to read the town's enthusiasm for folk dancing as Australian open acceptance of the Filipino women in Australian multicultural society, I am more inclined to raise the question: Is it acceptable because it reinforces the Australian perception of these women as "other"? Folk dancing performances keep Filipinos in their cultural category of "Filipino" rather than "Australian" (which at least the church activities may develop). It is also possible that Filipino enthusiasm is also a form of self-orientalization and of conforming to the Australian definition of them as "other." One indication of genuine "multiculturalism" would be the participation of white Australians in these folk dance activities (I ran a small folk dance group in Rockhampton, Queensland. We did have white performers dancing with Filipinos and while this initially raised criticism from both Filipinos and Australians [an indication that both groups still saw each other as "other"] it was accepted quite quickly).

THE SISTERHOOD

In a book entitled *Of Mines and Men*, Max Griffiths argued: "A mining town can be a place in which people become actively involved with their neighbours in community building, or a place of miserable isolation" (Griffiths 1998, 170). To illustrate this feeling of "miserable isolation," he described his encounter with a Filipina migrant for marriage in an undisclosed mining town:

She came from the Philippines. I had never inquired as to how and where she met her husband. Conventional wisdom had it that lonely Australian men, often previously married, went to Asian countries to find a wife. And conventional wisdom said a lot of other things about what subsequently happened to the women. But this women's (sic) husband wasn't like that. He was especially attentive when she became pregnant but she obviously wasn't happy, despite the politeness and smiles she afforded the other residents in the little mining community.

In the big mining community, 200 kilometers away, there were quite a number of Filipino women whose husbands worked in the mine. The so-called culture shock had been enormous when they first arrived in this remote, hot, dry town. But there were air-conditioned supermarkets, dress shops, a hospital and schools, and of course they had each other, meeting informally in their homes and greeting each other in the street.

But for the woman in this little mining community, things were a thousand times worse. A few houses, a small store, a resident nurse, and little else. Oh yes, there was a floodlit tennis court and a swimming pool, but she didn't play tennis and the constraints of her culture made swimming in public an embarrassment, especially when she became pregnant. Certainly the style and quality of houses were far better than she had ever known, but they all looked alike, inside and out, and she missed the busy crowded life of her own village. It was the first time she had been confronted with an electric stove.

I watched her walk slowly across the open space that separated the store and the nurse's clinic from the residences. When she reached her front door, she turned and looked at the flat featureless country which stretched out to every horizon, searching for one sign of familiarity. There was none. As she turned and entered the door, I thought I had never seen a more lonely person in my life. (1998, 161)

How do the Filipina migrants cope with life in Mount Isa? While reinventing themselves from "wife" to "worker" is one obvious strategy, bonding with the sisterhood/sisterhoods is clearly essential as well. Almost all those interviewed (with the exception of two) admit that socializing with other Filipinos (mostly women) is essential to their happiness and well-being. The sisterhood is a source of moral support and camaraderie. (While most of the sisterhoods are between exclusively Filipino women, some Filipino women did form sisterhoods with the white women in the town in activities such as bowling, gambling, or civic work. This was not as common as the exclusively Filipino sisterhoods.) The added bonus was that it also provides the locus for entertainment in a town that offers little outlets for amusements. Female groups gamble together: one group plays *mahjong*, another plays the poker machines in the Irish Club, and one group plays bingo together. Every Wednesday night, groups of women go the Irish Club for *karaoke* night. Only a few actually sing, but the others come to socialize. When I was there I noticed that there were several tables of Filipinas: each group occupied one table. Some were broken into linguistic/ethnic groups; that is, the Tagalog speakers sat in one table and the Visayans another. Not one single husband turned up. The absence of husbands was palpable with interviewees confessing that: "husbands doesn't wanna come" (Merlitta, interview July 1999), or "but in our group no husband goes with us anyway" (Tina, interview July 1999). There is a contrast between the group of single male contract workers who have their meals in the restaurant and the group of Filipino married women who come after dinner without their husbands to attend karaoke night. It is tempting to read this in a clearly feminist light and see it as the epitome of the sisterhood united and independent of male support. And indeed, the women enjoying an evening together rarely speak of their husbands and find happiness and solace in the atmosphere of fellow Filipino women.

One common insurance against loneliness is the almost daily "chicka-chicka" (to use Narelle's term) when women get together informally in each other's houses for small talk and to exchange stories. The town's fairly small population center means that it only takes fifteen minutes to drive from one end of town to the other, making regular visiting convenient. Furthermore, women also find other reasons or excuses to get together such as rehearsals for a modern dance group and a folk dance group (these groups are almost exclusively female). Rehearsals usually take up one hour followed by three hours of socializing. There are also two folk dance groups and one modern dance group in Mount Isa. One of the folk dance groups makes a very positive contribution to the social and cultural life of the town and it is constantly invited to perform for various events. When asked why they have a dance group the women interviewed claim that they enjoy dancing and enjoy the camaraderie that rehearsals and performances engender. The folk dancers are proactive in reinventing Filipino culture or translating Filipino culture to their children and to the Australian residents of Mount Isa. In this sense, these women redefine their own identities as Filipino Australians.[7] Although there are Filipino males in Mount Isa (the 1999 president of the Association was male), it is the women who dominate the Association's activities, perhaps in part because there are more of them (there are 69 males, 194 females, and 263 Philippine persons in the 1996 census though these figures seem far too small; see comments above, Australian Bureau of Statistics 1996).

The Filipino Association's main purpose is also to provide socials for the Filipinos in Mount Isa (in 1999 the Association was renamed the Filipino-Australian Association). This is the site where the women socialize with their husbands and families. The social events, which include Valentine's balls and beauty contests, become important social highlights of the women's lives there. According to Narelle, many women are so excited about the formal balls that they cannot sleep at night thinking of what to wear (interview 1999). These are social highlights shared with husbands and children—family activities that complement the regular meetings of the sisterhood/sisterhoods.

CONCLUSION

Before the end of the Wednesday night *karaoke* session, the vice-president of the Philippine-Australian Association of Mount Isa and two other members of one of the sisterhood groups approached me because they wanted to raise funds for an airfare to bring me back to Mount Isa. Now, my popularity with them had nothing to do with my research or the friendships that evolved from the research. They discovered that I used to be a professional dancer for the Bayanihan Philippine Dance Company (the leading folk dance company in the Philippines) and that I had run a small dance company of Filipino migrants in Rockhampton, Queensland, when I taught at Central Queensland University. They wanted to bring me back for a weekend workshop of folk dancing so that they could all learn a new repertoire for their local performances. It was clear from this discussion that the folk dance group was an important activity for the Filipino women in Mount Isa. The weekend workshop would be another female activity, planned and executed by the women so that they could meet and perform as a group. And yet it was going to be part of their civic work as the folk dance group performs (free of charge) for the many events in Mount Isa, including the home for the aged (the Laura Johnson Garden Settlement). The discussion on that Wednesday evening emphasized to me the significance of an all-women amateur folk dance group to the life of these Filipino women and to the town life as a whole. These women got excited over a "project"—a project that involved the sisterhood, fun, friendships, and civic work. Such an undertaking would also reinforce the bonds of sisterhood (to borrow Nancy Cott's phrase). Although in 1999 there was no overt or clear feminist element in the activities of the sisterhood/sisterhoods, there is the potential for a burgeoning feminist activism because women may discover that once women begin to get organized they become a force unto themselves. After all, it is the sisterhood that gives these women peer relationships that balance the predominantly patriarchal relationships in their marriages and provide support that facilitates their resistance against racial discrimination. The sisterhood/sisterhoods in Mount Isa have already begun the long process of empowering a marginalized group. It has close political connections with the local MP. It has subtly gained employment for its members and through their civic work (especially fund-raising, political campaigns, and folk dancing) has become part of Mount Isa's invented traditions. Mount Isa social events would not be complete without the visible presence and participation of Filipino women. Several months after my fieldwork in Mount Isa, Kim rang me to ask if I could help them write a history of the Filipino community there. The sisterhood has begun the campaign to write Filipino women into Mount Isa's collective memory.

NOTES

This research was made possible through a grant from the Center for Social Science Research, Central Queensland University. I would like to thank Associate Professor Daniela Stehlik for encouraging me to do research on Filipino women in Mount Isa, for her input in the grant proposal, her intellectual support, and administrative help for the project. I am grateful for the assistance given to me by my associate investigator, Associate Professor Soo May Cheng, The University of South Australia. Ms. Trinidad Kreutz was the model research assistant who not only arranged all the interviews but also gave her moral support, her personal enthusiasm, and her valuable friendship. My colleague Dr. Anne O'Brien very kindly recommended secondary literature on sisterhood and female friendships, and made some useful suggestions on an earlier draft. Associate Professor Beverley Kingston also read an early draft and gave some important criticisms. Archivist Renato Perdon and Adrian McMinn (UNSW library) were invaluable in the search for statistics. Finally, I have *utang na loob* (debt of gratitude) to all the women (and four men) interviewed who gave the project their valuable time and genuine enthusiasm.

1. *Mail-order brides* is not an appropriate term to use here because the women themselves object vociferously to the label, which has derogatory overtones. Also, few are technically mail-order brides. Many women married to Australian men met their husbands through Filipina friends or relatives who were also married to Australians. Some met their husbands when these bachelors were in the Philippines on a holiday while some met their husbands when they themselves were in Mount Isa visiting relatives who were married to Australian men. *Mail-order brides* was a term constructed to refer to women who met their husbands through pen-pal agencies or those who met and married Australian men after a very short period of courtship.

2. The "sisterhood" therefore is almost exclusively a "Filipino sisterhood" (although some individual Filipino women have joined Australian (white) women's social or civic organizations in Mount Isa). The groups are often organized according to regional dialect (i.e., the Cebuano speakers one group, Tagalog speakers another for example), reflecting women's interests to speak their language together as a group as well as a shared culture and identity. In the Philippines all women's organizations with interests in civic work in particular are a common cultural dynamic (see Mina Roces, *Women, Power and Kinship Politics: Female Power in Post-War Philippines* [Westport, Conn.: Praeger, 1998, Metro-Manila: Anvil Publishing, 2000]).

3. The studies on migrants and the government support or welfare services, or even those specifically addressing migrant women and support services, invariably focus on the migrant's accessibility to those services. In all cases the conclusions show the migrant's disadvantaged position in the use of these services and discuss policies that would rectify such an imbalance. See Chauvel (1985), Whiteford (1991), Evans (1984), Cox (1982), and Moss (1993). Others investigate demography and the patterns of migration (see Hugo 1992; Hassan and Tan 1990). There are no published studies of immigrant women making contributions to support services or community services save one short chapter I published in 1996 (see Roces 1996). There is one dissertation by Francis Chan (submitted January 2002) that examines Filipinas in Queensland focusing on their adaptation to life in Australia by doing an ethnography of their food, religion, language, and dance. See Francis Chan, *Dancing Their Way to Acceptance: Filipinas in Two Queensland Communities*, Ph.D. diss., Northern Territory University, 2002.

4. For a study on cultural constructions of the feminine and Filipino migrants for marriage in Australia, see Roces (1998a).

5. Five Filipino women married to Filipino men were interviewed. Two arrived in Australia as married couples, one couple met in Mount Isa and two other couples met when their bachelor husbands (already Australian migrants) returned to the Philippines to find a 'bride'.

6. I have borrowed the term *everyday resistance* from political scientists James C. Scott (James C. Scott, *Weapons of the Weak Everyday Forms of Peasant Resistance*, New Haven: Yale University Press, 1985) and Benedict J. Tria Kerkvliet (Benedict J. Tria Kerkvliet, *Everyday Politics in the Philippines Class and Status Relations in a Central Luzon Village*, Berkeley: University of California Press, 1990).

7. See Roces (1998b).

REFERENCES

Ang, I. "I'm a Feminist but . . . 'Other' Women and Postnational Feminism." Pp. 57–73 in *Transitions New Australian Feminisms,* edited by Barbara Caine and Rosemary Pringle. Sydney: Allen & Unwin, 1995.

Australian Bureau of Statistics. CD-ROM C-Data, 1996.

The Australian Encyclopaedia. Vol. 6. Sydney: Australian Geographic Pty. Ltd., 1996.

Boer, C. *Are You Looking for a Filipina Wife? A Study of Filipina-Australian Marriages.* Sydney: General Synod Office, 1988.

Brown, P. M. "For Wedded Bliss: Satisfaction of Migrant Partners of Australian Residents." Paper presented to the Asian and Pacific Women as Migrants Conference, University of Melbourne, 1994.

Cabigon, J. "Recent History and Politics of Australian-Filipino Marriages." Paper presented to the Asian and Pacific Women as Migrants Conference, University of Melbourne, 1994.

Cahill, D. *Intermarriages in International Contexts. A Study of Filipina Women Married to Australian, Japanese and Swiss Men.* Quezon City: Scalabrini Migration Centre, 1990.

Chauvel. R. *Migrants and the Commonwealth Employment Service.* Australian Institute of Multicultural Affairs, 1985. Anzus Conference, pp. 1–41.

Chuah, F., T. D. Chuah, L. Reid-Smith, and A. Rice. "Does Australia Have a Filipina Bride Problem?" *Australian Journal of Social Issues* vol. 22, no. 4 (1987): 573–83.

Cooke, F. M. "Australian-Filipino Marriages in the 1980s: An Exploratory Study of Reasons for Marriage in Context of Australian and Philippine Socio-Economic Conditions." Master's thesis, University of the Philippines, 1986a.

———. *Australian-Filipino Marriages in the 1980s: The Myth and the Reality.* Griffith University, School of Modern Asian Studies, Centre for the Study of Australian-Asian Relations, Research Paper 37, 1986b.

Cott, N. F. *The Bonds of Womanhood "Woman's Sphere" in New England, 1780–1835.* New Haven, Conn.: Yale University Press, 1977.

Cox, D. *Delivery of Welfare Services to Immigrants.* Melbourne: Department of Social Studies, University of Melbourne, 1982.

Cunneen, C., and J. Stubbs. *Gender, 'Race' and International Relations. Violence against Filipino Women in Australia.* Sydney: Institute of Criminology Monograph Series No. 9, 1997.

De Stoop, C. *They Are So Sweet Sir. The Cruel World of Traffickers in Filipinas and Other Women.* Belgium: Limitless Asia, 1994.

Elliott, J. *Mount Isa Portrait.* Brisbane: Boolarong Publications, 1988.

Escreet, M. *Survey of Filipino Women and Children (Developmental Years) in Mount Isa.* Mount Isa: Ethnic Childcare Resource Unit (unpublished ms), 1990.

Evans, M. D. R. "Immigrant Women in Australia: Resources, Family, and Work." *International Migration Review* vol. 18, no. 4 (1984): 1063–90.

Gibson-Graham, J. K. "Beyond Patriarchy and Capitalism: Reflections on Political Subjectivity." Pp. 172–83 in *Transitions: New Australian Feminisms,* edited by Barbara Caine and Rosemary Pringle. Sydney: Allen & Unwin, 1995.

Griffiths, M. *Of Mines and Men. Australia's 20th Century Mining Miracle 1945–1985.* Sydney: Kangaroo Press, 1998.

Hassan, R., and G. Tan. "Asian Migrants in Australia: A Socio-Economic Study." *Immigrants and Minorities* vol. 9, no. 1 (1990): 21–45.

Holt, E. M. "Writing Filipina-Australian Brides: The Discourse on Filipina Brides." *Philippine Sociological Review* vol. 44, nos. 1–4 (1996): 58–78.

Hugo, G. "Knocking at the Door: Asian Immigration to Australia." *Asian and Pacific Migration Journal* vol. 1, no. 1 (1992): 100–144.

Jackson, R. "Recent Migration to Australia from the Philippines." Pp. 136–55 in *Discovering Australasia. Essays on Philippine-Australian Relations,* edited by Reynaldo C. Ileto and Rodney Sullivan. Townsville: James Cook University, 1993.

Moss, I. *State of the Nation Report on People of Non-English Speaking Background.* Canberra: Human Rights and Equal Opportunity Commission, 1993.

Paredes-Maceda, C. "Filipino Women and Intermarriages." *Asian Migrant* vol. 8, no. (1995): 109–13.

Pendlebury, J. "Filipino Brides in Remote Areas." Occasional Paper No. 5. Darwin: Department of Social Security, 1990.

Perdon, R. *Brown Americans of Asia.* Sydney: The Manila Prints, 1998.

Population Flows: Immigration Aspects. Canberra: Australian Government Publishing Service, Department of Immigration and Multicultural Affairs, 2000.

Robinson, K. "Of Mail-Order Brides and 'Boys' Own' Tales: Representations of Asian-Australian Marriages." *Feminist Review*, no. 52 (1996): 53–68.

Roces, M. "*Kapit sa Patalim* (Hold on to the Blade): Victim and Agency in the Oral Narratives of Filipino Women Married to Australian Men in Central Queensland." *Lila Asia–Pacific Women's Studies Journal*, no. 7 (1998a): 1–19.

———. "Beauty Contests, Talent Quests and Folk Dancing: Gender and National Identity among Filipino Diasporic Communities in Australia." Paper presented at the Asian Studies Association of Australia Conference, The University of New South Wales, 1998b.

———. "Filipina Brides in Central Queensland: Gender, Migration and Support Services." Pp. 145–52 in *Futures for Central Queensland*, edited by Denis Cryle, Graham Griffin, and Danni Stehlik. Rockhampton: Rural Social and Economic Centre, Central Queensland University, 1996.

Saroca, N. "Filipino Women, Sexual Politics, and the Gendered Discourse of the Mail Order Bride." *JIGS (Journal of Interdisciplinary Gender Studies)* vol. 2, no. 2 (1997): 89–103.

Scaramella, M. *The Situations of Filipino Brides in Northern Areas of Western Australia.* Perth: Postgraduate Diploma in Counseling, Curtin University, unpublished paper.

Simons, N. "The Males who 'Order' the Brides: Masculinities and Australian Men Married to Filipinas." BA (hons) thesis. Curtin University of Technology, 1998.

Smith, A., and G. Kaminskas. "Female Filipino Migration to Australia: An Overview." *Asian Migrant* vol. 5, no. 3 (1992): 72–81.

Smith, A., and J. Boileau. "From Manila to Manjimup: Female Migration to Australia." Paper presented to the Asia and Pacific Women as Migrants Conference, University of Melbourne, 30 September–2 October 1994.

Vogels, J. G. *An Analysis of Some Studies Made on Filipino Women in Australia. Proceedings of the Seminar on towards a Better Life: The Profile of a Filipino Woman.* Perth: Filipino-Australia Club of Perth, 1987.

Whiteford, P. "Are Immigrants Overrepresented in the Australian Security System?" *Journal of the Australian Population Association* vol. 8, no. 2 (1991): 93–108.

Yeoh, B. S. A., and L.-M. Khoo. "Home, Work and Community: Skilled International Migration and Expatriate Women in Singapore." *International Migration* vol. 36, no. 2 (1998): 159–86.

5

Gender, Marriage, and Skilled Migration: The Case of Singaporeans in China

Katie Willis and Brenda Yeoh

Within the field of demography there has been a great deal of work on the effect of migration on women's employment when married couples migrate.[1] While there are differences in spatial terms, and also depending on education levels, age, stage in the household life cycle, and so on, the general findings are that women's employment status tends to decline when couples migrate. This reflects the fact that migration tends to be initiated by male partners, and women follow (see, for example, Chattopadhyay 1997; Halfacree 1995; Shihadeh 1991; Smits 1999; Yeoh and Khoo 1998)

When single people's migration is considered, the tendency is to regard them as more mobile because of the lack of marital ties. While their spatial mobility may be constrained for other reasons (such as finance), marriage is considered only as an "absence" in this context. However, despite being single, marriage needs to be considered in terms of the timing of migration within an expected life course, this expectation being strongly influenced by the social norms of a particular society regarding the appropriateness of marriage. While migration is sometimes undertaken solely or primarily for the purpose of marriage, often marriage is an unforeseen outcome of moving to a new location. Migration (particularly international migration) provides individuals with opportunities to meet a broader range of potential marriage partners. The appropriateness of these marriage partners is constructed in ethnic, racial, and gender terms.

This chapter is unusual as it brings marriage to the forefront of a discussion on unmarried Singaporeans who have migrated to China to work in highly skilled professional and managerial positions as part of Singapore's "regionalization" drive. While marriage is certainly not the reason for moving overseas, we will show that "marriage" is still a consideration within migration decision making and the migration experience. The presence of marriage as an issue for unmarried migrants is a reflection of the social, political, and economic context from which the migrants derive. As we demonstrate below, Singaporean cultural norms regarding the importance of particular family forms and the centrality of marriage within them are strongly rooted and are reinforced by government policy in a range of spheres. In addition, there is a strong gender dimension to these policies and the nature of cultural expectations regarding marriage.

Migration can, it has been argued, provide opportunities for challenging preexisting identities and social relations (Van der Veer 1995). Thus, in gender terms, migration is sometimes presented as a way of breaking out of the "straitjacket" of behavioral conventions "at home," policed by family, social disapproval, or approbation, as well as state policies. However, such "transgressions" are not inevitable, as in many cases preexisting gender relations and social norms reemerge in new geographic locations (see Alicea 1997; Hondagneu-Sotelo 1992; Mitchell 1997; Yeoh and Willis, 1999). While marriage rates may be decreasing among certain groups within Singaporean society (see below), marriage is still part of the normative life-course expectations of the vast majority of Singaporeans and is a key part of state rhetoric and social policy.[2]

As the global reach of transnational corporations has expanded and intensified, the mobility of professional workers has increased (Findlay, Li, Jowett, Skeldon 1996; Salt and Findlay 1989). This so-called transnational capitalist class (Hannerz 1993; Sklair 1998), often associated with the producer-services sector, has been portrayed as a highly mobile group moving from one "global city" to another (Beaverstock, 1996a).

While the gendered nature of migration has been recognized (see Willis and Yeoh 2000a for an overview), it is unskilled migration that has received attention. Skilled international migrants tend to be discussed as if they are nongendered beings who do not form part of a household and whose migration experiences are purely related to paid employment (exceptions include Adler 1994; Beaverstock and Bostock 2000; Hardill 1998; Hardill and MacDonald 1998; Kofman 2000; Willis and Yeoh 2000b; Yeoh and Khoo 1998; and Lee and Piper, chapter 6).

SINGAPORE

Since gaining independence in 1965, Singapore has experienced high levels of economic growth,[3] with a high standard of living for a significant portion of the population. This growth has been closely directed by the Singaporean state that, while promoting the market, has also made strategic interventions not only into the economy, but also all aspects of Singapore life, including the family (Huff 1995).

For rapid rates of growth to be maintained, the Singapore economy has to keep diversifying. Resource limitations have led the government and private sector to view investment outside the national boundaries to be of crucial importance. While Singapore companies have always been involved, to some degree, in foreign investment, it is only since 1986 and particularly since 1992 that this policy has been heavily promoted. "Going regional" involves investment in South and East Asia and is an example of how the processes of globalization have led to an increasingly complex web of international economic flows. Singapore has become a node of a regional economy, acting as a conduit for non-Asian funds coming into the region, as well as Singaporean firms investing directly in South and East Asian economies (Perry, Yeung, and Poon 1998; Yeung 1999, 2000).

Figures for Singaporean investment in the region have experienced rapid growth and show great diversity across countries (Yeoh and Willis 1997). This overseas investment has been accompanied by a relocation of skilled personnel and their families. There are an estimated 15,000 Singaporeans in mainland China and Hong Kong (Willis 2001). These figures do not include the large number of Singaporeans who "commute" out to the region on a regular basis.

The Singapore government has been highly involved in molding social elements of Singapore society. Some of these, such as the education system and housing provision, can be directly linked to the aim of creating a happy and healthy workforce, but other aspects, such as policies toward the family, are related to wider perceptions of "appropriate behavior" linked to the promotion of "Asian values." "The family," defined as households consisting of married couples and their children and perhaps parents or parents-in-law, is a key unit within government rhetoric and policies regarding "Asian" values. While the importance of marriage is clearly felt by the majority of Singaporeans, government control over housing, education, and other social services is an important influence, as certain social groups (such as single people and unmarried mothers) are excluded from particular services.

As part of the drive toward economic success, women have been encouraged to enter the workforce. In 1957 less than a quarter (21.6 percent) of adult women were registered as employed (Wong and Leong 1993, 3), whereas the figure currently stands at 50.2 percent (Department of Statistics 2000a). However, this expansion has not been accompanied by a reformulating of attitudes toward the role of women within the family or a major increase in state involvement in reproductive activities (Quah 1993). In fact, both individual ministers within the Singapore government (most famously then Prime Minister Lee Kuan Yew in 1983, see Doran 1996; PuruShotam 1998), as well as the Singapore government in general, has expressed concern about the impact of women's careers on the nature of Singapore society, particularly women's "reluctance" to get married and to have children. According to the 2000 Census, over 25 percent of graduate women in their early forties are unmarried, compared to fewer than 10 percent of graduate men at this age (in *Straits Times* 2001).[4]

It is clear, therefore, that family policy, which as PuruShotam (1998) argues is intertwined with, and often indistinguishable from, policies toward women, is related not only to "morality," but also, like so many other government policies, related to producing an appropriate workforce. George (2000) argues that Singapore is best likened to an air-conditioned nation designed, first and foremost, for the material comfort of its inhabitants by means of a finely tuned, infrastructure-intensive central control system. Within this system the "normal family" (PuruShotam 1998) is a key unit, both in terms of protecting "Asian values" and because of its perceived benefits for the larger family—the nation.

As we have argued elsewhere (Willis and Yeoh 1998), regionalization adds another complication to the attempt to maintain "Asian values" and rapid economic growth based on capitalist activities. This chapter focuses particularly on the issue of marriage, comparing the experiences of single Singaporean men and women during their postings in China. Throughout the chapter, marriage is often portrayed as an almost inevitable and desirable life event, reflecting the realities of current Singapore society, where other options such as remaining single or cohabiting are frowned upon and may involve material problems because of government policies (see PuruShotam 1998). Marriage patterns may not always reflect these expectations, but it is important to recognize the weight of these expectations and the ways in which particular forms of social and family behavior are incorporated into state rhetoric of the nation.

METHODOLOGY

Between July and September 1997, 130 interviews were conducted with women and men, most of whom had lived, or were living, in China, either because of work or because they were accompanying their spouses who had been posted there. Interviews were conducted in Shanghai, Suzhou, and Wuxi, as well as in Singapore. From October 1998 to August 2000, 30 further interviews were conducted with Singaporeans in Hong Kong and Guangzhou. Interviewees were recruited through a snowball method using contacts in companies and government agencies. All interviews, except two, were conducted in English. We also interviewed eight individuals who did not migrate to China, but had spouses who migrated or who took regular business trips in the region, and thirteen people who worked for companies where relocation abroad was an option that they had not taken. A basic interview schedule was followed for each interview, although respondents were free to bring up any topic that they felt useful.

Suzhou and Wuxi are prime sites of Singaporean investment in China, with major infrastructure projects in the form of an industrial park at Suzhou[5] (see Ng and Tan 1996) and a private-sector initiative at Wuxi. Shanghai is also a major destination for Singapore investment, particularly in real estate projects. Although there are no official figures for Singaporeans in China, we estimate that 450 adults live in the Suzhou and Wuxi area, and 1,500 in Shanghai. Hong Kong and Guangzhou were selected because they are also important destinations for Singaporean migration. Hong Kong now has a Singapore population of about 10,000 people (including nonworking family members). Guangzhou's Singaporean population is a matter of about 150. Of course, the expatriate population is a very dynamic one and there are many individuals who commute between Singapore and China, but these figures provide a general indication of the numbers involved.

This chapter considers the forty-six Singapore unmarried migrants (thirty-one women and fifteen men) and five single nonmigrants (two women and three men). In all cases "single" refers to individuals who were not married at the time of migration,[6] although some of the cases referred to are individuals who married during their time overseas.

GENDER, EMPLOYMENT, AND OVERSEAS POSTINGS

Before discussing the role of marriage in both the migration decisions and the experiences of single Singaporeans, it is important to provide an overview of the kinds of jobs in which the migrants are engaged. For most migrants, the jobs they took overseas were either postings from their existing company or were in related fields. Given the nature of Singaporean investment in China, the jobs undertaken in China were either in the private sector, particularly in finance, property, and marketing/customer relations, or were in Singapore government-linked companies in infrastructure projects. There were no single migrants engaged in entrepreneurial activities, despite the importance of Chinese business networks within regional business development (see, for example, Yeung and Olds 2000).

Employment in China tends to show gender segmentation, with women concentrated in sectors such as office administration and secretarial posts, health and education (particularly nursing and teaching), and human resources management and customer service. Five of the single men sampled worked in the property sector, compared to only one of the single women, and other important sectors

for male employment were engineering, law, and management. Finance and ac-
countancy were significant sectors overall for both men and women, reflecting
the importance of such producer services to the employment mobility of
transnational elites.

The opportunity to live and work in China was often taken by both men
and women in order to improve their career prospects. In almost all cases, these
migrants were relatively low down the career ladder, and they saw the "overseas exposure" as a chance to gain important skills and experience, as well as a
larger salary. For recent graduate Zina, accepting a two-year posting in Wuxi
provided the perfect opportunity for her to gain skills rapidly and to progress
up the career ladder much more rapidly than she would have in Singapore. Peter, who has worked in the hotel industry in both Shanghai and Guangzhou,
said that the benefits package available was "just too attractive to resist," and
Gina, a nurse in Hong Kong for three years, said that nurses' pay in Hong Kong
was three times higher than in Singapore.

However, these career- and finance-related reasons were not the only driv-
ing force behind the move to China. For women, in particular, migration was
seen as an opportunity to experience the kind of independence and excite-
ment unavailable at home in both the family context and within wider Singaporean society. While Singaporean gender norms are constraining for both
men and women, the expectations and controls placed on women are regarded
as more restrictive. Jayne, a business administrator in Suzhou, had selected her
job because she wanted to travel in order to escape from what she saw as the
sheltered life and lack of independence. As soon as the chance was offered, she
volunteered to come to China.

In addition, all the Singaporean migrants were of Chinese ancestry, and for
some, again especially the women, living in China was a chance to explore this
heritage. For example, Sarah, a teacher in Suzhou, had worked in Singapore for
about eight years and had decided to come to China to enrich her life and find
out more about her roots. She described China as "big and beautiful" and saw
the initial two-year posting in China as an opportunity to explore the country. The more career-dominated reasons given by Singaporean men perhaps reflect the constructions of masculinity within the city-state (see Yeoh and Willis
2000 for further discussion).

MARRIAGE AND MIGRATION DECISIONS

Having outlined the main reasons migrants gave to explain their movement to
China, it is important now to consider the timing of this relocation and the
ways in which marriage fits into this. In making decisions to migrate, the fact

that these individuals are not married does not mean that marriage ceases to be an important consideration. For many migrants, both male and female, not having marriage ties gave them freedom to travel overseas. In addition, the migrants viewed the timing of the postings (the migrants were in their mid to late twenties) as their "last chance," because marriage would be a probable event in the foreseeable future (see Lee and Piper, chapter 6, for a discussion of how life-course stages influence autonomy in migration decisions). Many Singaporeans used their marital status as a reason why they had chosen to travel overseas at this particular point. For example, Janice, an accountant working in Suzhou said:

> [I] got [so] sick of the same kind of work that I decided to venture overseas and then I mean so much had been talked about regionalization so I thought "Why not! I'm still single!" It's easy to travel without any family burden.

Similarly, Josephine, who has worked in China since the mid-1990s and currently works in marketing in Guangzhou, stresses how her globe-trotting (she has worked in a number of overseas locations) and her career-woman lifestyle is possible because she does not have commitments to a spouse or children:

> I think being single—that's me you know—career always number one. Rather than balance in life and family, I guess career becomes the most important aspect of my life. So I feel it doesn't matter to me [being posted overseas] . . . cos I don't have any dependents.

However, for women migrants, marriage was perceived as marking the end of overseas posting opportunities, as they would either stay in Singapore because of family commitments or would only travel overseas if accompanying their husbands. (See Chee, chapter 7, for a consideration of the ways in which women's status as mothers affects their paid-work opportunities overseas.) Maureen, a twenty-five-year-old management trainee in the banking sector, was fairly typical in her comments on what would happen if she got married:

> I think in every relationship there's a compromise. For myself, if I were to find a husband, very seriously I would not travel, because I think it's unfair to him, although he must support me. But personally I won't do it. But if he has to travel, I would support him. I will [follow him].

In contrast, men did not see marriage as marking the end of international mobility, many suggesting that overseas postings would be possible if their wives accompanied them or were willing to stay in Singapore to look after the children. For example, Sean, a property developer in Suzhou, said that marriage would not necessarily prevent overseas postings, but if there were children, he would want to return to Singapore so that the children could enter the Singapore education system at primary level. (See Willis and Yeoh 2000b, for a more detailed discussion of the impact of marital status on migration.)

PERCEPTIONS OF MARRIAGE

In Singaporean society there is a strongly held belief in marriage as an important cultural institution in which everyone should participate. This is reflected in the comments made by our interviewees, who often talked about "when I get married," rather than "if I get married." As outlined in an earlier section, government rhetoric regarding the importance of marriage is explicit and commonplace and in reality, most Singaporeans will indeed get married and will remain married for the rest of their lives,[7] although there are clear differences by education level and gender.

In the context of the regionalization process, what is particularly interesting is the perceived effect of migration on "marriageability" and the gender dimensions of this. As single migrants, these individuals' decisions were less bound up in the day-to-day realities of household strategies (housework, childcare, education) than married migrants (Willis and Yeoh 2000b). However, decision making cannot be regarded as a solely individual process, as most migrants took into account the opinions of other family members. As the vast majority of single migrants (male and female) regardless of age lived with their parents in Singapore,[8] the parental opinions were the most commonly cited. Because of the contributions, often financial, that adult children make to the household economy, decisions regarding changing employment could have an effect on other household members (Chye 2000).

Overall, female migrants reported objections to their mobility by family members more than male migrants (60 percent compared with just under 40 percent). In many cases, family members, particularly mothers, were concerned about the safety of their daughters. However, a particular element of parental worry relates to marriage. A number of women pointed out that their parents were concerned that living and working abroad would diminish their opportunities to meet an appropriate partner. There is growing concern in Singapore, including at a government level, regarding the declining marriage rates among women as they become more highly educated and enter highly paid jobs. Some parents believe that moving abroad will make it even more difficult to find a husband. For example, Priscilla's father was worried that her posting to Beijing would make it even harder for her to find a husband:

> I think the only thing is comes from my dad. His main concern is that you're going overseas that you aren't going to settle down. So I said "Well, fine. I may meet

a foreigner, Chinaman, and settle down." He said "Well it's fine with me as long as you settle down." That was the only question he raised.

In fact Priscilla, in her thirties, worked in Beijing for four years in the early 1990s and is still single following her return to Singapore. She says, however, that her older sister, who is forty-five, is single, so her parents are now used to this.

In addition, a number of women said that the length of their posting was affected by their need to return to Singapore. While the need to find an appropriate marriage partner was certainly not the only, or even the most important, reason for returning to Singapore, the desire to find a husband was certainly not insignificant for some women. Frances, who had spent a year as an office administrator in Suzhou, stressed the importance of coming back to Singapore:

> *Frances:* I think for girls, don't stay there too long. Even though not in China, or in some other place, because I believe that if you stay there for too long, you do not want to come back. Yah. Because I have friends, they work in Shanghai. They are there for five, six years and they don't want to come back. Then they are all single girls.
>
> *Brenda:* Right. And the career means that they are not likely to get married lah?
>
> *Frances:* I think so. Maybe they are committed to their lifestyle in China. So when I ask them, "you don't want to come back and get married?" they say not at the moment.
>
> *Brenda:* They got used to it. Do you think it's a freer lifestyle there?
>
> *Frances:* That's why the problem is . . . I don't agree people staying in a place for too long. Maybe if you plan to work in a place . . . for girl, I think 2 years to 3 years enough. Don't stay too long.

Since returning to Singapore, Frances has entered a serious relationship and says that now she would not accept a posting overseas.

No Singaporean men commented on the possible incompatibility between overseas postings and marriage. This does not seem to be because they expected to find a future wife overseas (although this sometimes happens as outlined below), but that their own, and Singaporean society's, expectations regarding possible marriage partners for men are much less restricted than for women.

MARRIAGE

Within our sample, there are four Singaporeans who married someone they met during their posting to China. In all four cases the Singaporeans are men and they married local Chinese women (one in Suzhou, two in Shanghai, and one in Hong Kong). The four cases represent just over a quarter of the "single" men in the sample. Throughout our fieldwork it has become very clear that this scenario is not uncommon, so there is a need to examine the reasons behind marriage pattern differences between Singaporean men and women.[9]

It must be stressed, however, that relationships and marriages between Singaporean women and Chinese men are not unknown. Two of the married female migrants interviewed were married to Hong Kong Chinese men. However, a number of points must be made about these cases. The first is that obviously Hong Kong is very different from mainland China in economic, social, and cultural terms. This highlights the importance of recognizing diversity within the PRC Chinese population. In all our fieldwork, we have not come across a Singaporean woman marrying a mainland Chinese man.

Secondly, for both marriages, the couples did not meet as part of a posting to Hong Kong. In one case the couple met while at college in Canada and in the other, the relationship started as a pen-pal relationship. Having investigated the ways in which Singaporean women socialize while on postings in China, the fact that these marriages have taken place in nonposting circumstances is not really surprising. In general, Singaporeans as a group tend to socialize a great deal with each other, but the exclusivity of socializing tends to be greater for women than for men. This tendency to socialize largely with other Singaporeans has not, however, led to high rates of marriage between Singaporeans who meet during postings. There were no incidences of this among our interviewees, and we did not hear any reports of marriages based on meetings overseas. This could be related to marriage norms outlined below.

In terms of marriage between Singaporeans and local Chinese, the first area of interest is in the ways in which local Chinese men and women are perceived as potential marriage partners by Singaporeans posted in China. Chinese women are often described by both male and female single and married interviewees with reference to their appearance, focusing on their beauty and their clothes. Before traveling to Suzhou, many Singaporeans had remarked on the reputation of Suzhou women as being incredibly beautiful, and this was also mentioned during our Suzhou interviews.

However, while praising their beauty, many Singaporean informants also viewed local Chinese women in urban China as predatory, using their female charms to ensnare unsuspecting foreigners. Priscilla described the local Chinese women who she saw in hotel bars in Beijing as follows:

> *Priscilla:* They hang around in hotels. They hang around in pubs, bowling alley, discotheque and all that. You can spot them very easily.
>
> *Brenda:* How would you know that they are up to no good?
>
> *Priscilla:* Oh well, if it's in winter a lady can be sitting at the lounge, alone by herself, in short shorts in winter. What can she be wearing shorts in winter for? And alone, sitting there for hours and things like that. Very easily you can spot

them. They are pretty, some of them are pretty. Tall, elegant, but when it comes to
social etiquette then you will be in for a shock.

Thus, for Singaporeans, local Chinese women are constructed as potential
marriage partners for Singaporean men because of their extreme beauty
and/or because, like Sirens, they entrap foreign men.[10] While each of the four
marriages between Singaporean men and Chinese women we came across had
their own particularities, what is interesting is the way in which the men
seemed to have internalized the general views of foreign-local liaisons and
were consequently self-conscious about discussing their relationships during
interviews. This was reflected in, for example, men stressing the fact that their
wives were highly intelligent and they had met them at work, and by the one
man who asked us to turn the tape off while he discussed his marriage. We
were present on a number of occasions when these men were being "teased"
by their workmates for marrying a local.

Of course, relationships between expatriate men and local women are not
restricted to single men. This adds to the view of local Chinese women as
"predatory"; they will pursue a foreign man, even though he is obviously married. A number of Singaporean men we interviewed talked about their "at-
tractiveness index" increasing the minute they got off the plane in China.
Peter, who has been working in Shanghai in the hospitality business for many
years, summarized this phenomenon when he said: "Let's say your handsomeness is 50 percent. When you come to China you automatically enhance your
index. Your handsomeness goes from 50 percent to 100 percent!"

At one lunchtime meeting with four Singaporean men who were working
in China, there was great hilarity when one of the men joked about another
having two MBAs (not only a Masters in Business Administration, but also
Married But Available).[11] On another occasion a married, middle-aged Singaporean manager posted to Guangzhou stated:

> All the girls come on to me. I say it's not because I am good looking, but because
> I am old and here they know that the older you are, the more cash rich you are.
> . . . Because they think that you have reached a certain age and your financial
> backing is very good. And that is a better fish to catch.

Compared to the constructions of Chinese women created by Singaporeans,
the discussions of Chinese men as potential husbands stress the negative. Singaporean women often described them as unattractive physically, but they also
stressed the disparities in wealth between themselves as expatriates from a
wealthy country and the local men. This brings us to a second gendered element of this discussion of marriage patterns—the norms of "marrying up" and
"marrying down." While this is certainly not confined to Singaporeans overseas,

or is found only in Singapore, it is an issue that has been highlighted in the debates about marriage within the city-state, particularly with the rise in women's education levels and economic status (see Perry, Kong, and Yeoh 1997, pp. 90–91). Social norms dictate that women should marry more educated men from higher social strata, while men's search for marriage partners should be in the opposite direction. This reflects norms regarding men's position as breadwinner and head of the household and helps explain the lower levels of marriage among highly educated women and also among men with low levels of education highlighted in the 2000 Census.

Wei Ying, general manager in an infrastructure company working in Suzhou, discussed relationships between Singaporeans and local Chinese:

> I agree with you that it's very unlikely that a Singaporean woman would go off with a Chinese man, leave the family for a Chinese man. . . . If they only earn S$200–300 a month, even if they earn S$1,000, to them it's a lot of money, but to us S$1,000 won't get you anywhere in Singapore. So it's very natural. But if you're talking about another country then maybe you'll have the single woman going astray.

Josephine, the marketing executive in Guangzhou, discussed how she sometimes socialized with Chinese male colleagues, but romance was never on the cards from her perspective, partly because of the chasm in income, but more importantly because she felt that she would not get the intellectual stimulation from someone who had a very limited worldview as a result of not traveling or being exposed to external ideas. There would also be travel problems; she loves international travel, but for most Chinese nationals, the freedom to travel, even if you have the economic wherewithal, is limited, although the numbers traveling overseas are increasing. She summarized her views on this topic as follows:

> I mean I go out with the local guys but you know you can't live in your cocoon, you got to mix around, but you know at the end of the day if you think that you want to marry somebody, you know it's not that. Because your lifestyle and outlook in life. I am so exposed internationally, certainly if I'm talking to someone who's never been outside of China . . . no idea at all what I am talking about. So intellectually, it's not that stimulating for me. . . . I try to expose myself so that culturally you can learn something for yourself, but don't expect too much from them. . . . Because, you know, using a knife and fork, they wouldn't even know properly. I have to teach them, months ago. But you see, if you bring them to a nice restaurant, they will embarrass you.

While women used economic disparities as an explanation for the lack of Singaporean women having relationships with Chinese men, and both men and women drew on economic explanations for the relative lack of socializing between Singaporeans and Chinese in general, economic and educational differences did not come into play in the discussion of Singaporean men and Chinese women.

As our research dealt purely with the Singaporean migrants, we cannot comment on the ways in which Singaporeans are conceived of as potential marriage partners by local Chinese men and women. However, we can make some mention of the perceptions that the Singaporeans believe that local Chinese have. The first is the conception that local Chinese men would not be attracted to Singaporean women because of their career-minded attitudes and greater education levels and income-earning potential, that is, that the patriarchal nature of Chinese society has also encouraged Chinese men to "marry down."[12]

The second explanation for the gendered marriage pattern was the fact that until 1999 Singaporean immigration law gave foreign-born wives right of entry, but denied foreign-born husbands. This reflected the patriarchal nature of much Singaporean legislation. For some Singaporeans, the fact that a Chinese man could not get a Singapore passport by marrying a Singaporean woman was a sufficient explanation for their lack of interest in Singaporean women.

Finally, Singaporean women are often regarded as "defenders of the nation," responsible for maintaining Singaporean "standards." Throughout the world, women's socially defined role in the domestic sphere has been conflated with the domestic sphere of the nation, stressing women's importance in socializing future generations into accepted norms and ensuring that other members of society (notably adult men) do not lead to the destruction of "traditional" norms and behaviors. Just as women are regarded as "nurturers" within the household, so too is the responsibility placed on women's shoulders of being the nurturer of the nation. In the case of Singaporeans in China, this role is taken on both by married women accompanying their husbands overseas and single women engaged in paid employment. As demonstrated earlier, there is a strong tendency for Singaporean women to distance themselves, both physically and behaviorally, from local Chinese women. The need to maintain "standards," based on the norms of Singaporean society, is reflected in Singaporean women's behavior in relation to marriage. While Priscilla's father was willing for her to marry a local Chinese man, as long as she married somebody, this rather open attitude to cross-national marriage is somewhat rare in Singapore. Because of this women may be unwilling to engage in relationships with non-Singaporeans (see Yeoh and Willis 1999 for further details and examples).

MARRIAGE AND CAREER PATHS FOR SINGAPOREAN WOMEN

To conclude this chapter we consider the longer term implications of the China posting to women's career and marriage paths. Within the larger sample of 150 Singaporeans, there were no cases of women who had traveled to Singapore when single and had then married on their return to Singapore. From this we cannot definitively conclude that migration per se is having a detrimental effect on the marriage rates of Singaporean women—regionalization is a very recent process so its impact on broader social trends is hard to evaluate. In addition, marriage rates for highly educated women throughout Singapore have been declining, causing concern (as highlighted above).

The decision to go overseas for career reasons seems to pay off for many single Singaporean women who, on their return to Singapore, are usually able to gain promotion as they can demonstrate new skills and experience. While none of the single women interviewed after their return to Singapore (eleven in total) ruled marriage out, and for many marriage and children were still very important goals, their careers remained very important to them. It seems, therefore, that migration to China could be another factor that contributes to declining marriage rates among career women in Singapore.

Finally, in some cases, there are signs of "career expatriates" among the single women interviewed. In order to remain "in the region" for more than a few years, singledom seems to be the norm. From our interviews it is impossible to assess whether these are women for whom marriage's importance was relegated because of career ambitions, whether these were women for whom marriage was never really appealing and overseas postings allowed them to fulfil other personal ambitions, or whether overseas travel provided an "excuse" for their nonmarried status. For example, Catrina, a project manager in her late thirties, travels frequently around China and Southeast Asia and says she has no intention of getting married as this would restrict her mobility. Hannah, a senior teacher in Hong Kong, is in her forties and describes herself as "adventurous and a traveler." Her posting overseas has given her the chance to develop some of her interests in natural history.

CONCLUSION

In this chapter we examined the interactions between gender, skilled migration, and marriage, using single Singaporeans who have moved to China for work as a case study. This case study has highlighted a number of conclusions in relation to the migration of skilled Asian men and women. Contrary to much research on unmarried migrants, this chapter has demonstrated that the prospect of marriage is an ever-present consideration in most migration decisions for both men and women, although the constraints of marriage on spatial mobility clearly affect women more than men. Secondly, marriageability is perceived to change on migration and in some cases this is used in the migration decision-making process. As with the effect of marriage on the ability to migrate for employment reasons, there are clear gender differences, with movement to China having greater negative effects on women's marriage prospects. However, this migration effect needs to be considered within the context of declining marriage rates among highly educated Singaporean women as a whole; thus migration per se cannot be regarded as the only factor explaining the migrants' marriage chances.

Finally, and reflecting these issues of marriageability and the intersections between gender and class in China, actual patterns of marriage show gender differences. Despite the physical movement out of Singapore and the highly educated and economically privileged status of the migrants, behavioral norms remain very strong. While these norms are likely to change as shifts in society become more widely acknowledged and accepted among current migrant groups, the expectation of marriage remains a key issue and concern within the migration experience, especially for single women.

NOTES

The 1997 fieldwork trip was funded by the Lee Foundation (Singapore) and an HSBC Small Research Grant administered by the Royal Geographical Society (with The Institute of British Geographers). The 1999 and 2000 fieldwork trips were funded by the Economic and Social Research Council (Grant No. L214 25 2007). The authors would like to extend their thanks to these funding bodies, as well as to all the Singaporeans who have helped them in this research and the postgraduate students in Liverpool and Singapore who have helped transcribe the interviews. Many thanks to Nicola Piper, Mina Roces, and Mark Seldon for their comments on earlier drafts of this chapter.

1. There has been far less work on the impact of migration on nonmarried couples. This is probably because many couples-focused studies use census information as the basis for their analysis.

2. A Social Development Unit (SDU) survey in 1996 revealed that 82 percent of the Singaporean graduates interviewed "considered marriage and starting a family as a desired life goal" (in Tarmugi 1999, 97). The SDU was set up by the government in the mid-1980s to promote marriage among graduates. This was a response to the worries about the declining birth rate, especially among more-educated members of society, and falling marriage rates among university graduates (Perry et al. 1997, 90–91).

3. There were great leaps in the GNP per capita throughout the 1990s, apart from the period 1997–1998 when there was negative growth due to the 1997 "Asian crisis." GNP per capita grew, on average, 8.7 percent per annum in the period 1991–1994 (Huff 1995). The figure for 1998–1999 was 3.4 percent (Department of Statistics 2000c).

4. The *Straits Times* report also highlights the fact that men with low levels of education are the fastest growing group of singles in Singapore.

5. The Suzhou Township project has not been as successful as anticipated, and the Singapore government has now formally withdrawn from plans for expansion.

6. There were no cases of cohabitation among the Singaporean interviewees.

7. According to the Census, 2.4 percent of adults in Singapore were divorced or separated in 2000 (Department of Statistics 2000b).

8. This is a reflection of housing policies in Singapore. In 1995 88 percent of households lived in Housing and Development Board flats (Department of Statistics 1996). Government restrictions on single people owning property means that for the majority who cannot afford a private-sector apartment, living with relatives until marriage is the most common arrangement.

9. This gendered pattern is also found among other expatriate groups, including British migrants (see Willis and Yeoh 2002).

10. Some interviewees intimated that companies prefer to hire women because they are less likely to become involved in liaisons with locals that could bring shame on the firm.

11. See Yeoh and Willis (2000) for a discussion of the constructions and negotiation of masculinity among Singaporean men in China.

12. Of course, some Chinese nationals have become rich as part of the economic opening-up process, but the perception of Singaporeans remains that Chinese nationals have lower income-generating potential than expatriate workers.

REFERENCES

Adler, N. J. "Competitive Frontiers: Women Managing Across Borders." *Journal of Management Development* vol. 13 (1994): 24–41.

Alicea, M. "'A Chambered Nautilus': The Contradictory Nature of Puerto Rican Women's Role in the Social Construction of a Transnational Community." *Gender and Society* vol. 11 (1997): 597–626.

Beaverstock, J. V. "Migration, Knowledge and Social Interaction: Expatriate Labour Within Investment Banks." *Area* vol. 28 (1996): 459–70.

Beaverstock, J. V., and R. Bostock. "Expatriate Communities in Asia-Pacific Financial Centers: The Case of Singapore." Paper presented at International Conference on Transnational Communities in the Asia-Pacific Region: Comparative Perspectives, Singapore, August 2000.

Chattopadhyay, A. "Family Migration and the Economic Status of Women in Malaysia." *International Migration Review* vol. 31, no. 2 (1997): 338–52.

Chye, E. *Love, Money and Power in the Singaporean Household Economy.* Unpublished D. Phil. Thesis, School of Geography, University of Oxford, 2000.

Department of Statistics. "Economic Characteristics of Singapore Resident Population." In *Singapore Census of Population 2000, Advance Data Release No. 4.* Singapore: Department of Statistics, 2000a.

———. "Singapore Census of Population 2000." Singapore: Singapore Department of Statistics Press Release, August 2000b.

―――. *Yearbook of Statistics Singapore*. Singapore: Department of Statistics, 2000c.

―――. *Singapore 1996: Statistical Highlights*. Singapore: Department of Statistics, 1996.

Doran, C. "Global Integration and Local Identities: Engendering the Singaporean Chinese." *Asia Pacific Viewpoint* vol. 37 (1996): 153–64.

Findlay, A. M., F. L. N. Li, A. Jowett, and R. Skeldon. "Skilled International Migration and the Global City: A Study of Expatriates in Hong Kong." *Transactions of the Institute of British Geographers* vol. 21, no. 1 (1996): 49–61.

George, C. *Singapore: The Air-Conditioned Nation; Essays on the Politics of Comfort and Control, 1999–2000*. Singapore: Landmark Books, 2000.

Halfacree, K. H. "Household Migration and the Structuration of Patriarchy: Evidence from the USA." *Progress in Human Geography* vol. 19, no. 2 (1995): 159–82.

Hannerz, U. "The Cultural Roles of World Cities." Pp. 67–84 in *Humanizing the City*, edited by A. P. Cohen and K. Fukuo. Edinburgh: Edinburgh University Press, 1993.

Hardill, I. "Gender Perspectives on British Expatriate Work." *Geoforum* vol. 29 (1998): 257–68.

Hardill, I., and S. MacDonald. "Choosing to Relocate: An Examination of the Impact of Expatriate Work on Dual-Career Households." *Women's Studies International Forum* vol. 21 (1998): 21–29.

Hondagneu-Sotelo, P. "Overcoming Patriarchal Constraints: The Reconstruction of Gender Relations among Mexican Immigrant Women and Men." *Gender & Society* vol. 6, no. 3 (1992): 393–415.

Huff, W. G. "The Developmental State, Government and Singapore's Economic Development since 1960." *World Development* vol. 23 (1995): 1421–38.

Kofman, E. "Invisibility of Skilled Female Migrants and Gender Relations in Studies of Skilled Migration in Europe." *International Journal of Population Geography* vol. 6 (2000): 45–59.

Mitchell, K. "Transnational Discourse: Bringing Geography Back In." *Antipode* vol. 29, no. 2 (1997): 101–14.

Ng, Y. P., and C. K. Tan. "The China-Singapore Suzhou Industrial Park." Pp. 111–28 in *Business Opportunities in the Yangtze River Delta*, edited by T. M. Tan et al. Singapore: Prentice Hall & NTU, 1996.

Perry, M., L. Kong, and B. Yeoh. *Singapore: A Developmental City State*. Chichester: Wiley, 1997.

Perry, M., H. Yeung, and J. Poon. "Regional Office Mobility: The Case of Corporate Control in Singapore and Hong Kong." *Geoforum* vol. 29, no. 3 (1998): 237–55.

PuruShotam, N. "Between Compliance and Resistance: Women and the Middle-Class Way of Life in Singapore." Pp. 127–66 in *Gender and Power in Affluent Asia*, edited by K. Sen and M. Stiven. London: Routledge, 1998.

Quah, Stella R. "Marriage and the Family." Pp. 20–85 in *Singapore Women: Three Decades of Change*, edited by A. Wong and W. K. Leong. Singapore: Times Academic Press, 1993.

Salt, J., and A. Findlay. "International Migration of Highly-Skilled Manpower: Theoretical and Developmental Issues." Pp. 159–80 in *The Impact of Migration on Developing Countries*, edited by R. Appleyard. Paris: OECD, 1989.

Shihadeh, E. S. "The Prevalence of Husband-Centred Migration: Employment Consequences for Married Mothers." *Journal of Marriage and the Family* vol. 53 (1991): 432–44.

Sklair, L. *Transnational Practices and Analysis of the Global System.* ESRC Transnational Communities Programme Working Paper No. 4. Accessed online: www .transcomm.co.ac.uk 1998.

Smits, J. "Family Migration and the Labour-Force Participation of Married Women in the Netherlands, 1977–1996." *International Journal of Population Geography* vol. 5 (1999): 133–50.

Straits Times. "Single in Singapore." 16 February 2001.

Tarmugi, A. "Higher Levels of Well Being through Marriage and Family." Pp. 66–70 in *Speeches: A Bimonthly Selection of Ministerial Speeches (Nov–Dec 1999),* edited by Ministry of Information and the Arts. Singapore: Ministry of Information and the Arts, Singapore, 1999.

Van der Veer, P. "Introduction: The Diasporic Imagination." Pp. 1–16 in *Nation and Migration: The Politics of Space in the South Asia Diaspora,* edited by P. Van der Veer. Philadelphia: University of Pennsylvania Press, 1995.

Willis, K. "End of ESRC Award Report 'Gender, Households and Identity in British and Singaporean Migration to China,'" unpublished document, 2001.

Willis, K., and B. Yeoh. "Introduction." Pp. xi–xxii in *Gender and Migration*, edited by Kate Willis and Brenda Yeoh. The International Library of Studies on Migration Volume 10. Cheltenham: Edward Elgar, 2000a.

Willis, K. D., and B. S. A. Yeoh. "Gender and Transnational Household Strategies: Singaporean Migration to China." *Regional Studies* vol. 34, no. 3 (2000b): 253–64.

———. "Gendering Transnational Communities: A Comparison of British and Singaporean Migrants in China." *Geoforum* 33 (2002): 553–65.

Willis, K. D., and B. Yeoh. "The Social Sustainability of Singapore's Regionalisation Drive." *Third World Planning Review* vol. 20 (1998): 203–21.

Wong, A. K., and W. K. Leong. "Singapore Women: An Overview." Pp. 1–19 in *Singapore Women: Three Decades of Change,* edited by A. K. Wong and W. K. Leong. Singapore: Times Academic Press, 1993.

Yeoh, B., and L.-M. Khoo. "Home, Work and Community: Skilled International Migration and Expatriate Women in Singapore." *International Migration* vol. 36, no. 2 (1998): 159–84.

Yeoh, B., and K. Willis. "On the 'Regional Beat': Singapore Men, Gender Politics and Transnational Spaces." Paper presented in the "Transnational Spaces" session, Association of American Geographers Annual Meeting, Pittsburgh, April 2000.

———. "'Heart' and 'Wing', Nation and Diaspora: Gendered Discourses in Singapore's Regionalisation Process." *Gender, Place and Culture* vol. 6, no. 4 (1999): 355–72.

———. "The Global-Local Nexus: Singapore's Regionalisation Drive." *Geography* vol. 355 (1997): 183–86.

Yeung, H. "State Intervention and Neo-Liberalism in the Globalizing World Economy: Lessons from Singapore's Regionalisation Programme." *The Pacific Review* vol. 13 (2000): 133–62.

———. "Regulating Investment Abroad: The Political Economy of the Regionalization of Singaporean Firms." *Antipode* vol. 31, no. 3 (1999): 245–73.

Yeung, H., and Kris Olds (Eds.). *Globalization of Chinese Business Firms.* London: Macmillan, 2000.

6

Reflections on Transnational Life-Course and Migratory Patterns of Middle-Class Women—Preliminary Observations from Malaysia

Michelle Lee and Nicola Piper

International investment and extended employment opportunities on a global scale have accelerated economic growth and expanded the middle class, particularly in some newly industrialized countries such as Malaysia (Stivens 1998; Embong 2000). This has encouraged transnational migrant workers to look for "greener pastures" overseas and to improve their socioeconomic status (Nash and Fernandez-Kelly 1983; Palma-Beltran and Dios 1992). The proliferation of international migration in the late twentieth century has created a substantial increase in transnational communities. The conceptualization of cross-border movements as "transnationalism" highlights the continuity between past movements and more complex contemporary transnational communities (Foner 1997). These communities possess fluid identities and give rise to new international networks. There are two major limits in mainstream transmigration perspectives, however: (1) in analyzing professional/skilled labor, they have mostly concentrated upon the mobility of men; and (2) discussions of women have typically been limited to unskilled or semiskilled workers. In addition, the exodus of labor has largely been analyzed from the perspective of economic push-pull factors (mostly from south to north) or sociopolitical security (Basch, Schiller, and Blanc 1994; Kritz, Keeley, and Tomasi 1983; Nash and Fernandez-Kelly 1983; Skeldon, 1997). As also observed by Willis and Yeoh and Chee (chapter 5), the main concern in existing scholarly work in this area has been on women as working class migrants. Little attention has been paid to women's mobility in the category of the well educated or skilled.[1]

To counterbalance existing studies of skilled migration that have mainly focused on intracompany transfers or the financial sector (Beaverstock and

Smith 1996) and multinational companies from the perspective of the male employee, this chapter focuses on cross-border migration of highly educated Asian women.[2] Although Asian women's involvement in migration has been extensively studied in recent years, with the majority of female migrant workers in Asia being positioned in semi- or unskilled jobs such as domestic helpers, sex workers, or "mail-order brides," it is not surprising that academic literature has almost exclusively focused on their experience. However, the exponential increases in intra-Asian investment, the expanding middle classes, and rising levels of education, together with reduced restrictions on travel, have resulted in increasing cross-border mobility of Asians as students and professionals. As opposed to men, elements such as constraints set by patriarchal characteristics of their "home" societies and gendered e/immigration policies have contributed to the relative disadvantage of migrant women in the transnational context.[3]

In addition to addressing the position of Asian highly educated or skilled migrant women in mainstream literature on workforce mobility, this chapter discusses marriage in the life of migrating women. Based on results of a pilot study, we tentatively put the argument forward that marriage migration of highly educated women needs to be contextualized with globalizing educational systems and labor markets, that is with rising international mobility of students and employees. Studying abroad in internationalized tertiary educational institutions often leads to meeting future spouses who are not "locals" themselves, but third country nationals. This type of scenario revolves around multiple transnational sites where different stages in the migrants' life course are lived out. The impetus (or reasons) for several cross-border migrations at different stages in a migrant's life often come from different sources or happen for different reasons. We have, therefore, thought a "transnational life-course perspective" as a useful framework that suggests that women can neither be described as purely "dependent trailing" wives nor as independent or autonomous migrants *at all times*. Rather, decisions to migrate are influenced by different levels of autonomy at different stages in the life courses of the women under discussion here.

We begin by providing a profile of the interviewees and methodological background information. In the section that follows, we outline the shortcomings of existing studies on skilled migration and transnationalism by referring to the specific experiences of our interviewees. The next section focuses on the present stage in the migrant women's life course (that is the "postmarriage, postmove to Malaysia" stage). Before we conclude, we briefly discuss the sociolegal construction of female migrants by receiving states with specific reference to Malaysia.

METHODOLOGY AND PROFILE OF THE INTERVIEWEES

This chapter is based on an ongoing research project of Asian skilled migrant women working in Malaysia. The interviews conducted so far are part of the pilot study that is to set the agenda for the larger project. This pilot study has been carried out in the Klang Valley, southwest of the Peninsula Malaysia, over a period of six months from October 2000 to March 2001.

Semistructured in-depth interviews were conducted with seven female Asian migrants. Their names used in this chapter have been changed to ensure confidentiality. Their ages range between twenty-nine and fifty-three years. Six of the seven women have university degrees, and the remaining woman holds a diploma. Four of the six university-trained women obtained tertiary education abroad, with the other two having university degrees from institutions in their home countries. These seven respondents include women who are currently working in professional or managerial jobs such as lecturer, investment consultant, stockbroker, and special project assistant; or previously worked in the corporate sector, but are currently working part time. Only one woman is at present a full-time mother/wife. At the point of the interview, they were all living in Malaysia, and all respondents, but one, were married. In one particular case, the Sri Lankan husband of one woman, also a Sri Lankan national, moved with her to Malaysia (a trailing husband!). Both had never lived outside of Sri Lanka prior to migrating to Malaysia. The experiences of those latter two "cases"—the single woman and the woman in a mononational marriage—are however, eliminated from further discussion in this chapter.

The remaining five respondents interviewed, upon whose experience we focus, were all at the same stage in their life course: postmarriage to a Malaysian citizen and postmigration to Malaysia. Their move to Malaysia is related to this being their husbands' country of origin. For all five, Malaysia is not the first country they have migrated to and it is also not the country where they originally met their husbands. The husbands were all born in Malaysia and are either Chinese Malaysians or Malays.[4]

The semistructured interviews were conducted either in the respondents' home or workplace. Therefore, the interviewer was able to observe the respondents' interaction with relevant social environments and individuals (household members, colleagues, and so on). The broad questions were guided by the so-called biographical approach in which the whole life of the respondent is investigated, including future plans to ensure that all life stages were covered.[5] Comments on future plans often constitute vague ideas, but they indicate an attitude or way of thinking shaped by previous (migration) experience and thus represent valuable information. This interviewing method assisted us in developing a new angle to the concept of transnationalism.

MIGRATION OF THE HIGHLY EDUCATED
AND TRANSNATIONALISM

In a review article by Kofman (2000) on the reasons for the invisibility of women in studies on skilled migration, she points to the highly heterogeneous groups subsumed under the category of "skilled" or "professional" workers. Apart from addressing the general lack of research on skilled migrant women in mainstream literature on labor mobility (as done by Willis and Yeoh, chapter 9), we concentrate on the specific context of student migration that can be seen as the first step toward leading to further, or prolonged, migration patterns.

In the specific context of Asian *women*, it is not surprising to find that so little research has been done on their skilled or professional migration, as until recently relatively few women participated in higher education in general as well as abroad, with even fewer migrating independently as students (Kofman 2000). Apart from a study by Findlay, Li, Jowett, Brown, and Skeldon (1994) on student migration in which it is argued that initial studying abroad often leads to further migration and thus more often turns into what conventional studies would consider "labor" (or work-related) migration, the issue of students studying overseas as a subcategory of skilled migration is a highly underresearched area (Li, Findlay, Jowett, and Skeldon 1996). Existing studies have shown that female proportions of the overseas student populations are increasing, as in the case of Japanese women, for instance (see Ono and Piper 2001), if absolute numbers are not even exceeding their male counterparts (Kofman 2000, 48). In the East and Southeast Asian context, this reflects women's increasing presence in institutions of higher education in general and the growing numbers of dual-income or dual-career households. It is surprising then to find that studies by feminist scholars still tend to treat women as un- or semi-skilled workers only or as dependents.

Although student mobility across national borders has traditionally not been considered by studies on work-related international migration, attention has begun to be paid to this particular phenomenon more recently. The latest OECD SOPEMI report, for instance, has a section on student migration, remarking upon the constant growth of student mobility facilitated by developments in communications and faster information flows on the one hand, and growing internationalization of education systems on the other (2001, 112). It is acknowledged that "student flows represent a form of migration of qualified labour and also a precursor of subsequent migrations" (OECD 2001, 93).

It is not surprising that most students coming from countries with a different language chose to go to the English-speaking countries, reflecting the dominance of English in practically all global matters. The United States figures as the largest receiver of foreign students (34 percent in 1998), most of whom originated in Asia-Oceania (65 percent), followed by the U.K. (16 percent), Australia (8 percent), and Canada (3 percent). In terms of enrollment in OECD countries of students from among non-OECD countries, Malaysia (which is the country of origin of all husbands of the women in our sample) has the highest figure for students studying abroad (118 per 1,000 students), followed by Indonesia (12.2 per 1,000), and Thailand (11.4 per 1,000). Malaysians also constitute the largest foreign student community from Asia in Australia. The Japanese show an enrollment rate of 14 in 1,000, with over 90 percent of them studying in the United States. Asians, thus, dominate the foreign student populations in the United States, Australia, and also New Zealand. Unfortunately, the statistics published in the OECD report do not provide a gender breakdown. Based on the statistics that are available, however, we can say that the cases of our interviewees who studied abroad follow exactly these patterns: they all studied in English-speaking countries; the women originate from countries well represented in these statistics (Thailand, Japan, Korea) and so do their Malaysian husbands whom they met while studying abroad.

When women graduate from a university abroad, they might stay on because employment opportunities are opened up to them and often also because of marriage. With increasing internationalization of tertiary education, growing numbers of marriages occur between foreign students/graduates. These types of relationships then often lead to further migratory movements at the next stage in the women's lives and ultimately to what we refer to as "transnational life course." Life-course studies are built upon the argument that the contemporary diversity and difference in people's lives do not follow any predictive single pattern.[6] Women's life-course transitions among educational institutions, the family, and work (Brinton 1992) are processes that do not only take place on a national level, but also increasingly transnationally. A crucial element in this "transnational life-course perspective" to multiple migration movements is that it distinguishes itself from so-called return migration or repeat migration, which are phenomena typically studied in the context of semi- or unskilled migrants who eventually return to their country of origin. Even when repeating migration in the search for work, this usually occurs to the same country (such as Filipino entertainers going to Japan repeatedly) or it eventually leads to returning to the country of origin. The specific context of these "return" or "repeat" migration movements is usually contract work. What we refer to, however, is migration that does not involve returning to one's country of origin at all (as far as the women are concerned) or of which returning to one's country of origin is only one stage among a number of different migration destinies. More-over, our cases are not overseas contract workers, compelled to return because of end of employment. A student visa could be seen as a type of "contract," but in most English-speaking countries such as the United States and Australia, it is an easy and straightforward process to swap a student visa for a work permit (OECD 2001).

Existing studies on transnationalism have mainly discussed migrants' lives from a "community" or "diasporic" perspective. Basch and colleagues define transnationalism as the processes undergone by migrants to "forge and sustain multi-stranded social relations that link together their societies of origin and settlement" (Basch et al. 1994, 7). Transnational migrants maintain social net-works and contacts with their families, relatives, and friends in and from the place of origin across geographical borders. In such context, these socioeco-nomic links transcend political boundaries and hence render places of origin and settlement a singular field for interaction. In the transnational field of in-teraction, migrants and their networks/contacts exchange telephone calls, let-ters, e-mails and parcels; not least, remittances and emotions. Of course, this does not make immigration policies and/or residence/citizenship issues trivial. Indeed, these issues have been problematic in many receiving countries (Kof-man 1999; Cobb-Clark and Connolly 1997).

Although we largely agree with Basch and colleagues' definition, it appears that most studies on transnationalism have focused too narrowly on cultural/social aspects on the microlevel, neglecting political, legal, and institutional (i.e., macro- and mesolevel) issues. Moreover, studies on transnational communities or diasporas have almost exclusively discussed the linkages between a migrant's country of origin and the new country of settlement, ignoring the fact that certain types of migrants have multiple migration experiences. Our case stud-ies of skilled migrants show that a first-time experience of migration can hap-pen as a student or employee, followed by further migration as a spouse. Not a few have the intention of moving across borders in the future—moves often related to concerns for their children's education. They potentially become "once a migrant, always a migrant." In the case of our interviewees, however, this is a phenomenon that cannot be seen as more than a mental attitude be-cause we cannot predict their future. This represents nonetheless an extension of transnationalism as understood so far. In this context, the connotation of "home" entails more than the country of origin where one was born and/or raised. Transmigrants may locate their home or homes in different areas or life stages in connection with birth, settlement, ownership of land and/or real es-tate properties or financial foundation, education, and working life. In the case of our research, respondents conceive of their homes in relationship to their marriage and the formation of a family, but also with the place where their natal families are (away from the place of the migrant's settlement). At the same time, they often contemplate moving back to a place that constituted a previous home (such as the country where they studied). This is indicative of their conception of "multiple" homes.

More importantly we employ the concept of transnationalism to develop the idea of a "transnational life-cycle" perspective to counterbalance studies that have focused on the "trailing wife syndrome" by depicting such women as purely passive. By highlighting the fact that women migrate at different stages in their lives for different reasons, we show that although there may be stages in a woman's life when she decides to follow her husband, necessitating compromises with her own career, during other, particularly early, stages, she may have made decisions to migrate that were quite independent of husband or marriage. Moreover, however important at a given stage, future migrations may be less structured by concerns for the husband's career and more by concerns for children's educational advances and children's well-being (as also discussed by Chee, chapter 7).

To sum up, highly educated woman migrants expand the opportunity to cross borders for their careers and families at different stages in their lives—a process that often involves more than just their country of origin and one country of settlement. In this sense, we are not only talking about a "transnational," but also a "transstagional" phenomenon (in the sense of transgressing life stages).

The following section illustrates the above points by referring to the five case studies. The nature of transnational marriage entails specific transitions from women to workers, wives, mothers, or dependents.

MOVING TO MALAYSIA: TRANSNATIONAL LIFE-COURSE PROGRESS IN PRACTICE

In the context of transmigration and formation of a family, women take on new roles as wives and mothers, in addition to being a migrant and worker (or student). The five respondents in this pilot study met their husbands outside Malaysia. For the women in our sample, marriage was the reason for migrating to Malaysia—the country of origin of their husbands. At the point of migrating to Malaysia, these couples were relatively young, most of them were university graduates, and among the reasons for returning to the husband's native country, the husbands' career and concerns for the newly formed families' economic advancement figure high. Moreover, there are cases in which the husband's natal family requested him to return, for example, to operate family businesses. In the cases presented here, the move to Malaysia coincided with, or triggered, the founding of nuclear families, leading to the children of the five couples discussed here being born in Malaysia.

The specific stage in the lives of the women under discussion here is post-marriage and postmigration for at least the second time. Most couples had met in English-speaking countries, which are often referred to as "traditional immigration countries" (such as the United States, Australia, and New Zealand), which are ethnically mixed and very open societies toward newcomers. To move from such environments to a country like Malaysia must bring about certain adjustment problems. Malaysia might be internationalized in terms of English being widely spoken and overseas companies with foreign personnel being present through intracompany transfers, but entering in the capacity of a spouse, the situation is different from other "expat" experiences. Being married to a local means for these women that they might have one foot in the expat communities, but the other foot is being immersed in local (family) life. Thus, living on the "husband's territory" has advantages and disadvantages. Previously, they both were migrants, now it is only the women who are, and with their children being born in their husband's country, this does have implications for the women's sense of (non)belonging and citizenship (see below).

The transformation from a migrant student or worker to a migrant wife and mother in a different cultural environment involves complex issues entailing sacrifices and accomplishments. This adjustment from the role of a student or career woman to mother/wife is never easy, but most certainly exacerbated because the women now live in a culturally different country where there are probably more traditional attitudes toward middle-class life (see Stivens 1998) than in a country like the United States. It would, however, be wrong to assume that moving to the husband's country of origin instead of to the wife's is simply rooted in traditional or patriarchal elements. The case of Ika (Japanese national) and her husband Chan illustrates this. They both studied in the United States, where they met. After graduation, Chan returned to Malaysia to take up a job in the information technology sector—a vast growing and very lucrative industry. They lived apart for a few years while Ika went back to Japan to also work in a fast growing company with high salaries. Chan eventually applied for a job in Japan, but failed to get it. The language barrier was one of the main reasons. Ika, by contrast, found it relatively easy to apply for a job in Kuala Lumpur. Although risking overinterpretation, Chan's unsuccessful job hunting could be seen as pointing to the relatively less accessible or more limited nature of the Japanese labor market for independent skilled migrants. In any case, it is not as if foreign husbands would not contemplate moving to their wives' country of origin.

Another reason for choosing the husband's country of origin is also the existence of ample job opportunities in either the area of the husband or the area of both spouses. In the case of Winnie (a Chinese born in Korea who holds

U.S. citizenship) and her Malaysian husband Ben (ethnic Chinese), the main reason for leaving the United States for Malaysia in 1994 was that the economic situation in Malaysia had rapidly improved in the early 1990s, providing a lot of choice for employment for Ben, an engineer, and Winnie, a stockbroker.

The cases we have examined highlight some of the difficulties faced by women who move to a new country just before or soon after they got married. Apart from being a stranger, they have to comply with their new roles as a wife, mother, daughter-in-law, and in some cases a new convert (to the husband's religion) in a totally new sociocultural environment. However, partly due to their previous migratory experience, and partly due to other coping strategies (such as a job outside the domestic sphere or satisfaction in their full-time role as mother as part of a large family in a stable economic environment), "our" women have managed to make the best of their present stage in their lives and do not show any regrets. Whether as a coping strategy or as a real intent, most of these women speak of plans to eventually leave Malaysia. Interesting is also that some women consider migrating again and even contemplate spending some time away from their husbands for work or further study. For instance, Ika considered at some point after moving to Malaysia earning a Ph.D. in the United Kingdom (where her best friend is currently studying). However, with children—or expecting a child—such ideas are usually put on hold or abandoned. This does, however, not mean that women in their roles of wives and mothers do not aspire to renewed migration after establishing a family. Ika, for instance, does not see Malaysia as her last place of abode. She has talked to her husband, Chan, about wanting to move to somewhere else in the future, possibly England—an idea that he shares—for their children's education.

Take the case of Winnie: she is very satisfied with her situation in Malaysia, but nevertheless keeps an eye open for other opportunities. In her own words, "there are many opportunities, better job offers are everywhere." She envisages a better living standard abroad and access to a superior education system when her children are older. She and her husband, thus, contemplate moving back to the United States at some stage.

The wish to move on might also be stronger among women whose own country of origin are in some respects more advanced than Malaysia (Japan, for example) or who have had a long history of living in a highly advanced country (such as Winnie in the United States). These women talk about lower living or educational standards in Malaysia being among the reasons for wanting to move on or move back to where they had met their husbands. Others, like Valerie (a Thai national who met her husband in New Zealand) or Jazz (a Filipino who met her husband in Australia) are perfectly content with living and remaining in Malaysia, despite some initial adjustment problems. In Jazz and Lee's case, further migration would be complicated, if not impossible, due to Lee's working for his family's business.

The reasons for migration and remigration are multiple and complex, rooted in individual personality, aspirations, and previous and present experiences. What can be seen, however, is that early migration experience as students to highly popular countries such as the United States or Australia often do lead to aspirations to migrate yet again and not necessarily in the form of return migration to either spouse's country of origin.

SOCIAL CONSTRAINTS AND STATUS OF FEMALE MIGRANTS

Highly skilled or professional wives of internationally mobile men are not usually considered to be labor migrants by researchers in mainstream migration studies. The majority of them enter as dependents in male-headed households or through family reunion (Kofman, Phizacklea, Raghuram, and Sales 2000). Receiving governments too typically treat such women as dependents of husbands by means of immigration policies and visa categories. By law, in many countries the rights of dependent migrant women are derived from their husbands during a certain number of years after entry. In some countries, this lasts for the whole of the women's lives as residents in the host country. Only very few countries grant the foreign spouse full residence and employment rights immediately upon entry (Kofman et al. 2000).

In the specific context of marriage migration and the formation of a family, issues of residence permits or citizenship are often part and parcel of settling overseas or the reason for the desire to move on yet again to a more accommodating country. The very nature of such legality is an integral feature of transnationalism. The reiteration of this subject by the interviewed migrant women indicates a great concern about their own and their children's nationalities (in the sense of identity and emotional attachment) and legal status (i.e., citizenship).

In Malaysia, there are no published statistics on foreign spouses, and the number of foreign skilled (but not unskilled) workers is classified as confidential by the Human Resources Department. On an individual basis, foreign women are legally allowed to migrate as skilled workers, but the women in our research entered Malaysia as wives and are, at least initially, treated as dependents by the authorities and not individuals in their own right. Although the initial path of entry is via the spousal visa, our research shows that this does not prevent professional women from pursuing or prolonging their working lives. This does not always happen in the specific type of career path they had embarked upon prior to entering Malaysia, nevertheless some are able to find not only paid employment, but also jobs that they perceive as satisfying. In other words, despite their legal/official visa status as dependent, they are legally allowed to gain employment from the moment they have entered Malaysia.

In the parlance of immigration policies in Malaysia, the term *expatriate* is used to refer to skilled or professional foreign workers; and *migrant worker* or *immigrant labor* are the phrases used for semi- or unskilled foreign workers. Such categorization indicates the unequal socioeconomic status and treatment accorded to these workers of different "class" background. This is far from being a uniquely Malaysian phenomenon. Foreign spouses, however—who in most cases are foreign wives of Malaysian male citizens—are not treated as expatriates (i.e., as a migrant female worker in her own right), but rather as dependents. It is in fact stated in the *Malaysian Immigration Act 1959/63* that a Dependent's Pass may be issued to "the wife or dependent child of the holder of a valid Employment Pass to enable such wife or child to accompany or join such holder and remain with him."[7] Relevant to this is the dependent's pass/visa for foreign wives and her children (not fathered by the Malaysian husband). Here the assumption clearly is that the migrating spouse is female. This means that women (who migrate to Malaysia with their husbands) are accepted as dependents with their status as wives directly locked to their husbands. When the husband leaves the country, his employment pass expires, or a divorce occurs; women have no (legal) status in the Federation of Malaysia and would have to leave the country too. In the case of divorce, if a couple's children are born in Malaysia and are Malaysian citizens, the foreign mother would face difficulties in taking them with her for good when leaving Malaysia, unless the custody of children is legally processed. This would invariably take a long time and impede women's immediate exit (out of the country) after the divorce.

The status of being a "foreign" wife to a Malaysian husband has at least two major implications. The first concerns the residence status. The foreign wife can supposedly apply for residence permit after five years of continuous residency. In the meantime, she holds a dependent's visa. The second concerns the work permit. When a foreigner is married to a Malaysian citizen, he or she can apply for a work permit or can get a previous permit extended as long as the employer agrees to further the employment. However, this limits the immigrant's scope of career development. In other words, job hopping is problematized by the difficulties in getting a new work permit, as each work permit is directly connected to the employer/institution. Hence, when the migrant's employment terminates and he or she intends to engage in a different job, it is necessary to apply for a new work permit directly linked to the new employer.

Some of the respondents complained about the long and tedious procedures of visa applications and extensions. In the case of Jazz, the complicated process of receiving a visa extension and a residence permit has created a lot of inconvenience and frustration. After almost a decade of residing in Malaysia, she still has not received a permanent resident permit. She claims that her husband gets agitated every time he has to drive her to the immigration office. Jazz herself is very angry too and feels that it is unreasonable for the immigration authorities to take such a long time to grant her permanent residency. She said, "I have been here almost ten years. My husband is here, my children are here. They (the children) go to school here, where else can I go if not stay here? Why can't they see that?" Being the only one in the family who does not hold Malaysian citizenship, she feels excluded and marginalized.

According to Ika and her friends, there are foreign wives married to Malay men who have received their permanent residence permit or citizenship within five years; whereas for wives of Chinese male residents, it takes seven years and for wives of Indian men, nine years. However, our interview with a public relation officer at the Malaysian immigration office revealed that the official and published requirement for the application of entry permits (applicable to foreign spouses) is a continuous stay of five years in the country. When the permit is issued, the foreign spouse will be given a red identity card (Malaysians' ID is blue); thus, a differentiation of legal and civil status in terms of a "born" and a "resident" Malaysian. When we informed him about Jazz's case, he replied that this was impossible and offered to look into the case as soon as he could. Nonetheless, similar statements as those coming from Ika were also made in the Japanese context—for instance, claims were made about the existence of highly arbitrary practices at immigration bureaus, often favoring one type of nationality over others (Kokusai Kekkon o Kangaeru Kai 1996). This suggests that the process of converting foreign women's status from that of a dependent to a resident in their own right is also based on ethnic differentiation.

An exceptional case, however, is that of Valerie, who migrated to Malaysia at a much earlier point in time than the others. She has been in Malaysia for more than twenty years (since 1980). She explained that because there were not many foreigners in the country then, relevant immigration policies were not as complicated as they are at present, and she was granted citizenship within two years and obtained a Malaysian identity card (blue). The government behaves in a contradictory manner: changing regulations so that it encourages foreign investments and import of skilled "expats" to train locals as well as the intake of foreign "cheap" labor; but at the same time, rules and procedures for visa application are increasingly being tightened and visa as well as work permit taxes on migrant workers (both skilled and unskilled) are constantly on the increase.

CONCLUSION

In this chapter, we attempted to contribute to existing studies on labor migration and transnationalism by discussing marriage migration of highly educated women at a specific stage of their life course. The growing mobility of women outside their national boundaries and the rising cases of international marriages have to be contextualized with student migration as many highly educated couples meet as students and often in third countries (which are neither spouse's country of origin). Hence, there is even more reason to broaden the study and theorization of women's heterogeneous lives in an era of increasing international mobility and marriage.

The findings in this research so far have shown that transnational marriage is a crucial reason or channel for transmigration and career switch at a certain stage in migrant women's lives where they switch from an independent female student or worker to a married woman about to start a family life in yet another cultural environment. Although in our research cases this involves "no choice" or making sacrifices on the part of some women, others found expanded job opportunities not only for their husbands, but for themselves too. Transnational marriage in the context of a cross-border life-course history can, thus, be an incentive for women to give up or postpone career concerns for setting up a family in an unknown and new environment—the husband's country of origin. In the cases we have examined, men are clearly at advantage being on their own territory while their spouses are foreign women who are unfamiliar with the culture and do not speak the local language. The decision to migrate to his native country is, however, not always primarily determined by considerations for husbands' careers.

Malaysia emerges as a facilitator for international family life as well as a less desirable country of residence, depending on the origin of the women and/or their previous migration experience. Malaysia is a multiethnic society in which English is widely spoken among the elite, particularly the international business class—which may facilitate entry for a multinational couple to start a family. Each of the respondents planned to have a family at some stage, and several soon had children. All others of these educated and skilled women with international work experience envisaged a future including both work and family, and several were living that dual life. Malaysian society offers "assistance" in the form of extended family members helping out and the possibility of hiring affordable domestic helpers, the latter available only to the super rich in Europe, the United States, and Japan, for example. At the same time, others view Malaysia as inferior to countries like the United States and expressed the wish to move on when the children grow older. Hence, several informants plan future migrations that are not tied to husband's careers, but are made out of consideration for children's education and perhaps in some instances their own careers. Such an attitude ("once a migrant, more often a migrant") constitutes a continuation of the migration process.

Highly educated or skilled woman migrants have thus in some instances been able to expand the space and opportunity across borders for their careers and families. Further in-depth studies are needed to fully comprehend the constraints set by sociocultural adaptation and immigration rules under which these women operate. These include the extent and nature of conflict within the household with regard to the timing of marriage, job switches, when and where to have children, and citizenship/s of children and parents. All these are woven into the fabric of multiple migration experiences as part of a transnational life course. To further the notion of a transnational life-course perspective, longitudinal studies and cross-generational studies would be beneficial.

State policies should reflect the experience of such professional migrants by being more sensitive to the circumstances of women's multiple statuses as worker, wife, and mother, and also potential changes in the nature of their family life, including from wife to divorcee or widow. In fact, the contribution of women's skills in the labor market deserves recognition that is absent in societies like Malaysia that treat them exclusively as dependents. In other words, national policies pertaining to immigration need to be more concerned with the variation of transnational marriage or family reunion, family flows and residence, and gender issues in relation to individual status (woman or man, worker, mother, or spouse, and so on). The construction or reconstruction of identities of female migrants and their self-perception in the context of transnational marriage are, therefore, influenced by the limitations posed by state policies in the host country pertaining to entry pass, residence, or family reunification.

Therefore, in the context of this research, the boundaries between a marriage of mixed nationalities and work/family are fabricated by immigration rules and regulations, the nature of legal residency permit, employment policies, and the complicated knit of cultural or ethnic/racial differences. All these affect migrant women's choices concerning marriage, family, work, and relationships with others in the host society and the intention to move on yet again.

NOTES

1. Exceptions are Willis and Yeoh (2000) and, in this volume, Taylor and Napier (1996).

2. Earlier "brain drain" literature has focused on movements from developing to developed countries. More recent studies, by Findlay and Li (1998), for example, have investigated professional Hong Kong Chinese going to Canada or the U.K.

3. See Lee (2000); Chant (1992).

4. The third main ethnic group in Malaysia is comprised of Indians, but none of the women in our sample was married to a man from this ethnic group.

5. For a detailed discussion on this approach, see Halfacree and Boyle (1993).

6. In this way, the life-course approach distinguishes itself from the life-cycle approach that is a development model outlining social changes encountered as a person passes through predictable stages (Bilton et al. 1996, 518).

7. Lee's personal experience in dealing with expats' work visa/permit was that it could take from a few months to a few years, depending on how specialized the position is, how far an expat is required in the position, and the availability of local personnel in that field.

REFERENCES

Basch, L., N. G. Schiller, and C. S. Blanc. *Nations Unbound: Transnational Projects Postcolonial Predicaments and Deterritorialized Nation-States*. Switzerland: Gordon & Breach, 1994.

Beaverstock, J., and J. Smith. "Lending Jobs to Global Cities: Skilled International Labour Migration, Investment Banking and the City of London." *Urban Studies* vol. 33, no. 8 (1996):1377–95.

Bilton, T., K. Bonnett, P. Jones, D. Skinner, M. Stanworth, and A. Webster. *Introductory Sociology* (3rd ed.). Basingstoke: Macmillan, 1996.

Brinton, M. "Christmas Cakes and Wedding Cakes: The Social Organization of Japanese Women's Life Course." Pp. 79–108 in *Japanese Social Organization*, edited by Takie Sugiyama Lebra. Honolulu: University of Hawaii Press, 1992.

Chant, S. "Migration at the Margins: Gender, Poverty and Population Movement on the Costa Rican Periphery." Pp. 49–72 in *Gender and Migration in Developing Countries*, edited by Sylvia Chant. New York: Belhaven Press, 1992.

Cobb-Clark, D. A., and M. D. Connolly. "The Worldwide Market for Skilled Migrants: Can Australia Compete?" *International Migration Review* vol. 31, no. 4 (Fall 1997): 670–94.

Department of Statistics, Malaysia. *Labour Force Survey Report*. Kuala Lumpur, Malaysia: Department of Statistics, Prime Minister's Department, 1999.

Embong, A. R. "Perindustrian, Peranan Pemerintah dan Pembentukan Kelas Menengah." Pp. 83–115 in *Negara, Pasaran dan Pemodenan Malaysia*, edited by Abdul Rahman Embong. Bangi: Universiti Kebangsaan Malaysia, 2000.

Findlay, A. M., and F. L. N. Li. "A Migration Channels Approach to the Study of Professionals Moving to and from Hong Kong." *International Migration Review* vol. 32, no. 3 (1998): 682–703.

Findlay, A. M., F. L. N. Lin, A. J. Jowett, M. Brown, and R. Skeldon. "Doctors Diagnose Their Destination: An Analysis of Length of Employment Abroad of Hong Kong Doctors." *Environment and Planning A* vol. 26 (1994): 1605–24.

Foner, N. "What's New about Transnationalism? New York Immigrants Today and at the Turn of the Century." *Diaspora* vol. 6, no. 3 (1997): 355–75.

Halfacree, K. H., and P. J. Boyle. "The Challenge Facing Migration Research; the Case for a Biographical Approach." *Progress in Human Geography* vol. 17 (1993): 333–48.

International Law Book Services. *Immigration Act 1959/1963 (Act 155) and Regulations and Orders & Passports Act 1966 (Act 150),* 1995.

Kofman, E. "The Invisibility of Skilled Female Migrants and Gender Relations in Studies of Skilled Migration in Europe." *International Journal of Population Geography,* no. 6 (2000): 45–59.

———. "Female 'birds of passage' a Decade Later: Gender and Immigration in the European Union." *International Migration Review* vol. 33, no. 2 (1999): 269–300.

Kofman, E., A. Phizacklea, P. Raghuram, and R. Sales. *Gender and International Migration in Europe.* London: Routledge, 2000.

Kokusai o Kangaeru Kai. *Kokusai kekkon handobukku* (Handbook about International Marriage). Tokyo: Akashishoten, 1996.

Kritz, M. M., C. B. Keeley, and S. M. Tomasi (Eds.). *Global Trends in Migration: Theory and Research on International Population Movements.* New York: Center for Migration Studies, 1983.

Lee, W. Y. *Female Transmigration in Southeast Asia: Filipina Domestic Helpers in Malaysia.* Unpublished Ph.D. thesis, UCL: London, 2000.

Li, F. L. N., A. M. Findlay, A. J. Jowett, and R. Skeldon. "Migrating to Learn and Learning to Migrate: A Study of the Experiences and Intentions of International Student Migrants." *International Journal of Population Geography,* no. 2 (1996): 51–67.

Nash, J., and M. P. Fernandez-Kelly (Eds.). *Women, Men and the International Division of Labour.* New York: State University of New York, 1983.

Palma-Beltran, M. R., and A. J. de Dios (Eds.). *Filipino Women Overseas Contract Workers: At What Cost?* Manila: Goodwill Trading, 1992.

OECD. *Trends in International Migration—SOPEMI 2001.* Paris: OECD, 2001.

Ono, H., and N. Piper. "Japanese Women Studying Abroad—The Case of the United States." Paper presented at the Joint East Asian Conference, University of Edinburgh, April 3–5, 2001.

Skeldon, R. "Of Migration, Great Cities, and Markets: Global Systems of Development." Pp. 183–215 in *Global History and Migrations,* edited by G. Wang. Boulder, Colo.: Westview Press, 1997.

Stivens, M. "Sex, Gender and the Making of the Malay Middle Classes." Pp. 87–126 in *Gender and Power in Affluent Asia,* edited by K. Sen and M. Stivens. New York: Routledge, 1998.

Taylor, S., and N. Napier. "Working in Japan: Lessons from Women Expatriates." *Sloan Management Review* vol. 37, no. 3 (1996): 76–85.

Willis, K., and B. Yeoh. "Gender and Transnational Household Strategies: Singaporean Migration to China." *Regional Studies* vol. 34, no. 3 (2000): 253–64.

7

Migrating for the Children: Taiwanese American Women in Transnational Families

Maria W. L. Chee

It is generally assumed, mistakenly, that Asian women migrate to Western countries because they can earn a better income there. And indeed, many of the studies discussed in this book reveal women actively making the decision to seek employment overseas precisely because the wages overseas are significantly better.[1] Some of these women migrant workers are married (see Pe-Pua, chapter 8 and McKay, chapter 1). The choice to live apart from their husbands and children often impacts significantly on their family life. These working wives have extended the concept of working outside the home to its maximum potential—working overseas. But a case study of women who migrate to California from Taiwan (also known as the Republic of China) illustrates a contradictory trend. Most of these women initially migrate in their capacity as "mothers" who accompany their children to study in the United States, while financial support is provided by the father who remains in Taiwan as the breadwinner. Income is then remitted in the opposite direction from the typical transnational migrant family: from Taiwan to the United States.[2] In this sense, Taiwanese[3] women who move to the United States do so primarily to privilege "motherhood" over "wifehood," some giving up their previous careers as working professionals in Taiwan.

This chapter examines nonworking-class women in transnational families split between the United States and Taiwan. I define two terms used in this chapter: (1) Nonworking class refers to the group of people who are business owners or skilled professionals and their family who do not perform manual labor for a living. (2) By transnational families I mean households split in two separate countries, with a spouse and child(ren) living in the United States and a spouse in Taiwan.[4] This chapter focuses on the main motivations that spurred most of these families to become transnational, and analyzes the impacts such arrangement might have had on these women as workers and wives. California is the logical area for a case study because it holds the largest concentration of immigrants from Taiwan within the United States.

I argue that most of these women initially migrated to the United States in search of better educational opportunities for their children, in order to improve their children's future socioeconomic positions, which would have been impossible had they remained in Taiwan. To do so, some women who were full-time professional workers in the labor market gave up their own careers and reverted to the traditional role of mother to care for children full time at home. Meanwhile, husbands worked in Taiwan to support their wives and children. While women and their husbands adopted the transnational family strategy to maximize benefits from productive and reproductive labor, some women—in privileging motherhood—compromised their roles as wives or paid workers. In the following sections I set out the theoretical framework with reference to relevant literature, describe the methods used in this study, and introduce the phenomenon of Taiwanese American transnational families. Next I discuss the main reasons for the families' migration and the subsequent impacts on women as professional workers and wives. This is then followed by a conclusion with the summary and findings of this study.

TRANSNATIONALISM

Current transnational studies on women and families have concentrated on connections between the United States and Latin America or the Caribbean, on working-class wives who are left behind by migrant husbands, and on women who migrate as productive laborers, including nurses and domestic workers from the Philippines. This research aims to uncover the impact on nonworking-class women when they move to the country of destination mainly for a reproductive purpose of helping children obtain educational benefits in the target nation, while husbands remain in the country of origin and send remittances to support them. Because it offers a stark contrast to the stereotypical transnational family, this research contributes to theoretical literature on the class and gender dimensions of international migration and provides comparative perspectives for the study of migration concerning women and marital relations in the Pacific Rim region.

Instead of the unilineal and bipolar patterns that study migration from country of origin to that of settlement (Uzzell 1976), transnationalists examine the social relations maintained between two or more countries by migrants, who are now transmigrants. Transmigrants build ties that transcend geographical distance and political boundaries and develop multiple relationships that may be familial, economic, social, cultural, religious, and political (see, among other works, Glick Schiller, Basch, and Blanc-Szanton 1992; Rouse 1991; Smith and Guarnizo 1998). These relationships are regular and sustained over time (Portes, Guarnizo, and Landolt 1999, 219). The split families from Taiwan are transnational kin whose social relations connect their countries of origin and settlement over extended periods. As transmigrants they are disciplined by national boundaries and jurisdictions, as well as sometimes by conflicting ideologies of family and kinship. The impact of migration on the individual necessarily involves an appreciation of gender in the process (Pessar 1999). Transnationals are gendered often in contradictory ways. In this case, women as workers and wives are situated in family forms constructed in one milieu yet expected to operate and remain unproblematic in another (Buijus 1993).

Dealing with working-class transnational families in the United States and Latin America or the Caribbean, scholars theorize that husbands' migration away from home constrains women and adds to their burden, as effective heads of households, as solitary persons in the in-laws' households, or as abandoned wives and mothers (Ahern, Bryan, and Baca 1985; Georges 1992, 91–92; Hondagneu-Sotelo 1994). Studies have also shown that female migration away from the home country frees them from local ideological and practical constraints and permits them to negotiate power (Grasmuck and Pessar 1991; Kibria 1993). On the other hand, Pessar (1995) demonstrates that some Dominican immigrant women in the United States revert to traditional ideology that confines women to the home in order to elevate social status for their families. These studies concentrate on women migrants who initially came to the United States as productive laborers, including mothers who work as domestic helpers to support kin back home (Hondagneu-Sotelo and Avila 1997; Parreñas 2000). How about nonworking-class women who migrated to the United States primarily for reproductive purposes, such as some women from Taiwan? Before pursuing this question, I outline my methodology in the following section.

METHODOLOGY

The primary sources for this case study came from surveys, and semistructured interviews with women who were currently or formerly wives of transnational families. I identified potential interviewees from organization-based questionnaire surveys at a married woman's retreat in southern California in 1999; and again in 2000 at a public school with adult education facilities that offered classes in English as a second language. I also contacted three churches with a large following from Taiwan. The survey questionnaire was written in Chinese because these women were far more proficient in this language than in English. Some women then introduced me to additional snowball samples. Further, I attended single-parent support group meetings to look for more interviewees.

From June 1999 to August 2000 I interviewed thirty wives and mothers in southern California. The ages of these women ranged from forty to the sixties (one woman), with the majority of women in their forties. Most of them were legal immigrants sponsored by family members who were American citizens. At the time of the interviews, sixteen women had all or some of their children older than age twenty-one but they continued to live here. The children were mostly in high school. The youngest ones were in grade school when they migrated. Prior to migration, twenty-three of the women had completed junior college, university education, or graduate studies, indicating a mainly educated sample. Of the thirty women, nine who worked as professionals before migration became housewives after that. I did not interview any husbands during this research period as the husbands were living in Taiwan.

I am Chinese American and speak fluent Mandarin, the official language of Taiwan and its language of education. All interviews were conducted in Mandarin. All except four interviews were completed in the homes of the interviewees in southern California. All the names used in this chapter are pseudonyms in order to protect the identities of the people interviewed.

BACKGROUND

Immigration from Taiwan to the United States began to rise in 1980. "In 1991, a total of 106,914 Taiwanese immigrants were residing in California" (Tseng 1995, 38). By zip code regions, 74 percent of Taiwanese immigrants to the United States went to the San Gabriel Valley area of Los Angeles County in southern California between fiscal years 1983 and 1990 (Horton 1995, 23). Others are dispersed in urban areas mostly on the East Coast such as New York and Maryland, and in the south such as in Texas. In 1986, out of those indicating Los Angeles as intended destination for residence, 63 percent worked in professional and executive occupations before migration and another 24 percent in teaching (Immigration and Naturalization Service, Public Use Samples from Tseng 1995, 40). These figures point to a largely nonworking-class socioeconomic background and preference for southern California. In some cases, the whole family emigrated in the first instance, then the husband/father commuted across the Pacific Rim and the family subsequently became transnational. Although there are no available statistics that give exact figures, there are significant numbers of such Taiwanese American transnational families. Typically, the wife and children live in United States, while the husband continues to work in Taiwan. He visits them in the United States once every few months, or the wife and children visit him in Taiwan during Christmas and/or summer vacations. On rare occasions, it is the husband and children who live in the United States while the wife commutes across the Pacific Ocean.

The thirty women in my sample gave the following causes for their emigration from Taiwan to the United States. Since they gave as many reasons as applicable, the total number of responses exceeds thirty:

For children's education	17
Political threat from China	5
To join natal family	4
For business opportunity	3
Dissatisfaction with the Taiwan government	3
Deteriorating natural environment	3
Deteriorating social environment	2
Taiwan's ethnic tension	2
To avoid son's military service	2
Others	3

A significant factor emerged from the above responses: Children's education was by far the most cited reason, given by seventeen respondents, trailed by political threat from China given by only five. Hence, many women migrated with children for their education in the United States. In the following sections, I show that the mothers did so to rid their children of a rigid educational system, to give their children other educational opportunities or a second chance.

MIGRATING FOR CHILDREN'S EDUCATIONAL PURPOSE

Unlike Caribbean and Latin American working-class women or Filipinas who migrate for paid labor outside their homes, many of these educated and professional women from Taiwan made the move primarily for their children's education in the country of destination. One woman's remarks reflect this characteristic: "If there were no children, there would be no need to make the move to come here." A woman named Ling indicated that she and her family did not migrate here for economic reasons. "In my case, I came for my child's education, and then for a better living environment." In fact, in most cases only those with economic ability migrated to the United States. Ling offered an anecdote that illustrates this situation: "Let me tell you one story that tells the economic backgrounds of the people who immigrated to the United States from Taiwan. I always told my daughter to keep a low profile at school. She acted and dressed like any other in her class. Then one day when she told her classmates that she was emigrating to the United States, they all oohed and aahed and exclaimed: 'We did not know that you are wealthy!' I would not say that we are so very wealthy, but we are certainly not poor. We had not moved here for money." Mothers migrated with children to give them better educational opportunities in order to reproduce their socioeconomic position in society or for upward mobility.

Studies show that education is the paramount factor affecting occupation and status in Taiwan. The higher the level of education achieved, the higher the rank of first job and salary (Sun and Wu 1993; Chang, Shi, and Wang 1996). In turn, first jobs directly influence the kind and level of one's future occupation. Education therefore is the primary instrument for social mobility (Wang, Chen, and Chang 1986). One study demonstrates that "Taiwan's stratified educational system functions as a sorting and allocating mechanism. In conditions of excess demand, higher educational credentials confer a higher return of occupational status" (Tsai 1998, 466). Most jobs specify the minimum educational requirement, and the salary is usually commensurate with the educational credential (degree) of the successful applicant. Hence Taiwan practices equal work for unequal pay: the higher one's educational qualification, the higher one's salary for the same job. These credentials are the results of successfully passing highly selective qualification examinations.

The educational system in Taiwan is extremely competitive—much like Japan, for instance. After nine years of compulsory education, students are tracked into academic education or vocational education systems. The academic track prepares students for regular university education in liberal arts, sciences, and professional schools such as medical school. Vocational track prepares students for vocational or technical training. Higher scores in citywide examinations place one in the academic track and in better schools. At the end of the twelfth grade, there is another tight round of entrance examinations for university or technical college education. A very few get admitted by special selection based on outstanding achievement such as excellence in sports by national standard. The vast majority sit in the selective entrance examinations.

The level and kind of education completed greatly determine one's opportunity in the job market, hence his or her future socioeconomic status. In general, there is reverence for academic excellence. In this hierarchy, the academic educational system is preferred to the vocational system. It is also more prestigious. This pyramidal examination selection process causes a lot of pressure and anxiety for both students and parents. Students often continue with private tutoring school in the evening after regular school, and a school day is not finished till 9:00 or 9:30 in the evening.

Some parents use migration as a strategy to counteract the rigid educational system and established channels of occupation attainment that condition future socioeconomic position. Families migrate for a child's better educational opportunities in preparation for a higher occupation and status than possible in Taiwan given the child's scholastic aptitude and inclination. Women as mothers facilitate this process by abandoning their own career in the interest of the children's future career development, in the hope of helping them reach a certain desired socioeconomic level. In a study on the relationship between education and mother's supervision in Taiwan, it is found that generally mothers positively influence their children's academic success (Lin 1999).

One of the women, named Yen, told me that her family immigrated primarily for her younger child's education. He had excelled in art and drawing, but not in academic subjects. By Taiwan's educational standard, he would most likely end up in technical school with a dim outlook for high-income future employment prospects. This also meant a diminished social status. Yen put it this way: "Here in the United States, students could be artistically inclined, and still be considered worthy when they continue artistic pursuits in art schools or performing arts. This is the major reason for my family's decision to come here."

One mother described her son's experience as follows: "He was right in the middle rank in a class of about forty students, he felt taunted and belittled. The teachers openly ranked the students in front of everybody. Some parents also told their children not to play and socialize with my son since he was not among the top. It hurt his self-esteem. He felt bad about himself and he did not want to return to school." The mother migrated with the son to begin senior high school in the United States. As it turned out, this youngster eventually got accepted into an Ivy League university.

Another woman's two teenage children had always ranked in the bottom of their classes. A friend believed that these two teenagers had to go elsewhere for a second chance, because they would never make it in Taiwan. The family had been approved for immigration to the United States for some time. They finally migrated so that the two youngsters could begin their ninth grade in the States. Another woman's two teenage daughters also needed this second chance. According to the parent, the older sister had always been a slow learner since kindergarten. Her performance continued to be less than mediocre in the eighth grade. To avoid being tracked into vocational school, the mother migrated with the two girls so they could continue with regular academic education. A mother commented that her child did not do that poorly in school: "But I wanted him to have a broader perspective. Taiwan is a small country. One easily becomes a big fish in a small pond. The United States is a big country with lots of people from many different parts of the world. It would give him a bigger window to the world. A wider horizon."

Instead of migrating for better economic opportunities, the above examples demonstrate that these nonworking-class mothers did so to give their children a better educational opportunity in the target country. Nine of the mothers were paid professionals in Taiwan before migration. International migration changed some of these women's positions as paid professionals in the labor market to full-time mothers who stay home for domestic responsibilities. They reacted to the change in different ways. The following section discusses some of the women's experiences with such transition.

MIGRATION: FROM FULL-TIME PAID PROFESSIONALS TO ALL-TIME STAY-HOME MOTHERS

Lin had been a business executive for many years in Taiwan. In the 1980s, Lin's parents sponsored Lin and her family to immigrate to the United States. Her husband went with them for the first few weeks, but then returned to Taiwan to continue working in his family business. He sent money to support the wife and children in the United States. Her husband would come to visit them once a year, for about one week each time. This arrangement lasted seven years before the family reunited. During the seven years, Lin stayed home as a full-time mother and homemaker. She seemed to welcome the opportunity to give up paid employment: "Some women have to work. They have no choice. I have a choice. I don't have to work if I don't want to. I enjoy staying [at] home as it is now." Another woman, Yen, was a nurse in Taiwan. She also taught nursing part time. Because Yen's nursing license was not valid in California,[5] and because she was not proficient in English, she just stayed home after migration. One consequence of abandoning her career to be a housewife was the loss of her income for more discretionary funds. She had to practice thrift. When I asked her if she considered this a sacrifice, Yen replied as follows: "NO! As parents, we want to give the best to our children, to the best of our ability."

By Taiwan's traditional values, as in Japan and South Korea (see Gelb and Palley 1994, among others), a woman's higher accomplishment comes primarily from her roles as mother and wife. If a woman neglects her expected responsibility of these roles in order to advance her own development or career, then it is considered selfish and a major flaw (Wu 1992). Although in recent decades women in Taiwan have managed both work and children in various ways, studies have shown that women's own value centers around family needs. Generally women wish to adjust their own labor participation in accordance with family development stages and needs; family needs take precedence and priority in the event of conflicting demands (Lu 1982; Chien and Hsueh 1996). The professional women in my sample discontinued their own career to migrate for their children's education in the United States. Such rupture had not passed with ease for all women. Some also talked about the conflicts and struggles over the decision to move. The following experiences exemplify the difficulties that some women underwent.

Lily had completed her university education in Taiwan. She worked as a top executive in a large private corporation. Her husband held a very high position in a large corporation and taught part time as a university professor. Each made about the same amount of money. In Taiwan they had a chauffeur, servants, and lived in one of the best areas in town. They also socialized with influential people. Lily felt that her profession prior to migration gave her a good sense of accomplishment. She was respected by her subordinates and appreciated by her boss. Lily considered her family elites in Taiwan. She knew that to start fresh in a new country they would not retain the same socioeconomic status and social life, and that she would stay at home as a housewife, at least in the beginning. Lily said: "I wanted to migrate rationally, but at heart I resisted it."

In Taiwan, women with higher education appear to have a greater commitment to career, compared to women with only a high school education. The former tend to insist on maintaining the dual roles of mother and professional worker. Despite emphasis on family roles they are found to be unwilling to totally give up their professions. Their ideals and goals are to keep both family and career at the same time (Lu 1982, 147). On the other hand, as shown by another study, "in the case of family care-giving, wives from higher income families are more likely to quit jobs or change employment patterns to adapt to the role of care-giving, with a higher value on family time rather than market time" (Lu 1997, 3). Family needs to migrate conflicted with Lily's individual career path. The struggle thus created is well expressed in her words above.

Wah, another highly educated woman, gave up her profession before retirement age for her child. Her son wanted to go to junior high school in the United States, but her husband had a well-paying and high-ranking position in Taiwan. To get the best of both worlds, Wah took early retirement from her professional job to accommodate her child's wish. The family bought a house in the States near her relatives and the son went to school in the neighborhood. The husband continued to work in Taiwan. Wah spent most of her time with her child and the husband flew to the States to be with the wife and son twice a year for about ten days each time. The mother and child returned to Taiwan during his summer vacation.

Wah was glad that she was able to take early retirement to be with her child in the States, but it was not without difficulty. "I did have a conflict," she admitted. She was very successful in her career, heading many well-funded projects at the institution where she worked. She said: "I was well-known and respected. I was efficient, hardworking, and energetic. I retired early. I gave up my career. I felt empty. I felt that I had nothing left. All of a sudden I was good for nothing. I felt contradictions and struggles. I was a successful professional, well respected, a modern woman. But when it comes to my family, I am expected to do all the domestic chores."

In Taiwan, married women's participation in the labor market has increased in the past few decades, from 31.9 percent in 1979 to 45.1 percent in 1994 (Chien and Hsueh 1996, 113), but in the eyes of society the husband is considered the main, or even sole, breadwinner. Women's income is looked upon as secondary. Women often discontinue work with childbirth or marriage, although they may reenter the labor market later in their life cycle. In addition, mothers still hold the responsibilities of supervising and educating children. According to Lin (1999), a mother's role in children's school performance far exceeds that of a father, and the father's primary responsibility is to provide financial support for the family. Husbands often support women's participation in the labor force out of economic needs, but women's career development is subject to men's own (Wu 1992, 83). Moreover, society expects women to fulfill their traditional roles and responsibilities, and women participants in the labor market are still charged with the bulk of household chores (Lu and Yi 1999).

Most of the professional women interviewed are caught between modernity and tradition, between personal aspirations and the benefit of the family. These modern-educated women were successful professionals in the workforce, yet they were constrained by the traditional roles and expectations of mothers and wives held responsible for childcare and housework. While Taiwan's modernization educates and prepares women to be contributing workers, tradition dictates that women remain as primary caregivers for their children. Women are therefore caught between the desire to have a professional career and the pressure to fulfill traditional motherhood roles. In the case of these transnational families, the woman suppressed her personal desire as an individual, to succumb to the expected responsibility of a mother opting to migrate to give her children a better education. This sacrifice is made for the sake of their children's future career prospects, a move that is seen as necessary to reproduce their current socioeconomic class position for the children.

TRANSNATIONAL SPLITTING OF FAMILIES

While the women in my sample migrated to care for the children in the United States, their families eventually became transnationally split between Taiwan and southern California. Transnational families from Hong Kong are also present in the United States, Australia, Canada, and New Zealand (see Pe-Pua, Mitchell, Iredale, and Castles 1996 and Man 1993, among others). These

Hong Kong families are termed "astronaut families" in the literature. Unlike transnational families from Taiwan, those from Hong Kong emigrated mainly due to the former British colony's retrocession to China (see, for example, Skeldon 1994, 1995). But families from both Hong Kong and Taiwan became transnational because of better economic opportunities in their countries of origin, compared to certain disadvantages encountered in their countries of destination.

Disadvantages have handicapped many new immigrants from Hong Kong and Taiwan who eventually formed transnational families. Some Hong Kong women and men accepted jobs below their qualifications and past work experiences, constituting what Skeldon (1994) has termed "downward displacement" due to disadvantages: their qualifications or prior work experience were not recognized; or they lacked fluent English proficiency; or because of discrimination. Even though Hong Kong was a former British colony and immigrants from Hong Kong are presumably more proficient in English than the new immigrants from Taiwan, nonetheless Hong Kong immigrants had learnt English as a foreign language. Their native tongue and the predominant language of communication is the Cantonese dialect. Their command of English is still less than adequate in an entirely English-speaking work environment. Immigrants with sufficient language proficiency, including Taiwan's former graduate students to the United States, may encounter other disadvantages such as glass ceilings that block their career advancement beyond midlevel management (see Woo 2000).

It may also be difficult for the new immigrants to start businesses because of different work cultures and the absence of established business contacts. In many cases, husbands (and occasionally wives) returned to work in Hong Kong to financially support the spouses and children in Australia or Canada because they could not obtain comparable or satisfactory employment due to nontransferable licenses, or lack of local work experience required by employers, and so on (see, for example, Pe-Pua et al. 1996; Man 1996a, 1996b). Similarly, among the women interviewed in this study, some husbands returned to Taiwan to assume the well-paid high positions they could not obtain in southern California, while others continue to run their businesses in Taiwan. They commute across the Pacific Ocean for family reunions.

One woman's husband was not sure if he should start his own business or work for someone else in southern California, so he first worked as an employee to learn about local conditions. Although he made about US$4,000 per month managing a warehouse, he was the one person responsible for all the work involved: office duties, locking up, janitorial service, and any necessary manual labor. He did not mind this kind of work, but his wife disapproved of his "downward displacement." She said: "In Taiwan he was the boss. He dressed up in suits and his subordinates respected him. Here he works like a manual laborer." After about two years in southern California, a former corporate employer in Taiwan contacted the husband with an opportunity for him to assume an executive position. The wife encouraged the husband to accept the offer, so he returned to Taiwan.

Another husband returned to work in Taiwan where his earning power was higher. His English was considered good in Taiwan, but not in the country of destination where he could not earn as much as he could in his country of origin. In addition, he was more familiar with Taiwan's investment environment. There he also had friends and business contacts who invested with him in business together. So he worked as a highly paid corporate executive, invested in the local stock market, and co-owned a few other businesses with his friends who acted as his managing partners. To maximize economic income or to further one's career potential, the skilled professionals returned to Taiwan where their human and social capitals could be better utilized. Thus, the husband worked in Taiwan while his wife and children lived in the United States. The separate residences across national boundaries led to the formation of transnational families.

The split-household transnational family phenomenon is also found among professional Korean immigrants in New York. Min (1998) presents three cases but their situations are somewhat different: two Korean men came as graduate students, got married, and established themselves in the United States; while one man came with his wife and two young children to work as an officer in an American company. After several years these husbands returned to Korea for better career opportunities but the wives and children remained in the United States. "In Korean transnational families, the wives participate in paid work while taking care of the children by themselves" (Min 1998, 112). Min's three cases indeed constitute a small sample; nonetheless they show that although separated from their husbands, these wives had established their families and careers in the United States without interruption by international migration. Perhaps because the husbands relocated across the Pacific Ocean and uprooted themselves instead of the wives, these Korean women could blend "woman as mother" and "woman as worker" more successfully than their Taiwanese counterparts in California.[6]

In transnational families women as mothers live apart from their husbands, and this physical separation between spouses affects women as wives in different ways. Several studies have investigated middle-class families split between Hong Kong and Australia or Canada (see Pe-Pua et al. 1996; Hui 1993; Lam 1994; Man 1993, 1996a, 1996b). Though lacking in analysis, these studies isolate the contradictory effects of the transnational split household on these women and their marital relations. They are: (1) loneliness, increased conflict and argu-

ments, discontent, and divorce; but also (2) positive and improved spousal relationship such as renewed love, increased appreciation, and stronger and closer
emotional ties; and (3) continuity where there is little change before and after
migration. Women with transnational families in the United States and Taiwan
report similar experiences as follows.

TRANSNATIONALISM AND MARITAL RELATIONS

How did migration affect a woman's relationship with her husband? One
woman's discontent was obvious in the early days after migration. I met Ying
and her family shortly after their arrival in southern California. At her husband's insistence, Ying reluctantly gave up her profession to migrate for her
children's education together with the husband. When they first immigrated,
Ying was upset about her career interruption. She was also constantly worried
about the household budget. They were not poor but she felt much less secure
after migration and the loss of her income. Husband and wife often argued.
She would blame the husband for the situation. He replied that if he could adjust then she should too.

After one year, Ying and her husband moved to an area near a community
with many residents from Taiwan, including some of Ying's former friends. She
ran into an old family friend who had left two teenagers to attend school alone
in southern California. Ying found out that without parental supervision and
support, those two kids felt abandoned and lonely and eventually ran into legal trouble. One even faced arrest and prosecution. Ying counted her blessings
that her own children were better adjusted. While Ying initially rejected the
move, she eventually came around with time and by learning about other,
mostly negative, experiences.

Ying also encouraged her husband to accept a job in Taiwan, thus instigat-
ing the formation of their transnational family. According to Ying, the split-
household arrangement actually improved their spousal relationship. With the
prospect of return to Taiwan in sight, Ying felt much better about her stay in
southern California. She commented: "After the children grow up to attend
university, I would be able to go back to join him in Taiwan and live the way
of life I enjoy. There is a purpose now. I have something to look forward to.
My life here in this country is not indefinite. There is hope." In addition, the
husband received a higher income in Taiwan than in the States. Ying no longer
felt the financial pressure and insecurity.

Now that the husband stayed in Taiwan most of the time, she also appreciated him more. She said: "He would do a lot of things when he was around.
He could go to pick up the kids, he could fix things around the house. When

there were problems he was around to discuss them with.....We argue less now, why waste money on the phone just to argue? Besides, if we start to argue and I don't like it I can just hang up!" Things actually improved for them! The new-found appreciation for one's spouse is also reported in studies on astronaut families in Hong Kong and Canada (see, for example, Man 1993).

The nurse Yen had a similar story. "Our family life has gotten closer-knit here after we immigrated. We are apart longer now. You don't want to waste your time together on arguments and bickering. We must depend on more tolerance, more understanding, love, and trust." Despite the longer separations, they frequently communicated by telephone. They spent "quality time" together as Yen put it: "Our family life is better here. It is a quieter life here. Children come home after school. When my husband comes home, every night the two kids would come and sit on our bed at night and we have heart-to-heart talks. He now has a better father-son relationship with the children." Her husband also preferred this lifestyle. Because her husband had always been a commercial pilot flying away from home on duty for several days, they were used to periodic separations. The only difference was spatial location of the family—home was now in the United States where the wife and children lived. Their mutual consideration for the children and family as a collective unit received priority over Yen's personal ambition and individual desire for a career.

Some women found no changes in the marital relationship before and after migration. Three women in their fifties attributed their marital stability to their age and the length of their marriage. One woman said: "We have been married for more than thirty years. Absence makes the heart grow fonder. We are happy to see each other after each separation. I feel sad about leaving him alone in Taiwan, but I am happy to see my daughters here. My older married children in Taiwan take good care of him so I don't worry about him too much." Another woman also reported no impact on her marital relationship. She said: "Our relationship is the same as before, there has been no change. We have been married a long time, over twenty some years. Old man and old lady." When husband and wife were apart, they would talk on the phone every day, and they were together often. Her husband visited the States every three or four months for about ten days each time. The wife would fly back to Taiwan every two or three months and stay with the husband for one to two months (the daughter and son were in college and capable of taking care of themselves). That means that they were never apart for very long in between.

The age of the spouses and their length of marriage seemed to help stabilize marital relations after migration. However, these women also traveled frequently to see their husbands. Personality, premigration emotional ties, family closeness, and frequency of togetherness appeared to bolster the bonds between husband and wife even when they were physically apart. In some cases, however, the separation destabilized the marriage or created distance and the marriage bond was threatened.

A woman named Yeh had immigrated with her husband and children in the early 1990s. While her husband made the decision to migrate, Yeh was one of the few women who commuted. She would stay for two months in Taiwan to take care of the business there, and stayed two months in the States with the family as wife and mother. Then one day she heard from her friends that her husband was having an affair with another woman. Yeh said: "He was at the age that he needed his masculinity reaffirmed, that he could still attract another woman. Since I was not around, and another woman offered. . . . Of course it took two to tango. But good sex is luring for men. Which man would refuse if a woman stood before him naked and wanting?" Then the other woman started to ask Yeh's husband for large sums of money. Little by little, he realized that what she wanted was his money, not him. In the end, he apologized to Yeh in front of the children. "I forgave him," Yeh said.

Shang's marriage also suffered from the separation. Her husband was ambivalent about moving to the United States because his entire family lived in Taiwan, and he held a good job there. Husband and wife and two young children immigrated to the United States together, but he did not find a job he liked. After they received permanent resident status, he took his son and returned to Taiwan to his former job, while the infant daughter remained with the mother. In the first year of the transnational arrangement, he came for two weeks every six months as is required to maintain one's permanent residency. Then slowly the frequency of contact and reunion decreased. After only one year of such arrangement, Shang could not locate him whenever she called. She went back to Taiwan to see her husband and her son. Her husband was cold toward her. He even slept in a different bedroom when she was at home.

Shang returned to southern California to care for her daughter; one year later the husband filed for divorce in Taiwan. A court in Taiwan finalized the divorce within three years of their separation due to the migration. Shang explained that his strong sexual appetite, wanting sex two or three times a night in her experience, might have been one reason. In addition, Shang admitted that her poor relationship with her mother-in-law might also have contributed to her husband's decision. She said: "I was at great odds with his mother. I disliked a lot of things that she did. I was young and tactless, and I said it as it was. She always had a lot of influence over him." While physical need might have caused the dissolution, her relationship with other family members could have contributed to the negative consequence of Shang's transnational family experience.

Although the above examples portray the man as the cause of deteriorated marital relationship, I do not mean that only men get lonely or instigate affairs. Perhaps it merely reflects the bias of my sample. In a study on astronaut families where husbands work in Hong Kong and wives live in Canada with the children, Lam (1994) reports of a woman who became very alienated in her new environment. She felt devalued as an individual, rejected by her teenage children, and frustrated by her husband. She was driven to a more active social life that eventually led to involvement with a local widower. When the husband and children found out about the relationship, she asked for a divorce. One of the women I interviewed put it bluntly: "If men have their needs, so do women. Women in Taiwan don't talk about their needs. It is a big unforgivable crime if women have extramarital affairs, yet it is acceptable if men do. Women have biological needs too!" This woman was forty years old, the youngest of all the thirty interviewees.

CONCLUSION

For several nonworking-class families from Taiwan, migration was a strategy employed to maximize their children's educational and future employment prospects. In doing so, they also negotiated a potentially better status position for the family in the future. To achieve these family-oriented goals some women in my sample sacrificed their professional lives as career women when they made the transition to full-time domestic mothers. Some women thrived in these new changes, while others grappled with the conflicting desire to continue being a professional and the pressure to conform to traditional Taiwanese patriarchal definitions of woman as mother. In most cases, conflicts between a woman and the family were suppressed in the interest of future prospects for the family as a unit.

The transnational family arrangement affected women in different ways but changes and ruptures in family relations were not always the norm. In direct contrast to the women who migrate to become workers and thus forfeit their chances to be true mothers (their own children are usually left behind, see Pe-Pua, chapter 8), these Taiwanese women left their country of origin in order to be ideal mothers and fulfill their motherhood roles. In prioritizing their children's lives (the next generation) over career or spouse (since they are separated from their husbands), these women privileged the woman as mother over the woman as wife, sometimes with dire consequences on their marital relationship.

NOTES

In its various stages as part of a larger project, this chapter was partially funded by the Pacific Cultural Foundation (1999–2000), the Fulbright Foundation (2000–2001), and the Pacific Rim Research Program of the Office of the President, University of California (2000–2001). The Institute of Ethnology at the Academia Sinica of Taiwan hosted me from September 2000 to June 2001, during which time this chapter was written.

The Institute provided me with the research support facilities needed. Gratitude is due to all the women interviewed who generously shared their experiences that made this chapter possible. I thank Dr. Yi Ching-chun, Dr. Lu Yu-hsia, and Dr. Chang Chin-feng at the Institute of Sociology, Academia Sinica, who shared their own research findings with me; and Dr. Maria S. M. Tam at the Chinese University of Hong Kong for her assistance in obtaining some reference materials. I also thank Dr. Christine Gailey at the University of California, Riverside, for her support and suggestions for the initial conception of this chapter, and the editors Dr. Nicola Piper and Dr. Mina Roces who provided an insightful critique on an earlier draft.

1. Many immigrants from Taiwan have returned to Taiwan from the United States beginning in the 1980s for higher income and better career opportunities. However, they are mainly male professionals.

2. This pattern is also found between Taiwan and Australia, Canada, or New Zealand.

3. In this chapter, the term *Taiwanese* refers to people from Taiwan irrespective of ethnic or provincial origin.

4. The definition as used in this chapter excludes Asian or Taiwanese children sent by parents to attend elementary or high schools in the United States, away from both parents on a long-term basis, and are not discussed in this chapter. These children are termed *parachute kids* in the literature. For a discussion of this phenomenon in the United States see Min Zhou, "'Parachute Kids' in Southern California: The Educational Experience of Chinese Children in Transnational Families," *Educational Policy* 12, no. 6 (1998): 682–704 in English, and Shiu-yu Kuo, *Taiwan's Parachute Kids in the United States* (Taipei: The Institute of European and American Studies, Academia Sinica, 1991) in Chinese; for those in Australia from Hong Kong see Rogelia Pe-pua, Colleen Mitchell, Robyn Iredale, and Stephen Castles, *Astronaut Families and Parachute Children: The Cycle of Migration between Hong Kong and Australia* (Canberra: Australian Government Publishing Service, 1996).

5. The problem of skill accreditation is quite common. For more details see Robyn Iredale, *Skills Transfer: International Migration and Accreditation Issues* (Wollongong: University of Wollongong, 1997).

6. Transnational families resembling those discussed in this chapter are also found recently between Korea and southern California where wives immigrate with children for their education and husbands work in Korea. This phenomenon appears to be on the increase but as of this date, no known local research has been conducted or published on this population (personal communication, Chang [2002]).

REFERENCES

Ahern, Susan, Dexter Bryan, and Reynaldo Baca. "Migration and La Mujer Fuerte." *Migration Today* vol. 13, no.1 (1985): 14–20.

Buijs, Gina. "Introduction." Pp. 1–19 in *Migrant Women: Crossing Boundaries and Changing Identities,* edited by Gina Buijs. Oxford: Berg Publishers Limited, 1993.

Chang, Ying-hua, Cheng Tai Shi, and Yi Chih Wang. *Educational Tracking and Socioeconomic Status: Policy Implication on Technical and Vocational Education Reform* (text in Chinese). Taipei: The Executive Yuan Education Reform Committee, 1996.

Chien, Wen-yin, and Cherng-tay Hsueh. "Employment of Married Women in Taiwan: Its Patterns and Causes" (text in Chinese). *Journal of Population Studies* vol. 17 (1996): 113–34.

Gelb, Joyce, and Marian L. Palley (Eds.). *Women of Japan and Korea: Continuity and Change*. Philadelphia: Temple University Press, 1994.

Georges, Eugenia. "Gender, Class, and Migration in the Dominican Republic: Women's Experiences in a Transnational Community." Pp. 81–99 in *Towards a Transnational Perspective on Migration: Race, Class, Ethnicity, and Nationalism Reconsidered*, edited by Nina Glick Schiller, Linda Basch, and Cristina Blanc-Szanton. New York: New York Academy of Sciences, 1992.

Glick Schiller, Nina, Linda Basch, and Cristina Blanc-Szanton. "Part I. Introduction. Transnationalism: A New Analytic Framework for Understanding Migration." Pp. 1–24 in *Towards a Transnational Perspective on Migration: Race, Class, Ethnicity, and Nationalism Reconsidered,* edited by Nina Glick Schiller, Linda Basch, and Cristina Blanc-Szanton. New York: New York Academy of Sciences, 1992.

Grasmuck, Sherri, and Patricia R. Pessar. *Between Two Islands: Dominican International Migration*. Berkeley: University of California Press, 1991.

Hondagneu-Sotelo, Pierrette. *Gendered Transitions: Mexican Experience of Immigration*. Berkeley: University of California Press, 1994.

Hondagneu-Sotelo, Pierrette, and Ernestine Avila. "'I'm Here, But I'm There': The Meanings of Latina Transnational Motherhood." *Gender & Society* vol. 11, no. 5 (1997): 548–71.

Horton, John. *Politics of Diversity: Immigration, Resistance, and Change in Monterey Park, California*. Philadelphia: Temple University Press, 1995.

Hui, Y. F. "Astronaut Family." *The Hong Kong Journal of Social Work* vol. 27, no.1 (1993): 59–68.

Iredale, Robyn. *Skills Transfer: International Migration and Accreditation Issues.* Wollongong: University of Wollongong Press, 1997.

Kibria, Nazli. *Family Tightrope: The Changing Lives of Vietnamese Americans*. Princeton: Princeton University Press, 1993.

Kuo, Shih-yu. *Taiwan's Parachute Kids in the United States* (text in Chinese). Taipei: The Institute of European and American Studies, Academia Sinica, 1991.

Lam, Lawrence. "Searching for a Safe Haven: The Migration and Settlement of Hong Kong Chinese Immigrants in Toronto." Pp. 163–79 in *Reluctant Exiles? Migration from Hong Kong and the New Overseas Chinese*, edited by Ronald Skeldon. Armonk, N.Y.: M.E. Sharpe, 1994.

Light, Ivan. "Disadvantaged Minorities in Self-Employment." *International Journal of Comparative Sociology* vol. 20, nos.1–2 (1979): 31–45.

Lin, Sung-ling. "Effects of Mother on Her Children's School Performance: The Comparisons of Cultural Capital, Economic Resources, and Supervisory Role" (text in Chinese). *National Taiwan University Journal of Sociology* vol. 27 (1999): 73–105.

Lu, Yu-hsia. "Facilitation or Inhibition: Family Interaction and Married Women's Employment" (text in Chinese). Pp. 1–40 in *Taiwanese Society in 1990s: Taiwanese Social Change Survey Symposium Series II (part 2), Monograph Series No. 1*, edited by Ly-yun

Chang, Yu-hsia Lu, and Fu-chang Wang. Taipei: Institute of Sociology Preparation Office, Academia Sinica, 1997.

———. "Women's Role in Taiwan's Family Enterprises: A Preliminary Research" (text in Chinese). Pp. 177–211 in *Population, Employment and Welfare.* Taipei: Institute of Economics, Academia Sinica, 1996.

———. "Women's Labor Force Participation and Family Power Structure in Taiwan." *Bulletin of the Institute of Ethnology, Academia Sinica* vol. 56 (1983): 113–43.

———. "Value Extension of Modern Women's Role Attitudes" (text in Chinese). *Thoughts and Words* vol. 20, no. 2 (1982): 135–50.

Lu, Yu-hsia, and Ching-chun Yi. "Employment and Family Status of Women in a Changing Society: Allocation of Household Chores" (text in Chinese). Paper presented at Chinese Family and Its Relationship Conference, Taipei, Taiwan, 1999.

Man, Guida. "The Experience of Middle-Class Women in Recent Hong Kong Chinese Immigrant Families in Canada." Pp. 271–300 in *Voices: Essays on Canadian Families,* edited by Marion Lynn. Toronto: Nelson Canada, 1996a.

———. "The Experiences of Women in Middle-Class Hong Kong Chinese Immigrant Families in Canada: An Investigation in Institutional and Organization Processes." Ph.D. dissertation, Department of Education, University of Toronto, 1996b.

———. "Astronaut Phenomenon: Examining Consequences of the Diaspora of the Hong Kong Chinese." Pp. 269–79 in *Managing Changes in Southeast Asia: Local Identities, Global Connections. Proceedings of the 21st Meetings of the Canadian Council for Southeast Asian Studies. The University of Alberta. October 15–17,* edited by Jean Debernardi, Gregory Forth, and Sandra Niessen. Edmonton, University of Alberta: Quality Color Press, 1993.

Min, Pyong Gap. *Changes and Conflicts: Korean Immigrant Families in New York.* Boston: Allyn and Bacon, 1998.

Parreñas, Rhacel Salazar. "New Household Forms, Old Family Values: The Formation and Reproduction of the Filipino Transnational Family in Los Angeles." Pp. 336–51 in *Contemporary Asian America: A Multidisciplinary Reader,* edited by Min Zhou and James V. Gatewood. New York: New York University Press, 2000.

Pe-Pua, Rogelia, Colleen Mitchell, Robyn Iredale, and Stephen Castles. *Astronaut Families and Parachute Children: The Cycle of Migration between Hong Kong and Australia.* Canberra: Australian Government Publishing Services, 1996.

Pessar, Patricia. "Engendering Migration Studies." *American Behavioral Scientist* vol. 42, no. 4 (1999): 577–600.

———. "On the Homefront and in the Workplace: Integrating Immigrant Women into Feminist Discourse." *Anthropological Quarterly* vol. 68, no. 1 (1995): 37–47.

Portes, Alejandro, Luis E. Guarnizo, and Patricia Landolt. "The Study of Transnationalism: Pitfalls and Promise of an Emergent Research Field." *Ethnic and Racial Studies* vol. 22, no. 2 (1999): 217–37.

Rouse, Roger. "Mexican Migration and the Social Space of Postmodernism." *Diaspora* vol. 1, no. 1 (1991): 8–23.

Skeldon, Ronald. (Ed.). *Emigration from Hong Kong: Tendencies and Impacts.* Hong Kong: The Chinese University of Hong Kong, 1995.

———. (Ed.). *Reluctant Exiles? Migration from Hong Kong and the New Overseas Chinese.* Armonk, N.Y.: M.E. Sharpe, 1994.

Smith, Michael P., and Luis E. Guarnizo (Eds.). *Transnationalism from Below*. New Brunswick: Transaction Publishers, 1998.

Sun, Tsing-shan, and Wu Rong-chiao. *Social Resources, Cultural Capital, and the Changing Process of Status Attainment* (text in Chinese). Research Report. Graduate Institute of Sociology. Tai Chung: Tung Hai University, 1993.

Tsai, Shu-ling. "The Transition from School to Work in Taiwan." Pp. 443–532 in *From School to Work: A Comparative Study of Educational Qualifications and Occupational Destinations,* edited by Yossi Shavit and Walter Muller. Oxford: Clarendon Press, 1998.

Tseng, Yen-fen. "The Development of Taiwanese Immigrant Business in Los Angeles." *International Migration Review* vol. 29, no.1 (1995): 33–58.

Uzzell, Douglas. "Ethnography of Migration: Breaking out of the Bi-Polar Myth." *Rice University Studies* vol. 62, no. 3 (1976): 45–54.

Wang, Te-mu, Yu-chia Chen, and Wei-an Chang. "The Changing Educational Structure and Equal Opportunity in Education" (text in Chinese). Pp. 353–76 in *Social and Cultural Change in Taiwan,* edited by H.Y. Chiu and Y. H. Chang. Taipei: Institute of Ethnology, Academia Sinica, 1986.

Woo, Deborah. *Glass Ceilings and Asian Americans: The New Face of Workplace Barriers.* Walnut Creek, Calif.: AltaMira, 2000.

Wu, Wan-Yu. "Women under the Patriarchal System in Taiwan" (text in Chinese). Master's Thesis in Sociology, Tung Wu University, Taipei, Taiwan, 1992.

Zhou, Min. "'Parachute Kids' in Southern California: The Educational Experience of Chinese Children in Transnational Families." *Educational Policy* vol. 12, no. 6 (1999): 682–704.

8

Wife, Mother, and Maid: The Triple Role of Filipino Domestic Workers in Spain and Italy

Rogelia Pe-Pua

Married women who migrate as either undocumented or contract workers usually leave their husbands behind. But what if these women were allowed to petition their families to later join them through family reunion schemes? Are these women who reunite with their families in a better or more advantageous position than those whose families remain transnational? This chapter presents a case study of the gendered aspects of international labor migration and marriage by discussing Filipino domestic workers in the southern European context. It is atypical for two main reasons: First of all, the host countries (Spain and Italy) are distinct from other typical domestic worker–receiving countries in Asia and the Middle East by allowing family reunions of foreign contract workers. In addition, it seems that extreme cases of abuse or exploitation are rare partly because labor conditions are comparatively good in the host countries discussed here. This, however, does not mean that there are no other sources of hardship experienced.

The main objective of this chapter is to present a comparison between Filipino women who are separated from their families and those whose husbands and families joined them later on in the migration process. Furthermore, this study explores how the new status of women as main or sole breadwinners affects gender relations within familial everyday life. Because men have more difficulty in obtaining employment, whether the Filipino husband can join his wife or not, she becomes the primary breadwinner of the family. This has important ramifications in the marriage dynamics as both definitions of masculinity and femininity have to be altered to accommodate these new changes.

One major similarity with other studies on Filipino domestic workers is that these Filipino women labor migrants are not only de-skilled but ossified into

positions of "domestic helper" and are prevented from moving out of this designated "labor space" (see also McKay, this volume). Like the Filipinas in
Canada who are prevented from reinventing themselves as something other
than "carer" or "domestic helper," these domestic helpers or maids in Spain and
Italy also find it difficult to break away from this occupation. Unlike the cases
discussed by McKay of Filipinas who have resorted to marriage with "local"
men (i.e., Canadian nationals) as a strategy with which to escape from the category of "housemaid" (see McKay, chapter 2), this option is not usually chosen
by Filipinas in Spain and Italy who rather make use of the "family reunion
scheme."

Comparisons between two sets of women migrants—those who do not have
their families with them and those who have reunited with their families—
provides the organizational focus for this chapter. Certainly, both sets of women
experience advantages and disadvantages. I am interested in exploring the aspect
of relationship dynamics and shifting gender roles when the women migrate to
work abroad. Some of the women in split families have affairs with mostly other
Filipino men in the host countries (a unique study in itself as it is usually
the Filipino male or husband left in the Philippines who is guilty of an extramarital affair). Those who have their husbands and families with them are typically expected to wait on their husbands and children so much so that one
informant described her life and role as: "Sometimes I feel that I am reinvented
as a maid three times over: I am a maid to my employer, a maid to my husband,
and a maid to my children" (Pinay 3).[1] I therefore argue that although the Filipino domestic helper is transformed into the main, or sometimes sole, breadwinner of the family, this does not entail a gender role swap, but rather a triple
burden in her role as income provider, "serving" mother, and wife. The intri-
cate similarities and differences between the Filipinas who are apart from and
those who are joined by their husbands are demonstrated.

METHODS AND DATA

The material for this chapter is based on fieldwork in Spain and Italy conducted in 1999. The data were gathered by using various strategies within a
participant observation framework. Access to Filipino migrant workers was
provided through a snowball technique, starting with a few contacts established
prior to the fieldwork. My husband and I visited the homes of the workers,
and we were invited to social gatherings, where we interviewed both men and
women individually and in focus groups. I facilitated the all-women groups,
and my husband, Ed, facilitated the all-men group discussions (which was likely
to be accompanied by some beer-drinking; very typical of Filipino male inter-

actions). Both Ed and I are Filipinos, thus we speak the Filipino language (also known as Tagalog) fluently and are adept at maintaining an informal atmosphere conducive to sharing of opinions and self-disclosure on the part of both the research participants and us.

All interviews were done in the *pagtatanong-tanong* style (Pe-Pua 1989) characterized by informality and a two-way exchange of ideas and opinions between interviewer and interviewee/s. These *pagtatanong-tanong* sessions were held either one-on-one, or in natural clusters (made up of two to three respondents who knew each other very well), or in groups (for example, during parties where we got invited). Where permission was granted, interviews were taped. We were able to talk to approximately fifty Filipino migrant workers in both countries.[2] I also interviewed other Filipinos who worked in the Philippine Embassy/Consulates and associated offices (labor attaché, agencies that provide assistance to migrant workers, and so on), community (voluntary, nongovernment) organizations, and church groups. There were a few interviews with Spanish and Italian government staff from the respective Ministries of Labor.

The data presented in this chapter are those related to marriage and family issues involving Filipino couples only. Mixed marriage was not discussed because the situation in Spain and Italy is such that a Filipino woman would move away from the Filipino community once she got married to an Italian or a Spanish man, which makes them more difficult to access. Besides, the current number of mixed marriages is known to be small.[3]

FILIPINOS IN SOUTHERN EUROPE

The total number of Filipinos in Spain and Italy is the highest for the whole of Europe, there being currently more in Italy than in Spain. The Philippine Embassy in Madrid estimated that there were approximately 35,000 to 40,000 Filipinos in Spain at the end of 1998 (including those who have been naturalized). This includes those who have registered with the Philippine Embassy and an estimated number of undocumented Filipinos (POLO Madrid 1999). Nongovernment organizations' estimates are higher placing the population of Filipinos at 50,000 (CFMW and KAIBIGAN 1995). The high number of Filipino workers in Spain can be traced to the colonial ties between the Philippines and Spain. On the other hand, "the combination of demand for waged household work and the 'safety net' provided by the relatively large number of Filipino Catholic clergy in Rome" (Tacoli 1996, 12) accounts for the high number of Filipino workers in Italy. These are discussed later in the chapter.

There are more Filipino women (66 percent) than men in Spain. The majority of the women were aged twenty-five to forty-five years. Most Filipinos are working as domestic helpers in private households and in the hostelry industry (90 percent). A small number work as administrative employees (6 percent), factory workers (2 percent), teachers (1 percent), and professionals (1 percent). The Filipino community is considered the oldest group of immigrants of Asian origin in Spain. Filipinos have the reputation of being very well-organized and relatively stable (its solidarity evidenced by the existence of various organizations run by Filipino workers themselves (POLO Madrid 1999; Fact Sheet: Spain 1999).

The number of Filipinos in Italy is much higher. In fact, Filipinos ranked fourth in the Italian population register of migrant communities in 1995, next to Moroccans, North Americans, and Tunisians. Italy is the country with the biggest concentration of Filipino migrants in the whole of Europe. The Philippine Embassy in Rome's estimate as of the end of 1998 was around 65,000 to 80,000 overseas Filipino workers (OFWs) and 37,500 undocumented workers (the number of undocumented migrant workers in Italy is said to be due partly to endogenous reasons, such as not renewing their residency permits). NGOs place the figure at 200,000 Filipinos in Italy. In 1998 alone, 10,061 Filipino workers were deployed to Italy, representing 68 percent of the total deployment to Europe. There were twice as many women as men. Most women worked as domestic helpers. Men would find work in restaurants or in the electronics industry (CFMW and KAIBIGAN 1995; Philippine Embassy-Rome 1999).

Interesting to note is that both Italy and Spain have a relatively recent history as receiving countries of migrant labor. Until 1973 (the year of the general halt of official recruitment of foreign workers in western Europe), nationals from both countries were prominent among the "guest worker" flows to the northwestern destinations in Europe. However, by the 1980s, due to economic development and declining demographic growth, the situation reversed, with both countries beginning to receive migrant labor from northern Africa and Asia (Castles and Miller 1993). The large and increasing demand for domestic helpers is related to poorly developed welfare services in the south of Europe (in contrast to Scandinavia, for example) on the one hand, and improving educational and employment opportunities for women on the other hand (Kofman, Phizacklea, Raghuram, and Sales 2000). For all the above reasons, there is a constant demand for domestic workers in general, and Filipinos in particular, because of their good reputation as all-around workers.

Filipinas are notably atypical of all domestic helpers because of their better education and high occupational level compared to women in the domestic service industry.[4] For instance, 41 percent of Filipino migrant workers in Spain (majority of whom are women) have completed university studies, including degrees in commerce, education, economics, dentistry, medical technology, midwifery, and nursing. Many held professional jobs before leaving the Philippines. (Barber 2000; CFMW and KAIBIGAN 1995; Lobera 1993; Tharan 1989, cited in Zlotnik 1995)

Many of the Filipino workers in Spain and Italy have come through contacts already existing in these countries. Among the early migrants were members of the Catholic clergy, students who were scholars of the Spanish government, former domestic helpers of Italian nationals who traveled to the Philippines, and so on. In Spain, regularization programs (known as CUPO or *Contingente*, see below) have been a vehicle for the entry of a number of Filipinos we spoke to or who were mentioned by our interviewees. To help out a family member or a friend, a domestic worker already residing in Spain can find a prospective employer for them. Or, since the Filipino domestic workers are well regarded by their host employers, they can convince their employers to sign papers that guarantee work for their family members or friends. This gives others the opportunity to come and work in Spain.

Filipino men have more difficulties in finding work compared to the women who are in great demand as domestic helpers. The most common jobs for those who manage to find work is in the restaurant (as cook, waiter, or kitchen hand, for example) or in the hotel industry (in housekeeping, for example). Some of the interviewees work as couriers for jewelry stores or as office staff at the Philippine Embassy (clerk, computer programmer, or client support, for example), or work in the construction industry. There are some men who worked as domestic workers for a while, joining their wives in a live-in arrangement, but this is rare. Besides, many of them do not stay long in this job since they are not used to domestic work (and probably feel humiliated by it partly because domestic work is conflated with the feminine), preferring alternative jobs.

When asked about their reasons for coming to Spain or Italy, the overwhelming response of our interviewees was financial in nature—(1) to earn a better income than they did or would have the opportunity to do if they had remained in the Philippines; (2) to help their families who now depend on them for their subsistence; (3) to pay for the education of the children; and (4) to save up to buy property in the Philippines. Some of them aspired to bring their families to Spain or Italy so they could live a better life. In addition, Tacoli (1999) discovered (based on interviews with Filipinos in Rome) that the widespread networks between the Philippines and Rome and the "safety net" provided by the Catholic Church to Filipino migrant workers encourage further migration. Despite the high cost of transport, workers are able to borrow money from friends and kin who are already settled in Rome, or find accommodation and employment with their help.

FOREIGN LABOR POLICY IN SPAIN AND ITALY

Immigration and Residency Policies

The Philippines was a former colony of Spain (for more than 300 years) and, hence, there already exist special historical ties between the two countries. This is reflected in the benevolent attitude that Spaniards tend to have toward Filipinos. The Spanish immigration program grants the Philippines (and other former colonies) special preference in terms of accepting applications for immigrant status. Former colonial citizens can apply for naturalization to become Spanish citizens after two years' residency. A substantial number of Filipinos have availed of this privilege (Huntoon 1998; Fact Sheet: Spain 1999).

Because of this preferential treatment, until July 1985, Filipinos were allowed to enter Spain without a visa. They were also allowed to even change the status of their tourist visa and get a work permit. The *Ley de Extranjeria* (Law on Foreigners), implemented for the first time in 1985, altered all this.[5] It still gives preferential treatment to Filipinos who apply for work permits. This law also accords the following rights and liberties to foreigners with legal status: freedom of movement and choice of residence; right to education; right to form associations, the right to hold public meetings and demonstrations; and the right to join Spanish trade unions or professional organizations (Huntoon 1998; POLO Madrid 1999; Fact Sheet: Spain 1999). But while the law clarified the status of many Filipinos, it also had its drawbacks. It created difficulties for Filipinos who do not have the proper documents, or those who do not have the time to queue outside the police headquarters (because they would suffer a loss of income), or those who are not allowed by employers to leave the house on weekdays (for live-in domestic workers). Some are disadvantaged because they live far from the government office, while others do not meet the deadline due to neglect (e.g., forgetting to do so) (Lobera 1993).

Two major regularization programs (popularly known as CUPO or *Contingente*) were implemented in Spain in 1991 and 1996. Residence permits have to be renewed annually (Huntoon 1998). These allowed formerly undocumented workers residence and the opportunity to work legally. In 1999, another regularization program was implemented. With the introduction of these programs, all foreigners are compelled to have work permits to hold jobs or otherwise face deportation (POLO Madrid 1999). In accordance with the 1991 Regularization Program, employment of foreign workers is allowed only in private households and agricultural services, occupations that Spanish workers generally avoid (Fact Sheet: Spain 1999). Postregularization data in Spain show the official registration of 25,000 Filipinos in 1992. Before these regularization campaigns, about 75 percent of the community did not have legal status (CFMW and KAIBIGAN 1995). Thus, in isolating domestic work and farm labor as the only occupations designated to incoming foreign labor, the law in fact prohibits foreigners from moving to other occupations and ensures that the category of foreign workers continues to be defined as either "domestic helper" or "farm worker." Spain therefore prohibits foreign women from moving beyond this assigned marginal "space" in the private sphere.

The Italian government suspended the issuing of labor permits for domestic workers altogether in 1986, but implemented a regularization program instead in 1986, with other amnesties following in 1990 and 1997 to address the problem of undocumented migration in the country (Kofman et al. 2000). To qualify, applicants had to prove that they had worked for at least four of the previous twelve months or had a relative they wished to join who had lived in Italy for over two years and had sufficient means to support and accommodate them. Applications from Filipinos ranked third in the number received during these regularizations. If successful, applicants are given a legal residence permit (*Permesso di Soggiorno*), which also allows them to work (SOPEMI 1998).

Foreigners can bring their families to Spain and Italy through the Family Reunification scheme (called *Agrupacion de Familia* in Spain and *Ricongiungimento Famigliare* in Italy). This means that once they acquired legal status, foreign migrant workers may also be joined by their spouses, dependent children, and parents as long as they have the financial wherewithal to support them. In Italy, after residing in the country for over five years, foreigners (and their families) may be granted a permanent Residence Permit (*Carta di Soggiorno*) provided they meet certain other requirements (SOPEMI 1998).

Both Spain and Italy recognize the need for integrating migrant workers in their society, and this is partly the reason why they have passed laws allowing families to reunite. This is also partly due to their membership in the European Union[6] and legal obligations (such as the European Social Charter) to give migrant workers (whether documented or undocumented) basic human rights (in this case, the right to form a family or be united with an existing one).

Labor Policies

In Spain, work permits are a necessary requirement to be able to engage in legal employment. These permits come in the form of an identification card that states the approved occupation. To switch occupation, one must lodge another application. The laminated card bears additional security features to guard against proliferation of false identification cards among foreigners (Fact Sheet: Spain 1999).

The same labor laws that apply to Spanish citizens also apply to migrant workers. Filipinos who are authorized to work are amply protected by Spanish

Labor and Social Security laws. Migrant workers can bring any incidence of labor exploitation or injustice directly to the attention of the Spanish police or through NGOs. All workers are registered by their employers with the Spanish Social Security System, with both the employer and worker paying the dues, but with the employer shouldering most of it. Through this system, workers are entitled to medical treatment benefits, sickness and maternity benefits, permanent disability benefits, old-age and retirement pension, death grants and survivorship pension, unemployment benefits, and family benefits (Huntoon 1998; POLO Madrid 1999; Fact Sheet: Spain 1999).

Italy also applies the same labor laws to both their nationals and foreigners. Among these are the Law of Direct Hiring of Foreign Workers from their country of origin and the National Contract Law of Italy, which provides equal protection to both Italian and migrant workers in the domestic service. Workers are entitled to wages agreed upon, holiday pay, vacations, Christmas bonus, and others. "Even undocumented workers get similar benefits, except for social security coverage, and have resort to courts in case of non-compliance with minimum terms and conditions of employment. These favourable work conditions are in line with the Italian policy of according full protection to labor" (Philippine Embassy-Rome 1999).

In both Spain and Italy, there is no restriction on the opportunity of migrant workers to change occupation, as long as they follow the formal application procedures. In Italy, this was done by way of implementing the Martelli Act of 1990, which eased restrictions on working hours for foreign domestic workers as well as the ties to a specific employer (Kofman et al. 2000). Many Filipino workers (men and women) in our study dream of some day becoming a professional or doing something other than being a domestic helper or a waiter/cook, and the like. However, most of them are not willing to sacrifice their working hours in order to obtain the necessary qualifications. They claim they cannot afford to reduce their earning capacity because relatives back in the Philippines count on the regular remittances they send (see also McKay, chapter 2). The costs of further education can also act as a deterrent. In addition, some cited their long absence from such endeavors that to take it up now might be too hard because they are no longer used to studying. Language is another obstacle to obtaining further education. Moreover, competition in the job market is stiff, and host citizens are most likely to be more favored over foreigners.

Although Kofman et al. (2000) mention many grim accounts of domestic workers from both a physical and emotional viewpoint, on the whole, particularly when compared to other Asian and Middle Eastern receiving countries, very few major cases of abuse by employers in Spain and Italy have reached the Philippines. The lower number of cases of extreme abuse most certainly are linked to better regulation of labor.

FILIPINO WOMEN AS DOMESTIC HELPERS

Our interviews conducted in Spain and Italy confirm the predominance of domestic work as the occupation of Filipino women. This service is primarily carried out in private households for local families, although there is a significant number of jobs that involve working and caring for elderly in Rome in elderly people's homes. It is common among domestic helpers to accept a live-in arrangement for which the worker gets free accommodation and food, and sometimes toiletries as well. This arrangement has some negative consequences though, such as longer working hours since they are at the beck and call of their employers even outside their agreed working time ("You can't really rest, especially your mind," said one worker). This is why some women prefer going home to their own place at the end of the day so they can have shorter working hours, autonomy, and can still accept work from other employers. Also, the pay is supposed to be higher, although they get less of the bonus, and other benefits such as vacation pay are not available.

Workers we interviewed were relatively happy with their wages and benefits. The pay ranges from an equivalent of US$550–1,000 a month, which is better than the pay that Filipinos domestic workers get in Hong Kong and Singapore (which ranges from US$125–400). This is related to the high competition in Hong Kong and Singapore of Filipinos against Filipinos and other Third World nationals. Partly because of the geographical distance of Hong Kong and Singapore to the Philippines, the number of Filipino migrants is higher there than in Europe. Also, the Hong Kong and Singaporean governments exercise more control and restrictions over foreign workers (Pe-Pua 2000). In southern Europe, they also get bonuses (thirteenth and fourteenth month pay), social security, vacation leaves, and days off for the live-in helpers.

> One of the benefits of working here is that you could save money even if you work as a domestic helper only. I am contented with my life here because I could still spend for myself with the salary I get, even after sending most of it home. Unlike in the Philippines, it is always *isang kahig, isang tuka* (referring to a hand-to-mouth existence). (Pinay 2)

There is a consensus among our interviewees that employee abuse is rare. As mentioned above, host country laws provide protection and assistance to migrant workers, even to the undocumented. Some of the few abuses cited involve nonpayment of salary, the employer's withholding of the worker's papers/documents, demand for longer working hours beyond what the contract states, and ungenerous behavior toward the worker. The otherwise overwhelmingly positive treatment that Filipino domestic workers receive from Spanish and Italian employers is also verified by the Philippine Embassy staff in both countries.

The POLO Madrid (1999, 2) report, for example, states: "On the whole, Spanish employers are good providers and responsible, they respect the agreements made with the workers. The relationship between Spanish and Filipino is characterized by mutual respect and empathy—no doubt an offshoot of our historical and cultural links."

There is also a modicum of "prestige" that Filipino domestic workers enjoy. It is widely known in both Spain and Italy that employers have high regard for them. They are known to be hard-working, industrious, persevering, trustworthy, loyal, caring, and excellent house-keepers and child-minders in general. In fact, it is no secret that they are the highest-paid among domestic helpers in the main cities (compared to other foreign nationality groups). ("Only the rich can afford a Filipino *chica*," according to one interviewee in Spain.) Host employers trust Filipino workers; for example, they allow them to have the house keys. This high regard for Filipino workers is reflected in stories related to how host employers would "beg" their departing domestic helpers to stay and entice them with a salary increase, reduced working hours, and other incentives.

Filipina maids enable many Spanish and Italians to participate in the labor force and free them from domestic tasks. Filipinas tend to treat their employers' children like their own, especially when they are separated from their own children. Hence they also help their employer fulfill "motherhood roles." With their educational background, they are also able to help the children with their homework. Filipina maids are oftentimes "counselors" within the household, listening to the problems of household members, and offering advice when appropriate. In this way, they carry out a huge range of tasks. Research conducted by Chell (1997) in Rome confirms our findings and also reports that there is usually no additional financial reward for the provision of such specialized skills.

WOMEN'S WORK ABROAD AND MARITAL RELATIONSHIPS

Most women migrant workers from among my respondents were married when they arrived in Spain or Italy. Families become transnational because husbands and children are left in the Philippines. Others are able to sponsor their families to join them due to relatively less stringent laws in Spain and Italy. In both scenarios, women have embraced the new familial role as the main breadwinner. They accept this without complaint, albeit with a great sense of inner satisfaction. They are, however, very careful not to flaunt their newly found "superiority" over their husbands lest they (husbands) start feeling some loss of pride and start objecting to the wives' constant absence. One reason why there are so few single women is because most parents in the

Philippines would not allow them to go to such faraway places. If a single woman was to become a domestic helper, her parents would say: Why not go to Hong Kong, Singapore, or Middle Eastern countries that are closer to the Philippines and where most Pinays are known to go? Moving from being wives to maids has earned them a sense of greater control over finances. Many of them talked about living with very limited resources back home, and not being able to make ends meet, no matter how creative they tried to be in budgeting or in generating income.

Being the main breadwinner through their overseas work gives them a great sense of achievement and a belief that they are instrumental in ensuring a better future by supporting their families through remittances. This change of role of the women, however, poses a challenge to the traditional role of men as "providers," a role that defines masculinity in the Filipino context. Through overseas employment, the women experience more independence and freedom from their husbands. While in overseas employment (and when carrying out their responsibilities as domestic helpers) there are, however, different challenges in the marital relationships depending on whether the husbands stay in the Philippines or join their wives in southern Europe. This change has been widespread in recent decades with migration of hundreds of thousands of women, mainly throughout Hong Kong, Taiwan, Singapore, and other parts of East Asia.

Wives with Husbands

A common pattern is for the wife to come to Spain or Italy and work as a domestic helper, and then sponsor her husband and children to come under the Family Reunification program. The alternative course is for the family to come as tourists, overstay, and then apply for residency under the regularization program. Many couples, especially those with children, will be renting their own place, for it is not practical for the wife to take the "live-in" arrangement as domestic helper.

In Spain, an apartment that they rent (or own by some who have been there much longer) is called a *piso*. When foreign workers in Spain and Italy were allowed to rent apartment units, Filipinos, especially couples or families, or fellow domestic workers who are not live-ins, started getting their own place. Many of these are small units, but they become a haven for domestic workers on their days off. They can either rent a room from the regular leaser of the *piso* on a monthly basis (say, 10,000 pesetas or US$74) with the proviso that the room is booked for them on their days off. They eat, sleep, relax, and cook Filipino food there. Other Filipinos come to these *pisos* on those days to play cards (with *tong-its* as one of the most popular games), *mahjong*, or just tell stories and gossip (*kuwentuhan, tsismisan*). Sometimes, playing cards or *mahjong* would turn into heavy gambling, heavy losses, and fights. Nonetheless, the *pisos* become the center for bonding among Filipino workers, a place for recreating a sense of family and friendships, "just like back home." (Lobera 1993, found the same practice during her fieldwork in Madrid.)

In families where the husband manages to find work, financial stability is pointed out as a source of satisfaction with life in the host country.

> We have two children, aged five and seven. My husband works as a courier for a jeweler. I used to work full time as a live-in domestic worker before we had children. Since then I have been working part time. My working hours also changed when my children started going to school. We have just bought our *piso*, with 500,000 pesetas [US$3,700] as a down payment. Our monthly rent will go toward owning this place (thirty years). It's wonderful to be owning your own place. I think we will settle permanently here in Barcelona because of the children. They speak Spanish very well. (Pinay 1)

If the husband cannot find employment he spends most of his time at home. The wife expects him now to take over most of the household chores considering that the wife works as a domestic helper for six to eight hours a day. This is a new role for him. When he was still in the Philippines, while his wife was working overseas, he would likely be holding a job as well, and (even if he did not work) he depended on the extended family and/or hired help to manage the household (and chores). Thus, in the new environment, he is stripped of this social support, faced with this new role of being a "house-band." This has serious implications for men's masculine identity and can be a source of conflict as is discussed further below.

Wives without Husbands

For the wives who remain split from their husbands and children, everyday life means work only to generate as much income as possible. The majority of the "single" domestic helpers live in their employers' abodes. Some of them do more than just one single job.

> I still work on my day off, for example on Sunday. I would earn 1,000 pesetas (US$7.50) per hour and work six hours. Anyway, I don't have my family here; I don't have anything to do on my day off. If I don't work, I'll just spend the time thinking, and then end up ringing the Philippines. Time flies when you're working so I prefer to do that on my days off. Other times, I'm involved with the church choir. (Pinay 4)

This woman is one of hundreds of women who are active in the large Filipino Catholic community, assisting the clergy by undertaking church tasks such as the choir, preparing for the mass (before and after), organizing catechism (religious teachings), attending to employment and family problems of other parishioners, and participating in activities as directed by the parish priest and nuns. In both Spain and Italy, Filipino language masses are held by Filipino priests, surrounded by Filipino assistants, and attended by a full pack of Filipino workers and residents. Specific churches are clearly identified as "Filipino," such as the Catholic Church in Urbana in Rome, the Basilica Sant Justo in Barcelona, and the Parochia de Nuestra Sra. Del Espino in Madrid. Just like their sisters in the Australian mining town of Mount Isa (see Roces, chapter 4), the Filipina domestic workers in Spain and Italy are the pillars of the Filipino community, most visibly in the Catholic community.

One of the main worries of the women in regard to their marital relationship when being split is the specter of a husband's infidelity. This scenario haunts these women who dread the pain and betrayal should their worries be confirmed. There are in fact several stories circulating about affairs permeating the lives of overseas Filipino workers and their partners. An extreme one was documented by Yeoh and Huang (2000) about a domestic worker who worked in Singapore for four years. She sent practically her whole salary home, and upon return she found another woman living in the house built from her remittances, who in the meantime won not only the affection of her husband but of her own children as well.

My fieldwork provides evidence to show that these economically empowered women also get involved in extramarital affairs. Since there is a substantial number of Filipinos in both Spain and Italy, the formation of friendship circles naturally occur. On their days off, most domestic helpers get away from the constant demand of their employers (if they are live-ins), and socialize with other Filipinos, relax, and unwind. In the past, they used to congregate in public places (such as Plaza España in Madrid, or Roma Termini in Rome) until they were told not to "hang out" there as it gave Filipinos a "bad image." Other places that they go are to the churches and to some centers for migrants. The *piso* is also a common meeting place. It is also a site for a lover's tryst. Here, the women whose husbands are still in the Philippines meet and interact with Filipino men, some of whom are also married (with wives in the Philippines). The interaction begins innocently enough with playful bantering (*tuksuhan*), culminating in a romantic relationship or a full-blown affair. The women who are lonely and homesick could fall in love this way.

In social situations, Filipinos abroad tend to keep to themselves and not mingle too much with locals. This is a phenomenon found everywhere Filipinos go. Because of the collectivistic (versus individualistic) nature of Filipino culture, Filipinos abroad will always seek out fellow Filipinos to fulfill their affiliation needs, for them to feel like they are still in the Philippines, to fill the gap in terms of a supportive social network. They need to re-create the familial and community ties and structure that are very much part of who they are. This is the "*kapwa*" (shared identity) psychology of Filipinos. A Filipino will feel lost and isolated without the collective of family and friends; his or her identity will not seem "complete." Where there is not a large community of Filipinos, then this is when the Filipino abroad turns to non-Filipinos to fulfill this affiliation need.

Because men find it harder to get a job than the women, a number of them become involved with Filipino women who then end up supporting them financially. In fact, there were extreme cases of multiple affairs. This is when community members and church leaders worry about the loosening of the moral fabric.

> Everything you hear about affairs is usually true! Some are not ashamed to admit that they are having an affair. Some women even agree to share a man and discuss arrangements on this (specific days they can have him, for example). They just don't care that people are talking about them. (Community leader)

Extramarital affairs are seen by, for example, Catholic priests and the Filipino community in general as threatening the integrity of the family unit. Familial and spouse relationships break down. Some women contemplate not ever going back to the Philippines except to visit. Some think about bringing their children over and leaving their husbands behind. The number of illegitimate children is also on the rise, according to a parish priest. Even the staff at the Philippine Embassy were on occasions inadvertently dragged into the quagmire raised by an extramarital affair when the worker severs ties with the family in the Philippines. This happens when the family sometimes turns to the foreign post to trace the worker's whereabouts. Family members (back in the Philippines or in Spain/Italy) make demands to the Embassy to withhold certain legal documents or take some legal procedure to withdraw some services from someone allegedly involved in an illicit relationship (as a punishment for moral reasons or to get back at the "guilty" party). It is not uncommon, therefore, that Embassy staff are called upon to mediate in "love triangles."

Our own findings are also supported by a study carried out by Pingol (2000) who gives us an insight into the dual dynamics of extramarital affairs when couples are split, with either the wife being involved in an affair overseas, or the husband in the Philippines, or both. Either way, the marital relationship becomes precarious. Interfering mothers-in-law can sometimes aggravate the situation by informing the wife of the husband's affair, or by fabricating such an affair in order to establish her influence in her daughter's household. On the other hand, many husbands worry that their wives might turn to other men in the foreign land, having heard such stories. Some husbands simply continue to trust their wives, and try to avoid entertaining suspicions. Others would remind their wives that they would lose all their rights to their children if they commit adultery. In the event that news of an affair is confirmed and if the husband in the Philippines is the guilty party, the wife is likely to remain overseas. If the wife overseas has the affair, the husband is faced with the decision of whether to forgive her or not; but the wife has the choice of whether or not to return. The Filipino community sees these affairs through a gendered lens, a double-standard mentality. When the husband has an affair, it is explained in terms of the masculine sexual need; female infidelity, on the other hand, is considered a serious fault. Be that as it may, members of the nuclear and extended family are likely to intervene to the effect of a reconciliation, in most cases citing the children and the integrity of the family unit as factors to consider. Divorce as such is legally not possible in the Philippines.[7]

Masculine Identity

Pingol (2000) observes how globalization, which has led to the feminization of Filipino overseas labor, has contributed significantly to changes to cultural ways of communities, not least of these involving the reconstruction of masculinity. During the early waves of labor migration, it was the men who left the family to work overseas. During the last decade, more and more women took up this role. The wives' absence deprives men of the ability to become "virile partners" (an indicator of masculinity); their wives' greater earning capacity challenges their role as a good provider; and the absence of their children's mothers imposes a demand for them to become more nurturant as fathers, to play the "mothering" role.

My own findings confirm the observations made by Pingol (2000) about Filipino women who work overseas who gain status within the family through their new role as the main breadwinner and provider. They also gain greater freedoms, a feeling of higher self-esteem and self-worth. With this comes the possibility of being the dominant partner in the marital relationship. However, her more proactive role is usually confined to decision making with regard to the family's economic investments and to the children's education. The men remain dominant in the sexual sphere. Sometimes, women try to uphold the traditional value of male dominance by assuring their husbands' role as head of the family, by ostensibly demonstrating their husbands' authority, by pretending their own subordination, or by seeking their approval before extending their contracts overseas. All of these are in response to the process of reconstructing masculine identity.

When left behind in the Philippines, there are other challenges to men's sense of masculinity, as examined by Pingol (2000), who provides an excellent analysis of how the traditional perception of Filipino men as "good providers, virile partners and responsible fathers" (123) is shaken when wives are absent.

There are basically two types of men: those who try to adapt and make the best of the new situation by maintaining a positive, albeit changed, masculine identity, and others who cannot cope with the new demands posed to them.

For those who are able to reconstruct their masculinity in a positive way, they tend to focus on remaining in control. They endure sexual abstinence. They focus on the economic well-being of the family and the children's education that will secure it. They do not resist "female tasks . . . housework [for example] did not necessarily feminize men" (Pingol 2000, 132). They become efficient house managers and good fathers. Whether they continue to work or are unemployed, "men project a new masculine image of efficiency through managing remittances, remaining strong against temptation and becoming responsive to their children's needs. Ideally, they become adept housekeepers, chaste spouses and maternal fathers" (Pingol 2000, 125). Coming under the surveillance of the mothers-in-law (who play the role of looking after the interest of their daughters) puts additional pressure on how "house husbands" are expected to behave. Mothers are considered by the overseas daughters as reliable sources of information. Some husbands enter into politics to gain an alternative measure of masculinity, at least as far as the community is concerned (Pingol 2000). Philippine society, being a collectivistic one, gives importance to community's regard for individual members.

On the other hand, some husbands are not able to negotiate this new identity as successfully. They are thus likely to enter into an adulterous relationship, neglect work and their children, develop vices such as drinking—in the process, they believe they are projecting their masculinity, but in the community's perception, they are not able to cope with their wives' absence, thus eroding their own reputation and authority (Pingol 2000).

Pingol's analysis is obviously couched within traditional Filipino values. After all, her sample is from the nonmetropolitan Ilocos region where these "gendered" values are still strong despite the high level of globalization defined in terms of international migration. Thus, the analysis has a certain element of "moral" prescription of relationship and roles of husbands and wives. While there was no opportunity to explore in more detail the relationships in transnational couples in my study, I suspect that the moral values described by Pingol are relevant, especially with regards to the pressure provided by community perception (i.e., "proper" behavior). However, I detect a strong sense of assertiveness or empowerment among the women in my study who have come from Manila and other urban centers in the Philippines. These women have previously worked in jobs that are comparable with their husbands'. Thus they are less influenced by community pressures to be in a subordinate role.

MOTHER-CHILD RELATIONSHIP

Split/Transnational Families

The concept of transnational family is not a new concept in the Philippines. The long history of overseas contract migration saw the evolution of a family where members are separated, albeit only in a physical sense. When overseas employment opportunity presents itself, the family is willing to take the sacrifice for the sake of the long-term good, to fulfill family goals. Chan's (1997) metaphor about the family splitting in order to be together translocally (in the context of Chinese diaspora) says it very well for Filipino transnational families. The same with domestic workers in Singapore:

> What usually helps women who join the contract labor diaspora from being cast adrift from all that "home" is the belief that separation from the family is actually a rational strategy, a "mission" with an explicit "purpose" of securing the family's reproduction and strengthening its future. (Yeoh and Huang 2000, 421)

Thus, in spirit, it is believed that the family is intact, that is, if the separated members are able to negotiate their way through adjustments required of the special situation. Family members are still expected to fulfill their respective roles. Reciprocity and loyalty are expected despite changing conditions.

Some of the Filipina workers in our study chose not to bring their families to Spain or Italy for various reasons. Some did not have the means to do so (the savings had gone to building their house in the Philippines, to the children's education, to assisting the extended families in the Philippines). Others believed that bringing them over is not a wise move.

> My children wanted to come, but I thought, what work will they end up with? Domestic work as well? Having one domestic helper in the family is enough! This trend has to end! (Pinay 6)
>
> My eldest has finished his Computer Engineering degree in the Philippines. He is now training to go to Canada. My second has just finished high school. He applied for a scholarship at De La Salle University; we're still awaiting the results. I'm going home for his birthday and his graduation. My two other children are still in high school. I don't want them to come here because it would be a shame if they couldn't apply their education. The quality of education in the Philippines is better. (Pinay 5)

When Filipina domestic workers in Spain and Italy become mothers *in absentia*, they face different sets of challenges. There is concern over reports of children back home not being raised in the moral traditions that "only a mother would give" if she were around. This relates to discipline, serious study, respect for elders, debt of gratitude, and hard work, to name a few of these values. Thus, there are disappointments over the inability of the woman to fulfill this mothering role in person. On the other hand, some of our interviewees glow with pride when they talk about their children's achievements and how their children continue to reap the benefit of their overseas employment. A woman in this category, however, expressed a sentiment that is a poignant reminder of the dilemma some children in the Philippines feel about the status of the job of their parents—the feeling of "shame" concerning the occupation of their parent.

> I am close to my children. I ring them up often. If only you know how much I spend on phone calls. One time, my daughter asked me why don't I stop working as a domestic. Maybe they see my sisters and brother are professionals back home and their lives are okay. I could have been someone like that too if my husband has not insisted that I come to Spain. Anyway, I told my daughter that I will just see them through college. After they all finished, I will stop working as a domestic. (Pinay 4)

This Filipina was pursuing a university degree in chemistry in the Philippines when her husband decided to try his luck in Spain, having been encouraged by a friend. He was hoping to work as a jeweler, but ended up becoming unemployed. After one and a half years, he wanted her to come to Spain to work. She resisted because there was then a chance for her to get a scholarship to study in Australia, or even without that, she had just a year to go to finish her degree in the Philippines. Her father, who was sending her to the university, objected also and tried to convince her that a university degree was what she needed to secure her family's future. Nonetheless, her husband was persistent. She knew that if she did not follow her husband's wishes, they would separate and that would destroy the family. So she went and worked as a domestic helper in Spain. In the end, after a long saga of unemployment, underemployment, and illness, her husband returned to the Philippines while she stayed on to continue working as a domestic for more than ten years at the time of the study.

Understandably, the children could be feeling that the occupation of maids is not a dignified one in the Philippines. What they do not understand is how Spanish and Italian societies depend on them and treat them with more respect than in the Philippines. At least, this is also how the domestic helpers themselves feel.

Frequent visits to the Philippines are common among these women without families in the host country. These visits are yearly for some, and/or timed on special occasions such as graduation day, Christmas and New Year, birthdays, the christening of a child, and so on. Sending of remittances is almost an expected practice among these women (virtually universal among Filipino overseas workers). The money sent home would take care of all the needs of the family.

It is not uncommon for members of the extended family in the Philippines to take the child-rearing responsibility when mothers take up overseas employment. (When fathers go overseas, mothers depend on male kin for tasks that require manual skills, such as plumbing, repairs around the house, carrying heavy stuff, and so on, but not child-rearing.) This "fostering out" of children to kin is in fact an important factor that makes it possible for mothers to work overseas (Andall 1992). This practice, however, is quite different from traditional arrangements of informal adoption, which is still common in Philippine villages (for example, when a child lives with and cares for an aging relative and becomes part of that relative's family). In the context of global labor, the migrant workers would adopt-out their children to trusted kin, but would pay for all expenses of their children (plus an allowance for the carer) and provide better accommodation to the carer. This comes in the form of building a house from income earned overseas and asking their kin to live with the children in this house (Pertierra 2001). These are among the arrangements that my interviewees have made in relation to their children in the Philippines. In situations where the children are adults, they could also be living on their own, but nonetheless there is most likely to be an adult relative working as "maid" to assist with the household chores, or the children receive frequent visits from close relatives, such as aunts and uncles or grandparents.

The impact of labor migration on the children left behind was the focus of a study conducted by Battistella and Conaco (1998) among elementary school children of Filipino migrants. Comparing children from families where one parent is absent to those where both parents are working overseas, they found that the most disruptive impact is when the mother is absent. Fathers are not able to take on the mothering role effectively. Thus, the degree of involvement of other women in the extended family is an important determinant of the guidance that children can get. It was observed that "Where the mother is abroad, relatives become involved in approximately 60 percent of the cases, either by moving into the house of the migrant or having the migrant's family move to theirs."

The literature presents at best mixed evidence on the impact of the mother's absence on the children. What is obvious though is the ingrained view that women are main caretakers and have primary responsibility over the children, whether they are around or have gone overseas to work (Zlotnik 1995). They are therefore responsible for making arrangements for the care of the children left behind.

Reunited Families

The issue of mother-children relationships resumed after a prolonged separation is also a big problem faced by women when they bring their families to Spain or Italy. When the children were still in the Philippines, the mother would be sending money home. Her own mother or a close female relative (mother-in-law, an aunt, sister, or female cousin) would most likely help her husband look after the children, doing virtually all the cooking, cleaning, and providing much of the moral support. Depending on the parenting style of the surrogate mother, the children could be "spoilt" in terms of having their material wishes fulfilled, getting their own way, being "served" rather than being obliged to do any household chores, and so on. In other words, they would have been brought up differently had the mother not left for Europe.

After the initial joy of reunion, the mother is now faced with having to discipline children who are initially reticent to accept her role as disciplinarian, expecting her to buy them whatever they like (since their relationship with their mother in the past has been the infrequent visits in which the mother comes home from overseas with presents [*pasalubong*] for them). They also assume that they will be exempted from performing household chores. "Laki sa lola/lolo" (literally means, "raised by grandma/grandpa" who tends to spoil the grandchild/ren) is a Filipino term used to refer to such children.

> I have been working here [Rome] for a very long time now. I used to be alone. Recently I made my husband and two children (aged twelve and fifteen years) join me because we have been apart for so long. My husband has been unemployed for a year now. I continue to work as a full-time, live-in, domestic helper. I cannot afford to do otherwise because it is difficult not to have a secure job. We cannot afford it. My husband does not want to lift a finger around the house. On my days off, I have to do everything. My children are spoilt. They're not used to doing any chore. They're used to being served by caretakers back home. They also think that I can still buy them anything—shoes, clothes, toys, etc. They don't realize that I could hardly make my income enough for us. My husband even blames me for bringing them over, for his unemployed situation now. Sometimes I feel that I am reinvented as a maid three times over: I am a maid to my employer, a maid to my husband, and a maid to my children. (Pinay 3)

Once the family is reunited with their mother, there are new challenges linked to the husband's success or failure in finding employment. If both parents work, one such challenge is the lack of supervision of children. Another set of problems occurs when children are said to learn ways of the host culture and begin to answer back to their parents (versus the Filipino expectation of children being submissive to parents), criticizing their parents openly (sometimes in public), not respecting them (calling them by name for example, which is seen as impolite in Filipino culture) or other authority figures such as the teachers, or hanging around with friends that are perceived to have a bad influence on them, failing in school, and in worst cases, being involved in drugs ("but not in crimes," said one community worker). Some of those who have a hard time in school because of a lack of proficiency in the host language drop out and because they want to earn money right away also end up in domestic work. Their lack of language proficiency again is an obstacle for finding a good job in a place where unemployment is high and job competition is very strong.[8] Many parents eventually come to realize that the host country is not an ideal place for their migrant children.

On the whole, having their children around allows Filipina maids to fulfill their role as a mother by way of providing personal care and emotional support to their children. But being together also creates a dilemma, that of being primarily responsible for giving this care and support without the benefit of assistance from their extended social network in the Philippines. Thus, the contrast is such that, in the Philippines, they can be working full time and will probably have maids or other relatives help look after their children. In Spain and Italy, on the other hand, they are working full time, but still carry the full burden of family care without assistance. Certainly in some circumstances and respects, reunification actually makes life harder for these women. There are existing community support networks in Spain and Italy, but the focus of most of their work has been related to assisting in employment and legal issues.

CONCLUSION

Filipino domestic workers in southern Europe provide a distinctive case in the study of marriage and migration in so far as these women do not migrate for marriage with local men or end up married to local men. (These women are usually already married to Filipinos when they arrive in Europe.) The reason for this is that there is a critical mass of Filipinos in these two countries, consisting of men and women. Filipino men may be fewer but this actually enhances their "marketability" among Filipinas who still prefer Filipino men. Besides, most Filipinas who went there were married, and the sanctity of marriage is highly valued, plus there is the apprehension of being the subject of vicious rumors within the community in the foreign countries, as well as news that may travel back home! But alas, extramarital affairs still happen.

Against the backdrop of specific immigration and labor policies in Italy and Spain, the main objective in this chapter was to outline the differences between Filipino domestic workers who work abroad separated from their husbands and children and those who have opted for reunification with their families in the host countries. In addition, unlike the transnationally split families discussed by Chee (chapter 7), the Filipino women in this scenario have taken on the role of main, often even sole, breadwinner. This has serious implications for gender roles and the workings of the marital relationship.

The women become independent and achieve a considerable degree of dominance over the economic situation of their family life. But the outcomes of their overseas employment are not purely positive—neither in the "split" scenario nor in the "reunified" scenario; neither as mothers nor as wives.

These women workers have a choice of whether to bring their families over or not. Very few in fact choose to do so; most women decide that fulfilling the mother role from a distance (transnational motherhood) is the best way to capitalize on the overseas employment. These women who are separated from their husbands, although enduring the loneliness of separation from families, are perhaps the more "liberated" of the women. They become empowered due to their status as main breadwinner. Both choices have their own consequences that are positive and negative, depending on circumstances. The negatives are oftentimes reconstructed in the light of the greater good that overseas employment has done for the family.

A second argument relates to the transformation of the wife's role and husband's role. Both parties are transformed by the feminization of labor migration. The study showed the tenuous situation couples can find themselves in when they are separated and thus have to renegotiate roles vis-à-vis the family unit. As wives play a greater part in the traditionally male role of the breadwinner, they may threaten the husband's masculine role (and men have more difficulty readjusting to this new role reversal). The migration (whether with family reunion or not) shakes the very foundations of the family, which either has to cope with an "absent mother" or readjust to a new country, which generally keeps foreigners confined to the assigned space of "domestic help." Unless sociocultural attitudes are changing in the country of origin too, the overall burden on marital life remains great, with the result that women have to perform the triple role of wife, mother, and maid several times over.

NOTES

This research was made possible through a Special Studies Program grant from the University of New South Wales, Australia. The author would like to acknowledge the Philippine Embassies in Madrid and Rome, the various offices of the governments in Italy, Spain, and the Philippines (including the Philippine Consulate-General in Sydney), the various voluntary organizations and church groups for their assistance to this project,

Eduardo Pua for assisting in the interviews and documentation, and most of all, the Filipino workers in Spain and Italy who have shared their time and stories generously.

1. *Pinay* is a colloquial term referring to Filipino woman. I have used numbers to distinguish between the anonymous Pinay interviewees.

2. These fifty migrant laborers include male and female respondents. In Spain, we interviewed twenty-two women, twelve men; in Italy, fifteen women and six men.

3. I have not been able to identify a precise figure for mixed marriages. This statement is based on estimates by NGOs and church group interviewees.

4. Other domestic workers in Spain are Portuguese, Moroccans, and Latin/South Americans (Chile, Peru, Argentina, Colombia), from the Dominican Republic, Cape Verde, and Guinea Ecuatorial.

5. Prior to the introduction of the *Ley De Extranjeria* there was no other law. It was just simply assumed that former colonial citizens could come and go without visa requirements. The *Ley* was the first of its kind regulating incoming foreigners.

6. Italy was among the founding countries of the EU (previously EC, or EEC). Spain joined in 1986.

7. Annulment is as impossible as divorce, with only the very rich being able to afford an official annulment if they even know that such an arrangement exists or how to go about it. Legal separation is allowed under Philippine laws, but in this situation, both parties cannot remarry. Nonetheless, many would not even bother separating legally because of the bureaucratic requirements.

8. Unemployment for Spain was estimated at 22 percent in 1996 (Fact Sheet: Spain 1999). For Italy, the figure is 12.2 percent for 1997 (Fact Sheet: Italy 1999). Despite high unemployment, Spaniards are not willing to do domestic work partly because of higher employment expectations. This is the same in Italy. The need to import foreign domestic helpers is also due to the lack of childcare facilities in southern Europe.

REFERENCES

Andall, J. "Women Migrant Workers in Italy." *Women's Studies International Forum* vol. 15, no. 1 (1992): 41–48.

Barber, P. "Agency in Philippine Women's Labour Migration and Provisional Diaspora." *Women's Studies International Forum* vol. 23, no. 4 (2000): 399–411.

Battistella, G., and M. Conaco. "The Impact of Labor Migration on the Children Left Behind: A Study of Elementary School Children in the Philippines." *Sojourn: Journal of Social Issues in Southeast Asia* vol. 13, no. 2 (1998): 220.

Castles, S., and M. Miller. *The Age of Migration.* London: Macmillan, 1993.

CFMW (Commission for Filipino Migrant Workers) and KAIBIGAN. *Europe-Philippines in the 90s: Filipino Migration—the European Experience.* Manila: CFMW, March 1995.

Chan, K. B. "A Family Affair: Migration, Dispersal, and the Emergent Identity of the Chinese Cosmopolitan." *Diaspora* vol. 6, no. 2 (1997): 195–213.

Chell,V. "Gender Selective Migration: Somalian and Filipina Women in Rome." Pp. 75–92 in *Southern Europe and the New Immigrations*, edited by R. King and R. Black. London: Routledge, 1997.

Fact Sheet: Italy. Commission on Filipinos Overseas, Philippine Government, 1999.

Fact Sheet: Spain. Commission on Filipinos Overseas, Philippine Government, 1999.

Huntoon, L. "Immigration to Spain: Implications for a Unified European Union Immigration Policy." *International Migration Review* vol. 32, no. 2 (1998): 423–50.

Kofman, E., A. Phizacklea, P. Raghuram, and R. Sales. *Gender and International Migration in Europe—Employment, Welfare and Politics.* London: Routledge, 2000.

Lobera, M. "La Inmigracion Filipina en la Comunidad de Madrid" [The Immigration of Filipinos in the Community of Madrid]. Pp. 562–619 in *Inmigrantes Extranjeros en Madrid* [Foreign Immigrants in Madrid], edited by C. Romero. Volumen II, Madrid: Estudios Monograficos de Colectivos Inmigrante, 1993.

Pe-Pua, R. "Implications of Government Policies on Working Conditions of Filipino Workers in Hong Kong, Singapore and Taiwan." *Pilipinas* vol. 34 (2000): 63–90.

———. "*Pagtatanong-tanong*: A Cross-Cultural Research Method." *International Journal of Intercultural Relations* vol. 13 (1989): 147–63.

Pertierra, R. "Multiple Identities, Overseas Labor and a Diasporal Consciousness in a Local Community." Pp. 74–91 in *Going Global: Asian Societies on the Cusp of Change*, edited by A. Malay Jr. Quezon City: Asian Center, University of the Philippines, 2001.

Pingol, A. "Ilocano Masculinities." *Asian Studies* vol. 36, no. 1 (2000): 123–34.

Philippine Embassy-Rome. Philippine Embassy/POLO Report, 1999.

POEA (Philippine Overseas Employment Administration). Statistics. www.poea.org.ph/html/statistics.html (accessed January 26, 2001).

POLO Madrid. *Profile of Filipino Workers in Spain.* Report submitted to the Philippine government, unpublished document, 1999.

SOPEMI. "Italy." Pp. 124–28 in *Trends in International Migration*. Paris: OECD, 1997.

Tacoli, C. "International Migration and the Restructuring of Gender Asymmetries: Continuity and Change among Filipino Labor Migrants in Rome." *International Migration Review* vol. 13, no. 3 (1999): 658–82.

———. "Migrating 'for the Sake of the Family'?: Gender, Life and Intra-Household Relations among Filipino Migrants in Rome." *Philippine Sociological Review* vol. 44, nos. 1–4 (1996): 12–32.

Yeoh, B., and S. Huang. "'Home' and 'Away': Foreign Domestic Workers and Negotiations of Diasporic Identity in Singapore." *Women's Studies International Forum* vol. 23, no. 4 (2000): 413–29.

Zlotnik, H. "Migration and the Family: The Female Perspective." *Asian and Pacific Migration Journal* vol. 4, nos. 2–3 (1995): 253–71.

9

International Marriage through Introduction Agencies: Social and Legal Realities of "Asian" Wives of Japanese Men

Tomoko Nakamatsu

In the late 1980s "International Marriage Through Introduction Agencies" (hereafter IMIA) attracted enormous media interest in Japan. The topic rapidly became *torendo*, or a trend ("Mono, Kane no Tsugi wa Hito no Kokusaika!!" 1988, 58), following the involvement of rural local governments in arranging international marriages for their male residents in response to the problem of inability to attract Japanese brides to farm households. Media interest was enormous, focusing on rural farming families and the experiences of the brides from other parts of Asia who were referred to by a racialized[1] term, *Ajia no hanayome* (Asian brides). "Asian brides," the majority of whom were Filipinas, were consistently portrayed as economic victims of their homelands or as foreign workers disguised as brides. The extensive coverage on the rural cases in the media generated an impression that IMIA was exclusively a rural phenomenon involving Japanese farmers and was the sole explanation for the increase in the number of Asian women becoming the spouses of Japanese nationals. While in the early 1980s Asian women were mostly categorized as "entertainers," by the late 1980s public and academic discourse dichotomized "Asian women" as either "urban entertainers" or "rural brides" (see for example, Asahi Shimbun Shakaibu 1989, 107–50; McCormack 1996; Moeran 2000; Truong 1996). These dominant stereotypes obscured the existence of those who initially came to Japan for employment or educational purposes and later married Japanese nationals,[2] and also the activities of international marriage agencies in *urban* areas. Moreover, this derogatory picture of female foreigners disallows the view of these women as "active female migrants" (Kofman 1999), positively contributing to Japanese society by providing reproductive and productive work. In addition, these women are not short-term labor migrants, but

long-term settlers. As wives of Japanese, their strategies in the process of negotiating citizenship in Japan need to be investigated—a neglected area of academic inquiry so far.

This study counteracts the popular interpretation of these women as "not
respected as an equal human being," as described by Yoshizumi (1991, 42). It
also challenges the other prevailing understanding of them as pseudo laborers
from "a back door" (see for example, Kajita 1994, 39–41). It introduces a different perspective to the literature on so-called "mail-order brides" of Western
men, which depicts marriage experiences purely in negative terms (see, for example, Glodava and Onizuka 1994; Breger 1998, 134). The women in this research have demonstrated their autonomy and agency in a way that revealed
them taking responsibility for their own lives. International marriage for them
was not a form of "trade in women" (Truong 1996, 47), but rather a strategy
meticulously employed to fulfill their desire for marriage and family formation
in the context of socioeconomic stability. The analysis is based on interviews
with forty-five women from South Korea, China, and the Philippines who
married Japanese men (of whom only seven have farming as their main source
of income) through both rural- and urban-based international marriage-
introduction agencies. My informants arrived in Japan during the period of
1985 through 1995.[3]

This chapter explores the highly controversial and complex extent to which
one can talk of "commodification," "objectification," and "trade in women" on
the one hand, and the women's own decisions to participate in marriage introduction, as well as the processes of negotiating between productive and reproductive roles in a foreign country on the other. These women have to be
regarded as permanent settlers, which means that apart from their roles of
mothers, wives, and workers, their role as citizens has to be included in this discussion as an additional dimension.

IMIA—AN ISSUE OF "TRADE IN WOMEN"?

In Japan, IMIA has attracted the interest of activists and academics from vari-
ous disciplines. Some have approached this issue from the perspective of human rights (Yamazaki 1988; Nakamura 1988; Satô 1989), family sociology
(Matsuoka and Ueki 1995), anthropology (Sugaya 1995), and psychoanalysis
(Kuwayama 1995). Scholars in the fields of rural studies (Mitsuoka 1989;
Nakazawa 1996), migration studies (Kajita 1994; Kojima 1996), and adult education (Sasagawa 1989) have also examined this issue. Some scholars in the
West compared brides and entertainers of Asian origin to wartime "comfort
women" (McCormack 1996; Moeran 2000). These studies, despite different ac-

ademic orientations, assume economic determinates to be fundamental in their observations on the causes for such marriages for women. In addition, these Asian wives are typically depicted as poor, "using" Japanese men as a remedy to alleviate their economic problems.[4] The dialectics involved—that is, Japanese men "using" Asian women and vice versa—as well as the various levels or stages of agency on the part of the women are usually ignored. As a result, the meaning of marriage in the context of family life for the individual women, as well as their contribution as reproductive and productive workers to society at large, remain unexplored.

Because their political standpoint is to counter women's continuous and renewed subordination in the global economy, feminists and activist women tend to view Asian women migrants for marriage solely as "victims." For example, Yoshizumi (1991, 42), in her contribution to a fact-based book edited by two prominent Japanese feminists (Inoue and Ehara 1991), strongly criticizes the oppressive nature of the IMIA system, but does not recognize the women participants' own agency. Truong (1996), by making reference to the Japanese context, sees "mail-order brides" as female migrant reproductive workers along with foreign female sex workers and domestic workers. She argues that a cross-national transfer of labor in reproduction is a form of "social dumping," as reproductive work is cross-culturally devalued, and thus one must "foremost give recognition to the cruciality of reproduction" in order to halt this "trade in women" (1996, 47). Her approach, while useful for addressing structural problems in the global economy, trivializes the importance of marriage and family life in the experience of the women involved in international marriages by introduction, and devalues the marriage migrants' multiple and changing identities by depicting their marriage migration solely as a matter of trade. Based on a narrow view of these women as "reproductive labor" in the overall globalization of "trade," these perspectives tend to dehumanize these women's experiences. Reproductive work, even when undervalued and assigned to women in many societies, may nevertheless give fulfillment to some women because of its attachment to the family that serves as a source of affection and emotional comfort. Moreover, the description of the women involved in international marriage by introduction as purely reproductive workers is not confirmed by my data; as shown by my sample, these women also engage in productive work for a number of reasons and with varying levels of satisfaction (more detail below).

I would, therefore, argue—together with those feminist researchers who point out the unproductive binaries on theoretical sites between structure and agency (for example, Chancer 1998; Ortner 1996; Kofman 1999)—that it is essential to acknowledge rather than undervalue these women's agency in their decision to participate in marriage migration in male-dominated, economically stratified societies of Asia. Acknowledging marriage migrants who use the international marriage business not as "mail-order brides," "Asian brides," or purely "reproductive workers" but as active female migrants and new citizens, each with her own aspirations, strategies, and limitations, offers a useful contribution to studies of gender and migration.

Another related issue is that of there being different types of marriage agencies. Existing critiques of the "mail-order bride" business (for example, Wilson 1988) are based on agencies whose role is limited to advertising subscribed women (and men) on the Internet and in catalogs.[5] Japanese marriage agencies under discussion have a more involved role of assisting male clients to select women from their catalogs and organizing meetings in cooperation with their counterparts in Japan and overseas. It is more the traditional way of *miai* (introduction meeting) that is internationalized. Mapping international and domestic connections of marriage agencies therefore becomes an important issue for investigation. Marriage agents usually promote international marriage to individual men but some approached rural town and village officials whose major concern was depopulation and marriage difficulties of the male residents in their areas. While the media highlighted this collaboration of private agencies and local government bodies, the large majority of marriage agents mainly deal with individual—urban and rural—men, and their activities are by no means limited to rural areas. The marriage agencies I discuss in this chapter include both urban and rural based agencies.

GLOBALIZATION OF "THE MARRIAGE BUSINESS" IN JAPAN

In Japan, arranging marriages by go-betweens (individuals or agencies) was popularized since the Meiji (1868–1912) period. The business of arranging *international* marriages involving women from other Asian countries is a more recent phenomenon: it began in the late 1970s and expanded in the mid-1980s. As with most migration flows, the origins of marriage migration are also clearly "demand-driven." While its growth relates to changes in the domestic marriage market—particularly by women postponing their marriage and the demography of some rural towns and villages that have become seriously underpopulated—the actual operation of this type of business suggests that its development is a by-product of the globalization and economic integration of the Asian region. Many Japanese marriage agents were or had been engaged in businesses involving other countries in Asia, such as trade in products, restaurant enterprises, travel agencies, business consultancies, and language schools.[6] The agents based in Japan were often approached by individuals such as a Chinese overseas student, a Cambodian refugee, or a Japanese second-hand car exporter offering to act as recruiters. The web of intraregional marriage agencies thus displays the extent of Japanese economic expansion in the region, the accelerated movement of people and social integration between Japan and other countries in the 1980s, and their historical connections.

The global operation of Japanese marriage agencies is intricately linked with the operations and business connections of the existing domestic matchmaking industry. In many cases agencies with international connections acted as suppliers of foreign brides to other affiliated small-scale domestic agencies belonging to the same industry associations. Unlike the introduction business, which only sells members' information via printed or online catalogs, these international agencies incorporate the common style of *miai* (reminiscent of domestic matchmaking practices) as well as popular "group package" tours. Their services ranged from arranging introductions and a marriage ceremony overseas to assisting in the preparation of necessary immigration documentation. International marriage agencies for Japanese men therefore operate within a web of cross-border and local connections, accommodating the international marriage business to the needs of domestic consumption while internationalizing the domestic marriage business.

SOCIOCULTURAL BACKGROUND OF THE FEMALE PARTICIPANTS

A brief social profile of my forty-five informants (eighteen South Korean, nine Chinese, three Korean Chinese, and fifteen Filipino women) reveals the diversity of their backgrounds. At the time of their marriage to Japanese men, the average age was higher among South Korean (thirty-one years old) and Chinese (thirty years old) than Korean Chinese (twenty-six years old) and Filipino women (twenty-four years old). The overwhelming majority (93.7 percent) had secondary education including nine with university qualifications. Prior to immigration thirteen women had held professional or clerical jobs such as accountants, teachers, or secretaries. The Chinese women tended to hold higher educational qualifications, and hence were in skilled employment categories. Ten women were in the sales and service industries. Seven women were self-employed. Six South Korean owned small businesses such as clothing shops. Four others worked in textile or food processing factories; five had casual jobs; and six were not in the labor force. Filipinas showed the greatest diversity in their educational and occupational backgrounds—two factory workers, four with professional employment, and two university students among them.

Most women (82.2 percent) were never married prior to migrating to Japan, and fourteen women had sisters, female relatives, and friends living in Japan before or around the time of their arrival. Some of these family members and acquaintances had also married through introduction agencies, which may suggest the existence of chain marriage migration. The majority of the women in this study described their standard of life in their countries of origin as average. While six women mentioned growing up in impoverished households, eight revealed a rather affluent upbringing. Filipinas were most likely to express dissatisfaction with their economic situation, but the degree of hardship varied from "occasional shortage of food" to "not enough for going out, like to go to night clubs." Some reported variable economic statuses over time due to such variables as a parent's illness, the success or failure of a family business, and their own careers.[7]

CHOOSING INTERNATIONAL MARRIAGE INTRODUCTION— THE WOMEN'S PERSPECTIVE

Previous researchers attributed women's motives for international marriage in Japan solely to economic goals, such as the desire for a better life in Japan (for example Nakazawa 1996; Shukuya 1988; Sugaya 1995). The limited life opportunities for women in their country of origin were also highlighted (Sasagawa 1989) in the Korean context. Most of these studies failed to analyze the women's own definitions, and understanding, of "a better life" and how this is related to marriage migration across national borders. My findings suggest that women decide to marry internationally for multiple reasons, many of which are not directly related to economic goals. And even when the underlying desire for a more affluent life is the primary incentive for marriage migration, this was not an end in itself: the women aspire to affluence as married women within the context of a stable marital and family life. In my sample, the decision to enter international marriage was most commonly made after the women had experienced some setbacks or uncertainties in their lives: breakdown in relationships with boyfriends or partners, declining sales in a retailing business, resignation from a full-time job, divorce or failure to gain university entry. For example, a South Korean woman's engagement with a Korean man had been broken off because of his affair with another woman. Around the same time she incurred financial loss from her boutique business. She "wanted to have a rest" from the responsibilities of running a business by herself, thinking that to have "a stable ordinary family is the happiest," like her sister who had married a Japanese man through introduction.

Juxtaposed with the sentiment of wanting to escape from unpleasant situations was a sense of adventure for marrying and moving to another country. The image of the life of a middle-class wife in an affluent foreign country that is presented by marriage agents appealed to these women. Possible career advancement overseas for the women themselves contributed to the positive image of Japan as a destination and was particularly attractive to four Chinese women in their early thirties with university degrees. Cahill (1990) argues that due to inadequate employment opportunities in the Philippines, many Filipinas "felt forced to grab" other opportunities presented, "whether as overseas contract workers and/or as partners in an international marriage" (29). Filipinas as well as other women in my study, however, distinguished marriage migration from labor migration. International marriage projected the image of reinventing oneself as an affluent middle-class wife in an overseas setting with opportunities for self-advancement. The definition of "a better life" contained positive images of marriage—a caring, middle-class husband, children, affection, love, financial security, and personal career advancement—for the women believed these were less attainable in their countries of origin.

Some women were enticed by the chance of "being chosen" (as a bride) among other women. Some joined marriage agencies on their own accord, which often involved the paying of fees in the cases of some Korean and Chinese women. Others were either approached individually by agents or by persons acting for the agents, usually relatives or acquaintances, with a particular potential marriage proposal, or they attended introduction meetings organized by Japanese village officials and their intermediaries. The women who joined agencies showed their determination to marry a "desirable" person. For instance, a South Korean woman described her introduction situation as "he met three other women, a nurse, a post office clerk and a shop assistant. All of them were apparently good-looking, and all wanted to marry him. But he wanted me."

Six Filipino women who married through the initiatives of Japanese villages also expressed the euphoria of "being chosen." These women attended group meetings in a very casual manner, "for fun" or "as a joke," and saw many other "prettier" women: "I saw about twenty women at a meeting. When I was chosen, I felt like I was going to be a princess." Their statements confirm the overwhelming joy at being "selected" as well as their relative passivity in the process. A combination of subjection to the male gaze and the female fantasy of "being chosen" like a princess nurtured from the outset unequal gender relations between prospective husband and wife.

All women, however, were proactive in the decision-making process that ultimately culminated in marriage and migration. Many indeed laughed when asked "Who made the decision to marry?" often insisting they always made decisions concerning their own affairs. But their choice reflects ambivalence. Although these women challenged the family's authority over them and therefore could not be seen to be victims of the "family system" in their country of origin, they reveled at describing how they were "chosen" as brides by foreign men. Their dreams were inextricable from a life that focused on finding a man to marry. This suggests another layer of subjection in the gender-specific expectations associated with marriage by introduction and also reinforces patriarchal stereotypes. Although this chapter is reticent about interpreting this phenomenon as "trade" in women because it ignores the various stages in this process, the "business" aspect of the international marriage by introduction cannot deny that some elements of women (and men) as "commodities" still linger. Women are more vulnerable in the system because of the existing patriarchal construction of marriage institution and the fact that women move from their countries of origin to their spouses' countries. But as this very migration offers aspirations of a new life to women, to insist on the whole marriage by introduction process being a kind of "trade" denies these women agency. My study problematizes the one-dimensional view that relegates victim status to these women and introduces instead the complexities and ambivalences that predicate women's decisions that seem to both challenge and endorse patriarchal relationships.

MANAGING THE FAMILY AND NEGOTIATING THE REPRODUCTIVE ROLE

The couples married through international marriage agencies did not know each other before marriage. Their knowledge of each other therefore was fully played out within expectations of husband and wife relationships in socioculturally different contexts. At the beginning of their marital life, communication difficulties were felt most acutely. Limited proficiency in the Japanese language intensified misunderstanding, isolation, and tension thus producing a sense of frustration. Crying, throwing and destroying things, or refusing to talk was used to show dissatisfaction.[8] In the family domain, issues such as financial resource management, household duties, and child-rearing became focal points to be negotiated by migrant wives. For the majority of the thirty-six women who had lived or still live with parents-in-law, strong parental power complicated their relationships with their husbands and children.

The foreign wives attempted to establish their position in a family through performing their roles of wife and mother. One of the most contentious issues was the allocation and control of household finances. For women in this type of marriage by introduction, the management of financial resources symbolizes the growing trust between themselves and their husbands, as well as a sense of belonging as a family member. Control of household finance also built a solid power base. In the beginning of their marriage, some women received monthly allowances while others received part of their husband's salary for managing day-to-day living expenses. These practices disturbed women who interpreted the loss of financial control as a lack of trust undermining the self-image of a capable wife. The issue of control over household finances became even more complex for my rural informants who lived with an extended family. In their region, a young couple commonly handed over part or all of their income to their cohabiting parent/s, who managed the household budget and allocated an allowance for the young couple. The parents also handled the expenses of the couple's children. While combining resources of all the family members maximized the household's interests as a management unit, such tactics overlooked an individual's personal or specific needs. The majority of foreign wives in such a circumstance found the arrangement unacceptable and threatening, both to their status as a wife and to their autonomy as an individual. Intense disputes arose when a wife started working and was expected to hand over her entire salary to the household. The women commonly reacted by arguing for full autonomy over their own earnings. Such control contributed to their sense of independence. Three women who had acceded to control of the *ie no saifu* (household wallet) at the time of the interviews mentioned the difficulties of managing the household economy, recalling, ironically, the "easy days" of receiving an allowance from a parent-in-law. Full control over the household finances meant full responsibility for one of the most important household duties. This task created new challenges and opportunities for each woman. One Filipina expressed her dream: "I want to renovate our house. It's our time now. It may sound a cheap dream, but this is my dream." The control of resources signified the firm establishment of status in the family.

One strategy employed in the process of negotiating gender roles in the household was to raise the issue of cultural differences. One Chinese woman said, "Husbands do housework in China. But in Japan wives do everything and they don't complain." Similarly, a Korean person commented:

> Japanese wives don't complain about small matters to their husbands. But the wives over there [in Korea] regard complaining as also an expression of love. For instance, when my husband drinks alcohol and comes back late, I would scold him for being drunk and being late. Then he asks why I should scold him. People here think a wife should tolerate such small matters because men work [outside]. I can't get used to this idea. I ask my husband to phone me when coming back late, but he can't bother. I tell him if he can't accept that, he does not need to live with me. I would not stick to my opinion all the time, but he must cooperate because he is not married to a Japanese woman.

The use of the discourse of cultural "differences"—whether real or imagined— at times worked in defense of their interests.

Unfortunately the argument for cultural relativity was less effective over their parents-in-law. The confrontation between *yome* (daughter-in-law) and *shûtome* (mother-in-law) in the Japanese household system is a familiar theme. Ethnicity and cultural differences usually aggravated the potential for conflict. Some parents-in-law continued to regard their urban-oriented daughters-in-law as if they were from a backward country and frowned on cultural differences in child-rearing among other things. For example, the use of physical discipline by some wives was criticized by their mothers-in-law: "When my son does not listen to what I say, I smack him. Then my mother-in-law shouts at me that 'You people [in South Korea] use violence to bring up children.' Are all the Koreans gangsters?" Such disapproval did not deter her from using a form of discipline that she received when she was a child, but she nonetheless felt an encroachment on her autonomy in raising her own child. A mother-in-law's childcare role, which enabled the mother and other women to work outside, increased the sense of alienation for foreign wives. A Filipina expressed her lack of authority over her children: she was "just a mother figure, a decoration or something." But these foreign wives did not meekly submit to the pressure from in-laws. Instead, wives constantly confronted their mothers-in-law directly or through their husbands. One Filipina's divorce threat pressured her mother-in-law to initiate changes. Eventually she stopped interfering in matters of disciplining the children. In those extended families where the division and control of reproductive work had to be negotiated between a mother-in-law and a wife, the wife had to struggle to establish a "mother" position. In such a situation, ethnic identity became a liability because mothers-in-law were less tolerant about different child-rearing practices.

Precisely because some wives have to live with the extended family, the family in its extended form can be a site of female and racial oppression. The ideology of Japanese household structures where *yome* (daughter-in-law) are assigned low status in the family hierarchy combined with a rigid sexual division of labor was oppressive to the foreign wives, particularly when it was compounded with the myth of hierarchal ethnic relations between Japan and "Asia" in Japanese society. Nonetheless the experiences of the migrant women demonstrated that the women negotiated with the low status assigned to *yome* and "Asians" in general in Japan. The low status did not totally undermine their efforts to establish a family on their own terms.

The performance of traditional household roles often empowered women in the household economy. Two former South Korean small business owners metamorphosed into major players in the family farming business. Both women persuaded their families to diversify and value-add to their farming, introducing the making and selling of processed food using food from their own crops. These two women claimed that they eventually became the main decision makers in their household.

The possibility of changing family relationships was vividly illustrated by five women living in rural areas even where the extended family setting and the expectation of the first-born son's patrilineal responsibilities were still strong. Indeed, such expectations may have led to their husbands seeking foreign wives, as opposed to remaining unmarried. After a series of arguments these women successfully convinced their husbands to live separately from parents-in-law. These five women were fully aware that they were challenging a norm in the community. And yet they persuaded their husbands to join them in disputing the extended family system, which in their view worked to the disadvantage of a young couple, particularly a young foreign wife.

The examples showed that these foreign women—despite domestic conflicts—were not required to culturally assimilate in order to be recognized as legitimate wives and mothers. Thus, this data challenges studies that overemphasize conflicts between the "Asian" women and Japanese families (see for example, Nakazawa 1996; Ishii 1995), which view these women as marginalized forever in the status of an "outsider" and "foreign" wife.

FOREIGN WIVES IN PAID EMPLOYMENT

The marriage migrants' domain was not limited to the spheres of marriage and family. The women's attempt to expand their social space was evident in their participation in civic work, such as giving cooking demonstrations and performing cultural dances at various events organized by local governments and nongovernment organizations. Some of the women, both in rural and urban areas, actively participated in ethnicity-based women's groups (see also Roces, chapter 4; Suzuki 2000).[9]

Furthermore, all except four women have or had paid work in Japan. They participated in the paid workforce to obtain their own money, for self-development, to avoid conflicts with parents-in-law, out of loneliness, or to support the household economy. Because Chinese women commonly valued paid work over staying at home they identified self-development as the primary reason they sought paid employment. A former school teacher said, "I worked more than ten years [in China] so I don't want to be just a housewife." Filipinas and those who had left children by a previous marriage in their countries of origin usually sought wage employment in order to send remittances to their families in their countries of origin.[10] The remittances greatly contributed to the educational welfare of their younger siblings and children in their countries of origin. None of the women were pressured by their Japanese extended families to go out and get a job.

The general environment of the gender-segregated Japanese labor force that tends to assign part-time work to a married woman, compounded by ethnicity and the women's level of Japanese language proficiency, largely determined the types of work (and hence the wages) available to my informants. The residential status of foreign wives of Japanese nationals does not in theory restrict occupational opportunities. In reality, however, regardless of a migrant woman's qualifications and work experience the range of employment available to them is severely restricted. Even though a certain level of proficiency in Japanese language is acquired, full-time jobs available to foreign women are largely limited to manual labor in factories or marriage agencies. Other available jobs are confined to (1) ethnicity-related duties such as language teaching, or (2) working in a bar. The working hours were also another impediment.

The most common job category was production and processing work (59 percent), followed by managerial and clerical work (12.5 percent), hospitality (12.5 percent), farming (9 percent), and sales (7 percent). The employment status of the majority (73.6 percent) was part time or casual. Production and processing work was largely in textiles, electrical appliances, and food processing factories whose size varied from a family operated backyard company to large firms with over 150 workers. The part-time factory workers earned 70,000 yen to 100,000 yen monthly (approx. US$550 to US$850 in 1995/96) and their full-time counterparts typically around 150,000 yen. Six women took up manufacturing piecework at home. This type of work is one of the most feminized or "housewived" and thus one of the most severely underpaid forms of work in Japan as elsewhere. Managerial and clerical work included office work at marriage agencies, language teaching, and assisting foreigners at public community centers. These jobs required competence in Japanese language and social skills, and offered good hourly rates (as high as 5,000 yen) but only a limited number of working hours. Four women worked with the marriage agencies that had arranged their own marriages, performing administrative tasks and consulting with clients, earning on average 200,000 yen per month. The women in sales positions were all part time, whether in a supermarket or at stalls, and received slightly higher hourly wages than those in factories. The jobs in the hospitality industry included serving in a bar with an hourly wage of more than 1,000 yen.

Evaluation of Paid Work and Working Environment

Although involvement in the paid workforce offered wages and contact with the host society outside the family domain and "was better than staying at home," it did not contribute to occupational upward mobility for the migrant women. The women employed in factory work expressed the most dissatisfaction. One woman who had been an up-market dressmaker in South Korea was assigned to a menial assembly line job in a textile factory. Her requests for more complex sewing tasks were dismissed. For these women de-skilling was not uncommon. A Filipina, a former secretary, responded to my question about the level of work satisfaction, with: "I don't ask for enjoyment or worth [from my job]. Work is work. You work hard and receive money." Another person, a university graduate medical technician from the Philippines, said, "At least I am not [working as] a strip dancer." Filipino women sought consolation in the value of the Japanese yen, which allowed them to send remittances. De-skilling also meant a career dead end. After five years in factory work there were still no prospects for career advancement and promotion. Women were stuck in these "niches" that failed to maximize their talents (for the discussion of de-skilling of Filipinas in Canada, see McKay, chapter 2).

Work environment in the factories was unpleasant. Migrant women often complained about (1) the lack of respect for privacy, and (2) the perennial gossiping, which included the telling of dirty jokes by their colleagues (who were mainly married Japanese women in their thirties to fifties). Female Japanese workers may use gossip and sexual jokes as a form of resistance to tedious work, but these practices made the foreign women uncomfortable, further aggravating the already unfriendly atmosphere of the factory. The migrant women tended to identify their Japanese coworkers as "uneducated," "middle-aged," and "old-fashioned," reflecting their dissatisfaction with the work environment.

Furthermore, the majority of the women in factory work experienced overt or covert racism from their colleagues. While some chose to ignore it, others, like this Filipina respondent, confronted this hostility directly:

> Those Japanese *obasantachi* (middle-aged women), they can be mean. They know we are foreigners. They don't say but they don't like us. Once a woman accused me of not washing my hands [before starting to make sandwiches]. [So I said] "Who? Me? Did you see? I bet you didn't. I'm not a child. I knew all that [about hygiene]. You stupid idiot." Then this woman said "Oh! You understand Japanese." . . . So you see, they are mean when we don't understand Japanese. They treat us unfairly because we are foreigners. They won't stop if you keep quiet. It's no good.

This person emphasized the importance of responding with courage, because standing up for herself actually produced positive results. The Japanese women altered their attitude toward her. For one other person, a series of direct confrontations brought about the "stalemate": "They [the Japanese women] know me now, so don't say anything." Gender and class relations in Japan confined Japanese middle-aged working-class "housewives" to factory work. These same social structures likewise pushed married foreign women into gender- and class-based work, where their ethnic backgrounds often made them prime targets for discrimination. Paid work in Japan largely failed to offer the upward occupational mobility that some of the women desired before their marriage migration.

In the entertainment and marriage introduction industries the migrant women's ethnicities were an advantage over locals in terms of their employability. The entertainment industry is closely linked to Asian women migrant labor and officially regulated by the so-called entertainers visa. One Chinese woman confessed that she greatly enjoyed her bar work, attending "customers who talked politics and economics," compared with her previous factory work where she was "confined with middle-aged women colleagues." But because of the association of bar workers with sex workers and its stigmatized connotation on a married woman, she pretends to her customers to be an overseas student. The entertainment industry offers better payment and stimulus than factory work. But Asian women in the hospitality industry are more stigmatized in wider society than any other foreign worker.

On the other hand, these women who have immigrated through the marriage by introduction agencies scheme are ideally placed to work in marriage introduction agencies where their bilingual skills and personal experiences regarding marriage migration to Japan could be maximized. Agencies can also advertise them as successful examples of wives who have assimilated happily in Japan. Dealing with newly arrived brides can be part of their work. The four migrant women employed by marriage agencies all had "challenging office work" with reasonable salaries. One of them, a Filipina, was happy with her duties in a Tokyo-based agency, handling Japanese clients and corresponding with overseas contacts. She was also enjoying taking part in a computer course. However, one could argue that this type of job poses serious questions as to their own subject position: are these women participating in the "commodification" of other women who were lured into the marriage-migration market? Or are they helping these new migrants settle in Japanese society? Or does the job in an introduction agency merely highlight their ambivalence—they are both clients and marriage agents at the same time? In any case, the women's work at a marriage agency could be interpreted as part of their attempt to find a worthwhile career in Japan.[11]

MIGRANT WOMEN AS SETTLERS AND THE ISSUE OF CITIZENSHIP

An investigation into the meaning of citizenship to the migrant women is essential in examining the migrant women's lives in Japan. Migrants should have the liberty fully to participate in civic society on the ground of residence regardless of whether or not they acquire nationality in the host country. However, legal and practical aspects of citizenship often intersect and influence the lives of migrants in any country (Piper 1998, 78–80) and also in Japan where the notion of citizenship governing social and legal rights intricately overlaps with the concept of nationality with racial connotations. As Piper (1998) pointed out in the European context, this mingling of the concepts of citizenship and nationality is rooted in a symbiotic relationship of racism and nationalism.

While the migrant women in my study were not "forced to be naturalized" (Ishii 1995, 86) by their Japanese families, the women's perceptions of residential status were influenced by the impact of the Japanese *koseki* (family register) system that excludes non-Japanese nationals. The Japanese government in principle does not permit dual citizenships and registers its residents in two categories: Japanese nationals or non-Japanese nationals. The Family Registration Act (*koseki hô*) and the Residents Registration Act (*jûmin tôroku hô*) control the former, and the Foreigner Registration Act (*gaikokujin tôroku hô*) the latter. *Koseki* registers the family as a unit (up to two generations) under the head of a family, and, unlike the residential registration, which is based on one's current domicile, it records the individual family members' certain personal history such as marriage and residential areas.[12] In *koseki*, the marriage of a Japanese national to a foreign spouse is written in a column reserved for remarks (Sakakibara 1992, 168). A cross-cultural family whose members consist of Japanese and non-Japanese nationals is therefore in principle divided in separate registrations. The residential status of non-Japanese is directly regulated by the Immigration Law and the Nationality Law (Sellek 1997). When my respondents were deciding whether to apply for permanent residency or naturalization,[13] the social implication of *koseki* had considerable impact on their decision. A foreign spouse with permanent residency is not formally registered with his or her Japanese family's *Jûmin Tôroku* (resident registration) and *koseki* because these registrations apply only to Japanese nationals. This exclusiveness affected the social identity of my informants and their views on residential status (see McKay, chapter 2, and Pe-Pua, chapter 8, for the different situations in Canada, Spain, and Italy).

Among my interviewees, eleven women decided on naturalization; two had submitted the application for permanent residency; and of the remaining thirty-two women with spouse status, four mentioned their preference for naturalization, twelve for permanent residency, and sixteen were unsure. Those who preferred naturalization gave various practical benefits as reasons, including the establishment of their family life in Japan, concerns for the welfare of their children, and the convenience of having a Japanese passport. A sense of unfairness that *koseki* does not recognize foreign spouses was strongly expressed by these women. One Korean woman who was waiting for an outcome said:

> It makes me feel sad that *koseki* does not record my name. What's more, my husband cannot understand my feeling of loneliness because of this. . . . I am like a

cohabitant. I want to be [regarded as] a *real* wife on the *koseki* as well. My children are Japanese nationals and accordingly registered, but I am [treated as] a foreigner. I want to show that they are my children, and were born with a *proper* mother. (emphasis added)

Koseki divides a family by nationality and imposes outsider identity on a non-Japanese spouse. In other words, the state denies a foreign national a place in the family in terms of *koseki*. Applying for naturalization therefore had the women's status "properly" recognized, and the action of applying made them feel "stronger" in the country that differentiated them.

Adopting naturalization brought "half happiness and half sadness." Finally seeing their names in the family's *koseki* delighted all the women, but losing their original nationality brought to some a feeling of sadness. While the women stressed adopting Japanese nationality had little to do with their sense of ethnicity, some felt offended by a different understanding of naturalization between themselves and their Japanese acquaintances. One Korean woman who became naturalized was congratulated by a Japanese friend who said, "You truly have become Japanese now." Sellek (1997, 201), observing the Japanese government's preference for *Nikkeijin* (descendants of Japanese living overseas) as foreign workers, noted that the primary determinant of "Japaneseness" was lineage or "race." If "being Japanese" depends upon being member of the "Japanese race," then non-Japanese who take on Japanese citizenship are affected by ethnocentric overtones and become "pseudo-Japanese." The lack of a concept of citizenship independent of nationality, ethnicity, or race denies the diversity of ethnic identities of the marriage migrants.

The connotation of assimilation in the naturalization process affected some women, who preferred permanent residency for that reason. All who opted for permanent residency showed antipathy toward "becoming Japanese": "I am not ready to become Japanese" and "If I take up naturalization, I become Japanese, and I will be a foreigner in my own country when I would return." For these women, naturalization threatens their sense of ethnic identity and appears to limit their options of returning to their home country, even though they may never do so. Moreover they know that naturalization does not automatically grant full social citizenship in daily living. A Korean woman said, "I want to avoid changing nationality. Some people do it for the sake of the children. But others know that you are Korean even though you change your nationality. You cannot become Japanese." Adopting Japanese nationality does not seem to her to provide a practical benefit to herself and her child in daily living. Of the twelve women with spouse status who preferred permanent residency to naturalization, all except one were technically eligible to apply. These women appeared to have been postponing such action. When naturalization was not their option, remaining in spouse status had a similar effect on their daily lives as permanent residency did. As a result, the insecurity of spouse status—possibility of losing the status upon divorce or a husband's death—tended to be overlooked.

Japan favors foreign spouses of Japanese nationals on the grounds of marriage compared to other foreigners without such ties when it comes to residential status. Yet my respondents felt that the intricacy of immigration, nationality, and family registration policies denied them the right to retain both their ethnicity and their "rightful" place in the family and Japanese society.

CONCLUSION

Although feminists of all color and persuasions are likely to classify women who marry through the international marriage introduction system as "victims" of patriarchy's commodification of women, this case study shifts the perspective to one which interprets these women's actions as part of a complex and sometimes ambivalent process of negotiating strategies to fulfill their roles as wives, workers, and later as new citizens. While the notion of international "marriage" through marriage agencies does raise questions of "commodification" and "objectification" of women who are "chosen" as wives by men whom they had never met before, the same system offered the women opportunities to marry foreign men and live overseas. Further, once women become wives they begin to negotiate for their identities and independence as wives, as handlers of the purse strings (financial independence), and as working women with an independent income, not hesitating to challenge social norms concerning the Japanese family. Some of the women successfully cooperated with their husbands in confronting social norms. Strategies employed are: (1) the use of cultural differences to argue for a more equal marital relationship, (2) the control of the finances, (3) the entrance of women in the workforce, and (4) integration as a citizen. Though still marginalized in the workforce (through de-skilling), and facing discrimination from their families, the workplace, and the government, these women use marriage as a strategy in which to reinvent their roles as wife, mother, worker, and citizen. One Korean woman said to her visiting worried mother: "I may not look happy now, but just wait. I will make it happen." The women's aspirations for participating in IMIA and their struggles to be successful in marriage and migration on their own terms deserve full acknowledgment in the analysis of international marriage migration through introduction agencies.

NOTES

1. The term "Asian brides" referred to non-Japanese women from Asian countries. The term stressed their countries of origin as "Asia," which was often associated with poverty and backwardness in media reports on this issue.

2. In the case of the Filipino nationals, the number of those who changed their visa status to "a spouse or child of a Japanese national" from other residential status increased from 734 in 1984 to 910 in 1985, and 2,323 in 1987, suggesting the increase of Filipinas who initially came to work and later married Japanese men (Kojima 1996). The increase in this category occurred slightly earlier than those who entered Japan "as a spouse or child of a Japanese national," which peaked at 2,430 in 1989 from 915 in 1987 and 2,009 in 1988 (Kojima 1996).

3. The interviews took place in 1995 and 1996. At the time of the interview, thirty-five women lived in Yamagata prefecture, a relatively poor farming area in northeast Japan, and ten in or near Tokyo; eight women had been in Japan for eight years or more, eighteen for five to seven years, fifteen for two to four years, and four for one year or less. .

4. This was also observed by Piper (1997, 331).

5. As in the case of catalogs of "Asian brides" in America (Wilson 1988), the representation of the Asian women for the Japanese male audiences in the matchmaking business renders Asian women familiar yet different, without highlighting overt "Asian markers" (Wilson 1988, 119). This makes the women marriageable. For example, Japanese agents' advertisements emphasize cultural similarities between Korea and Japan, and at the same time highlight Korean women's humbleness and gentleness as the traits that Japanese women have lost. Further, the inclusion and exclusion of certain race markers is determined by marriageability, which is fundamentally constructed within conventional gender relations. "Poverty" of Filipino women is generally stressed in the agents' rhetoric as it places many Japanese men in the position of superiority. But when some agencies promote Filipino women to urban high-income earners, the women are assigned to have middle-class, educated, and English-speaking traits. Yet their portrayal retains submissiveness with no threat to Japanese men. Transcending differences between the races of foreign brides, their marriageability is determined by existing patriarchal gender relations.

6. The finding is based on my interviews with thirty-two marriage agents in Japan and on other secondary sources.

7. Most of the Japanese husbands of my informants were five or more years older than their wives; most completed secondary education, including three university graduates; and their main occupation at the time of interview included thirteen in the professional/clerical category, eleven construction or factory workers, nine skilled workers in trades, seven farmers, four in the transportation industry, and one small business owner.

8. The proficiency in Japanese language varies among the interviewees. Some of the women studied the language prior to their migration to Japan. In general, the Korean interviewees showed a higher proficiency, considering the similar duration of stay in Japan, then the Chinese women, followed by the Filipinas. The language proficiency helped women to negotiate various matters in the family, but this did not correspond to the level of their marital satisfaction.

9. The extent of my interviewees' involvement in civic work and its influence on their residential communities is more limited than the Roces account (chapter 4) of Filipinas in a mining town in Australia. This difference in my study would stem from the small number of the foreign women compared to the ratio of the total population

of the host communities; relatively short residential history of some of my interviewees; and religious and language factors limiting the participation opportunities for them. The women who participated in government and nongovernment-based events in my study valued their civic work. But they showed dissatisfaction to the repeated staging of culturally stereotyped activities (i.e., cultural dancing or cooking) requested by these organizers. Their role in the communities was valued most in narrowly defined gender and cultural bounds as a foreign bride. In other words, the women's civic work was appreciated "*because of*" their differences (emphasis in original, Ang 1996, 37).

10. Six women had children from their previous marriages. At the time of interview, two of the women's children were legally adopted by their Japanese husbands under the Japanese civil law and lived in Japan. Among the Filipino women, attitudes toward remittance varied. The issue of family obligation frustrated some, but also was a source of pride for others.

11. I do not have enough room to explore this issue in this chapter, but the relationships between marriage agents and their female clients are multifaceted. A woman is regarded as a commodity for an agent, but she is also a client. This agent-commodity/client relationship can be developed into that of employer-employee, collaborators, or competitors in the marriage business after a woman's migration to Japan. Dichotomizing marriage agents (exploiters, power holders, males) versus brides (exploited, victim, females) has serious limitations.

12. Although it is beyond the scope of my work, the *koseki* system has attracted criticism from feminists and human rights activists. Its entry of the family as a unit under the family head in effect puts the family ahead of the individual, and the head of a family above other family members (Sakakibara 1992). The entry of certain personal history conflicts with the protection of one's privacy as *koseki* is in principle open to the public if a certain procedure is followed.

13. The residential status of a Japanese national's spouse is initially permitted under the category of "Spouse or child of Japanese National" in the Immigration Law. A foreign spouse may lose this residential status in the event of divorce or if his or her Japanese spouse dies. He or she can then apply for *teijūken* (long-term resident status) with custody of the children strongly influencing approval. The acquisition of permanent residency or naturalization requires a certain length of residential history and many documents. The criteria for permanent residency do not specify the required residence history but indicate that five years' consecutive residency is the standard. It indicates fewer years for certain people, including spouses of Japanese nationals (Japan Immigration Association 1991, 156). Naturalization is open to those who have lived in Japan for five or more years. A spouse of a Japanese national is eligible to obtain naturalization when he or she has lived in Japan for three or more years consecutively, or has been married for three or more years and has lived continuously one or more years in Japan (Nationality Law Article 7).

REFERENCES

Ang, Ien. "The Curse of the Smile: Ambivalence and the 'Asian' Woman in Australian Multiculturalism." *Feminist Review*, no. 52 (Spring 1996): 36–49.

Asashi Shimbun Shakaibu (Ed.). *Chikakute Chikai Ajia* (Neighboring Asia). Tokyo: Gakuyô Shobô, 1989.

Breger, Rosemary. "Love and the State: Women, Mixed Marriages and the Law in Germany." Pp. 129–52 in *Cross-Cultural Marriage: Identity and Choice*, edited by Rosemary Breger and Rosanna Hill. Oxford: Berg, 1998.

Cahill, Desmond. *International Marriages in International Contexts: A Study of Filipina Women Married to Australian, Japanese and Swiss Men*. Quezon City: Scalabrini Migration Center, 1990.

Chancer, Lynn S. *Reconcilable Differences: Confronting Beauty, Pornography, and the Future of Feminism*. Berkeley: University of California Press, 1998.

Glodava, Mila, and Richard Onizuka. *Mail Order Brides: Women for Sale*. Fort Collins: Alakan, 1994.

Inoue, Teruko, and Yumiko Ehara. (Ed.). *Josei no Dêta Bukku (Women's Data Book)*. Tokyo: Yûhikaku, 1991.

Ishii, Yuka. "Kokusai Kekkon no Genjô: Nihon de Yoriyoku Ikiru Tameni" (The Present Situation of International Marriage: Towards a Better Life in Japan). Pp. 73–102 in *Teijûkasuru Gaikokujin* (Foreigners Residing Permanently), edited by Hiroshi Komai. Tokyo: Akashi Shoten, 1995.

Japan Immigration Association (Ed.). *A Guide to Entry, Residence and Registration Procedures in Japan for Foreign Nationals*. Tokyo: Nihon Kajo Shuppan, 1991.

Kajita, Takamichi. *Gaikokujin Rôdôsha to Nihon* (Foreign labors and Japan). Tokyo: Nihon Hôsô Shuppan, 1994.

Kofman, Eleonore. "Female 'Birds of Passage' a Decade Later: Gender and Immigration in the European Union." *International Migration Review* vol. 33, no. 2 (1999): 269–99.

Kojima, Hiroshi. "Firipin kara Nihon e no Jinkō Idō" (The Population Movement from the Philippines to Japan). Pp. 77–110 in *Rōdō Shijō no Kokusaika to Wagakuni Keizaishakai e no Eikyō: Ajia Taiheiyô Chi'iki no Rōdōryoku Idō* (Internationalization of the Labor Market and Its Influence on Japan's Economy: Labor Migration in the Asian Pacific Region), edited by The Japan Institute of Labor. Tokyo: The Japan Institute of Labor, 1996.

Kuwayama, Norihiko. *Kokusai Kekkon to Sutoresu* (International Marriage and Stress). Tokyo: Akashi Shoten, 1995.

Matsuoka, Akiko, and Takeshi Ueki. "Mogami Ken'iki ni okeru Kokusai Kazoku—Teichakusuru Firipin Hanayome no Jittai Chôsa" (International Families in the Mogami Region, Japan—Filipina [*sic*] Brides Settling into a New Life). *Kazoku Kankei Gaku* vol. 14 (1995): 63–75.

McCormack, Gavan. *The Emptiness of Japanese Affluence*. New York: M. E. Sharpe, 1996.

Mitsuoka, Kôji. *Nihon Nôson no Kekkon Mondai* (Marriage Problems in Japanese Farming Villages). Tokyo: Jichôsha, 1989.

Moeran, Brian. "Commodities, Culture and Japan's Corollanization of Asia." Pp. 25–50 in *Japanese Influences and Presences in Asia*, edited by Marie Söderberg and Ian Reader. Richmond, Surrey: Curzon Press, 2000.

"Mono, Kane no Tsugi wa Hito no Kokusaika!! Gekizôsuru Kokusai Kekkon wa Yome Kikin o Sukuerunoka?" (After Goods and Money, Now the Era of Internationalization of People. Can Increasing International Marriages Solve Bride-Famine?). *Sukora* (14 April 1988): 56–59.

Nakazawa, Shinichi. "Nôson ni okeru Ajiakei Gaikokujinzuma no Seikatsu to Kyojû Ishiki" (Experience and Views of the Foreign Wives of Asian Origin in Farming Areas). *Kazoku Shakaigaku Kenkyû*, no. 8 (1996): 81–96.

Namamura, Hisashi. "Japan Imports Brides from Sri Lanka: A New Poverty Discovered." *AMPO-Japan Asian Quarterly Review* vol. 19, no. 4 (1988): 26–31.

Ortner, Sherry B. *Making Gender: The Politics and Erotics of Culture*. Boston: Beacon Press, 1996.

Piper, Nicola. *Racism, Nationalism and Citizenship: Ethnic Minorities in Britain and Germany*. Aldershot: Ashgate, 1998.

———. "International Marriage in Japan: 'Race' and 'Gender' Perspectives." *Gender, Place and Culture* vol. 4, no. 3 (1997): 321–38.

Sakakibara, Fujiko. *Josei to Koseki: Fûfu Bessei Jidai ni Mukete* (Women and the Family Register: Towards the Practice of Different Surnames between Husband and Wife). Tokyo: Akashi Shoten, 1992.

Sasagawa, Kôichi. "Kankoku kara no 'Hanayome' to Ibunka Kôryû" ('Brides' from Korea and Cross-Cultural Exchange). Pp. 217–67 in *Mura to Kokusai Kekkon* (Villages and International Marriage), edited by Takao Satô. Tokyo: Nihon Hyôronsha, 1989.

Satô, Tôzaburô. "Nôson ni okeru Kokusai Kekkon no Mondaiten No. 1" (Problems of International Marriage in Rural Areas No.1). *Hôritsu no Hiroba*, no. 42 (1989): 84–86.

Sellek, Yoko. "*Nikkeijin*: the Phenomenon of Return Migration." Pp. 178–210 in *Japan's Minorities: The Illusion of Homogeneity*, edited by Michael Weiner. New York: Routledge, 1997.

Shukuya, Kyoko. *Ajia kara Kita Hanayome: Mukaerugawa no Ronri* (Brides from Asia: Logic of the Receivers). Tokyo: Akashi Shoten, 1988.

Sugaya, Yoshiko. "Kokusai Kekkon no Mura: Yamagataken Mogami Chihô kara" (A Village with International Marriage: From Mogami Region, Yamagata). *Imin Kenkyû Repôto*, no. 3 (1995): 1–25.

Suzuki, Nobue. "Between Two Shores: Transnational Projects and Filipino Wives in/from Japan." *Women's Studies International Forum* vol. 23, no. 4 (2000): 431–44.

Truong, Thanh-Dam. "Gender, International Migration and Social Reproduction: Implications for Theory, Policy, Research and Networking." *Asian and Pacific Migration Journal* vol. 5, no. 1 (1996): 27–52.

Wilson, Ara. "American Catalogues of Asian Brides." Pp. 114–25 in *Anthropology for the Nineties: Introductory Reading*, edited by Johnnetta B. Cole. New York: The Free Press, 1988.

Yamazaki, Hiromi. "Japan Imports Brides from the Philippines: Can Isolated Farmers Buy Consolation?" *AMPO-Japan Asian Quarterly Review* vol. 19, no. 4 (1988): 22–25.

Yoshizumi, Kyoko. "Kokusai Kekkon" (International Marriage). P. 42 in *Josei no Dêta Bukku (Women's Data Book)*, edited by Teruko Inoue and Yumiko Ehara. Tokyo: Yûhikaku, 1991.

Index

Page numbers in bold type (e.g., **8–13**) indicate detailed discussion of a topic.
Page numbers in italic type (e.g., *84–85*) indicate a table.

About the Contributors

Maria W. L. Chee is a sociocultural anthropologist educated in Canada and the United States and a Fulbright recipient 2000–2001. She is currently a doctoral candidate in sociocultural anthropology at the University of California, Riverside. Her research interest lies in the Pacific Rim and Asian America, in areas concerning globalization and transnationalism, migration, women, ethnicity, ethnic banking, and business.

Eleonore Kofman is professor of human geography at Nottingham Trent University. She has published widely on gender, citizenship and international migration, and feminist political geography and has coauthored a book entitled *Gender and International Migration in Europe: Employment, Welfare and Politics.* Her current interests include skilled female migrants, family migration, and contradictions of contemporary European migratory policies.

Michelle Lee is a Ph.D. graduate from University College London, University of London. She teaches in the School for Social, Development, and Environmental Studies, University of Malaysia (UKM). Her research interests include women and transmigration as well as transgenderism.

Deirdre McKay is research fellow in the department of human geography, Research School of Pacific and Asian Studies, The Australian National University. In 1999 she completed her Ph.D. at the University of British Columbia. Her dissertation explored gender and local ethnographies of development in the uplands of the northern Philippines. She is currently undertaking further research on Filipino migrant communities in Canada as well as transnational households and remittance landscapes in the Philippines.

217

Prapairat R. Mix joined Amnesty for Women, a human rights organization based in Hamburg, Germany, that fights against trafficking in women, as a social worker in 1991—initially in a voluntary position, but since 1993 as full-time staff member. She is one of the researchers and coauthors of the book *The Migration of Thai Women to Germany: Causes, Living Conditions and Impacts for Thailand and Germany*. She also wrote a number of articles about the situation of Thai women in Germany in a Thai circular aimed at the Thai community in Germany. She has lived in Hamburg, Germany, since 1991.

Tomoko Nakamatsu is associate lecturer in Japanese at the Asian Studies Department of the University of Western Australia. She completed her Ph.D. at the Department of Asian Studies, Murdoch University, Australia, in 2002, with a dissertation entitled *Marriage, Migration and the International Marriage Business in Japan*. She has published articles on gender relations in contemporary Japan. Her research interests revolve around sociology of gender and ethnic relations in contemporary Japan.

Rogelia Pe-Pua is senior lecturer at the School of Social Science and Policy at The University of New South Wales, Sydney. Her interest in migration research revolves around sociopsychological aspects of migration. The specific issues she has investigated are the experience of international students in Australian universities, street-frequenting ethnic youth, refugee families, Hong Kong immigrants in Australia, and the legal needs of ethnic residents in western Sydney. She was also part of an international research team looking at comparing ethnocultural youth identity and acculturation in thirteen countries.

Nicola Piper is researcher with the Regulatory Institutions Network, at the School of Social Sciences at The Australian National University. She holds a Ph.D. in sociology from the University of Sheffield, United Kingdom. In her research on international labor migration she has been specifically concerned with citizenship, labor/human rights, and gender in the European as well as East and Southeast Asian context. She has written *Racism, Nationalism and Citizenship— Ethnic Minorities in Britain and Germany* and coedited *Women and Work in Globalizing Asia* (with Dong-Sook Gills).

Mina Roces, a Ph.D. graduate from the University of Michigan, teaches history at The University of New South Wales in Sydney, Australia. She is the author of *Women, Power and Kinship Politics: Female Power in Post-War Philippines* and *Kinship Politics in Postwar Philippines: The Lopez Family, 1946–2000*. With Louise Edwards, she coedited *Women in Asia: Tradition, Modernity and Globalisa-*

tion. Her current research interests include postwar Philippines, gender and power in twentieth-century Philippines, and Filipino migrants in Australia.

Katie Willis is a lecturer in geography at the University of Liverpool. Her main research interests focus on the impact of macroeconomic changes on households and the gendered nature of these impacts. She has conducted research in Mexico and California, as well as in Singapore and China, and has published in journals such as *Gender, Place and Culture* and *Regional Studies.*

Brenda Yeoh is associate professor, department of geography, National University of Singapore. She teaches social and historical geography and her research foci include the politics of space in colonial and postcolonial cities, and gender, migration, and transnational communities. She has published a number of scholarly journal papers and books in these areas, including *Gender Politics in the Asia-Pacific Region* (with Peggy Teo and Shirlena Huang).